Russell

Daddy (64-15025) 4-29-65

The
Byzantine
Achievement

PLATE 1

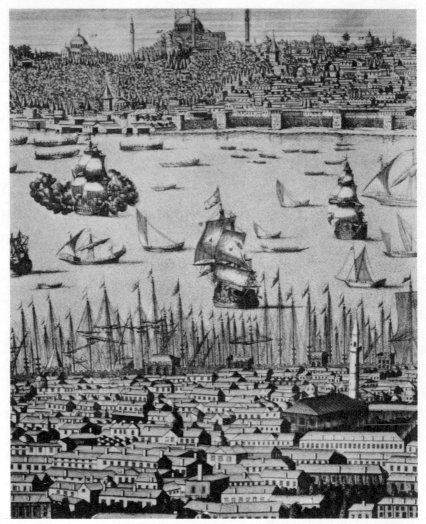

COMMERCE IN THE GOLDEN HORN

The
Byzantine Achievement
AN HISTORICAL PERSPECTIVE
A.D. 330-1453

ROBERT BYRON

NEW YORK

RUSSELL & RUSSELL · INC

1964

FIRST PUBLISHED IN 1929
REISSUED, 1964, BY RUSSELL & RUSSELL, INC.
BY ARRANGEMENT WITH ROUTLEDGE & KEGAN PAUL, LTD.
L. C. CATALOG CARD NO: 64—15025

PRINTED IN THE UNITED STATES OF AMERICA

IN CELEBRATION OF THE
PAST YEAR, TWENTY-FIFTH
SINCE THE WEDDING OF MY
FATHER AND MOTHER—R.B.

CONTENTS

vii

LIST OF ILLUSTRATIONS

Acknowledgements and relevant details will be found in the notes on the illustrations, page 313.

ix

LIST OF ILLUSTRATIONS

AUTHOR'S NOTE

THE proportion of emphasis in every book must vary with the measure of misapprehension in the popular imagination concerning the subject with which it deals. The history of the Levant, hitherto distorted by journalist and scholar alike to the furtherance of their private hypotheses, demands, in its present phase, an element of correction, which should result in the imposition of a foreground of recent fact upon a distant plane of historical analysis. The intention of this book was originally to present a history of the eastern Mediterranean between the years 1919 and 1923. But it became immediately apparent, upon a second and protracted exploration of the Greek seaboard in 1926, that to portray the events of those years without previous investigation of their historical foundations, were equivalent to offering the public the last act of a problem play without the first. The fault now committed, the offer of the first without the last is, I hope, the lesser. The extension in scope needed another two years' work. And an author's time, above all men's, is money. A manuscript once completed, he will as soon lock it in a box as a financier horde gold pieces in a vault.

The present volume is in no sense one of research among original sources. Its intention has been simply to gather the currents of the past into a single stream; and while indicating, with deference, a number of unexplored eddies in the spate of Western evolution, to enable a successor, if ever it is written, to show which forces have retained their vitality in the present time. Above all its intent is not didactic. It is hoped, simply, that the reader will in future experience some quickening of historical emotion, when next there obtrudes on his notice the seaboard of the Greeks and its capital city of Constantinople.   R. B.

" Of that Byzantine Empire the universal verdict of history is that it constitutes, without a single exception, the most thoroughly base and despicable form that civilisation has yet assumed. . . . There has been no other enduring civilisation so absolutely destitute of all the forms and elements of greatness, and none to which the epithet mean may be so emphatically applied. . . . Its vices were the vices of men who had ceased to be brave without learning to be virtuous. Without patriotism, without the fruition or desire of liberty . . . slaves, and willing slaves, in both their actions and in their thoughts, immersed in sensuality and in the most frivolous pleasures, the people only emerged from their listlessness when some theological subtlety, or some chivalry in the chariot races, stimulated them to frantic riots. . . . They had continually before them the literature of ancient Greece, instinct with the loftiest heroism : but that literature, which afterwards did so much to revivify Europe, could fire the degenerate Greeks with no spark or semblance of nobility. The history of the empire is a monotonous story of the intrigues of priests, eunuchs and women, of poisonings, of conspiracies, of uniform ingratitude, of perpetual fratricides."

An example of classico - rationalist criticism, from WILLIAM LECKY's *History of European Morals,* 1869.

PART I
THE HISTORICAL IMAGE

CHAPTER I

PRIDE of the masses in birth and circumstance, termed when racially manifest, patriotism, is habitually evoked in the defence either of institutions or ideas. Since his divergence from the lesser forms of creation, man has striven to maintain not only his social organisations, tribal, municipal or imperial, but also, on occasion, the less concrete principles of religion, honour and mental freedom. To-day, as a force in the second quarter of the twentieth century, patriotism is variously regarded. While it remains the opinion of many that immolation in the furthest desert to which their country's sovereignty extends, constitutes the highest form of human expression, there are others who, with parallel intemperance, dismiss every token of national existence as a kind of original sin dating from Louis XIV and George III. Mental patriotism, such as that which fought the Reformation and led England to declare war on Germany in 1914, is viewed by nationalists with less enthusiasm, by "little Englanders" with greater tolerance. But removed from these definitions is another form of pride in which the individual can permit the rest to share ; a form seldom felt, more seldom given words, which transcends the consciousness

3

of this or that tradition, the sunsets of an empire or the concept of a god; which surmounts the barriers not only of political, but of ethical, intellectual and spiritual disagreement. World-consciousness is a commonplace; European already a reality. But the supreme pride is measured not in terms of the existing earth, of temperament and social device, but in divisions of time, in terms of human development—that development, which, whether it prove ultimately progressive or retrograde, is continuous. The instinct is a pride, a patriotism in our age. Sons of fathers, fathers of children, we stand companion to a moment. Let the flag fly, not of lands and waters, morals and gods, but of an era, a generation.

In communion with this apotheosis of the age, this pride in the present's relation to the past and future, there emerges from the furthest antiquity of every country and every race, the science of historical analogy. This process, commonly a mere embellishment of popular writers, makes it possible, by sorting the centennially and millennially repeated incidents and trends of history, to surmise the actual moment of our progress. Civilisations are uncommon phenomena. They are to be distinguished from transitory cultural epochs such as those enjoyed by Periclean Greece and the Italy of the Renascence. Ours is barely come. But not only are we poised on the footboard of the encyclopædic civilisation now being launched; in addition, we are gathered to the brow of infinity by the initial achievement of the scientific revolution.

Thus, like Moses on Nebo, we occupy a vantage-
point: we look both ways: back to Darwinism,
daguerreotypes and railway trains; ahead to mathematical pantheism, television and the colonisation of
the stars. And it is this increasing systematisation
of intuitive analysis, standardisation of old form to
produce new, and interconnection of place, which
distinguishes the oncoming civilisation from its pre-
cursors. Its vitality will endure, as theirs did not,
from the scope and unity of its embrace.

Thus the historian, substituting for the methods of
the pedagogue those of the scientist and the philosopher,
is the high priest of the instant. To assimilate peace-
fully the forces of the advancing epoch, as yet but
faintly discernible on its distant horizon, the world
must revise its conception of the past, distilling from a
recoordination of essential fact, the elements that
have contributed to the immensity upon which it is
about to lay hold. It is the day of historical stock-
taking, when all peoples must bring their achievement
into line with the one universal development of the
future. (Until, when that is interrupted, some classic
Melanesian golden age shall raise a tiny cultured head
and start again.) In place of the presentation of an
unpalatable sequence of incident, sugared with romance
and moulded to the bias of particularist writers—in the
English language usually Protestant or Liberal—the
function of history in this moment of rapid evolution
resolves into a dual purpose: the general, to sift from
the past a philosophic and scientific understanding of

the present in preparation for the future; and in particular, to enumerate and render intelligible any series of events, the consequences of which are liable to affect ensuing generations in an immediate and perceptible manner. In the whole of European history, no moment offers more relevant comparison to our own than that in which Christianity became the state religion of the Roman Empire. A new civilisation was thus born, the nature and achievement of which have remained unintelligible in the centuries of Triumphant Reason that have followed its extinction. Hence, in a single, if yet uncompleted, enquiry, the alliance of Constantine's foundation with such incidents in its legacy as the sack of Smyrna in 1922.

CHAPTER II

As the sapphire and the aquamarine from the turquoise,
so differ the waters of the Ægean from the flat blue of
the Mediterranean whole. Sail from Italy or Egypt.
And as the rose-tinted shores of islands and pro-
montories rise incarnate from the sea, a door shuts the
world behind. Earth's emotion diffuses a new essence.
Who are we to cut the water and cleave the air with
prow and funnel?

Those who sit at home with their anthologies, their
Homers and Byrons, have long grown impatient of the
hackneyed eulogy. Travellers, on the other hand,
know that the poet has not lived who can hackney
the Greek sea itself. How lies it apart? What magnet
of our stifled love hold this blue, these tawny cliffs and
always the mountains framing the distance? Why
does the breeze blow with a scent of baking herbs
which the misty shores echo in their colours? What
is this element, hybrid of air and water, physical as a
kiss, with which the night enfolds us? The islands
float past, forming and reforming in good-bye, gleaming
golden white against the sharp blues, or veiled in the
odorous haze of evening. A silver sheen overspreads
the sea as the ship moves north; the sky grows mild,

hung with ſtationary clouds. Through the ſtraits, all day across the Marmora brings the shadowy cones of the Princes' Islands, and the mirage of Conſtantinople. Then down again beside the rich soil and undulating ranges of Anatolia, to the bay of Smyrna, Rhodes, and below, in the corner, Cyprus. At the foot lies Crete; on the weſt, Corfu. This is the radius of the elusive essence; Byzantium, the keyſtone of its arc. From the southern boundary of Albania to the Asia Minor littoral, the entity is definite as Great Britain or the islands of Japan. Within it, the divinity of earth moves to the brink of tangibility. And if, in the firſt migrations, its cuſtody was vouchsafed a people in whom the queſt of the divine, which diſtinguishes man from beaſt, was already conscious, small wonder that this people has played a significant part in the general evolution of civilisation. Who was this people, favoured above others? What has become of it?

It were futile to deny that, in Anglo-Saxon parlance, the term " Modern Greek " is flavoured with a suspicion of contempt as inevitable as that aroma of human perfeƈtion which attaches to Ancient. When it was discovered, in the opening years of the nineteenth century, that the wild tribes of the Peloponnese, among whom four centuries' alien misrule had rendered outlawry the only honourable profession, were not imbued with the heroic virtues so conspicuously absent in the contemporary ſtates of Weſtern Europe, the world of the Greek revival received the intelligence with pain.

Balm, however, was forthcoming in the writings of Fallmerayer, whose history of the Morea, published in the thirties, convinced a Europe anxious to believe it that the " Modern Greek " was of Slavonic origin. With sensation of relief, it was decided that the descendants of Pericles and Pheidias were extinct. The word degenerate, brandished with such potent futility by Gibbon, was borrowed from the ashes of the empire to decry the foundations of the kingdom. From then onwards the world at large, eyes riveted on the dead pillars of the Parthenon, has discounted the inhabitants beneath them as the unmoral refuse of mediæval Slav migrations, sullying the land of their birth with the fury of their politics and the malformation of their small brown bodies.

But within the last few decades there has arisen, in face of the prejudice of scholarship, the science of anthropology. It has therefore become possible to determine, without further question, the racial origins of Ancient, Byzantine and Modern Greeks.

In the early neolithic age the whole area of land between Great Britain and Somaliland was inhabited by a genus of delicately built brunets, which have been termed by modern scientists the Brown or Mediterranean race. Gradually the sphere of its predominance was encroached upon by Teutons in the north, Nubians in the south; till at length it survived only in a majority on the Mediterranean littoral. Subject to that limitation, it may be classified, speaking of physical characteristics, in four main families, of which the

Pelasgians—to borrow a name from Herodotus—inhabited Greece, the Archipelago, and the west coast of Asia Minor. That this people, or more accurately this branch, was possessed, before the advent of the Indo-European Hellenes, of a civilisation capable of high development and assimilation, is demonstrated in the artistic and domestic achievement of the Minoan era in Crete, for which it must have been mainly responsible. Additional, though less sophisticated, remains of its culture are to be found in the monuments of the Etruscans, a branch of the Pelasgians migrated to Italy.

At length, from that uncharted fount, the home of the Aryans, the magic Hellenes brought their powers of reasoning, their perception of form and their language. These they imposed on the Pelasgians. In the representational arts, the period of fusion, prior to the wholesale preponderance of the Hellenic culture, produced those coloured portrait busts, superior to anything that formerly came out of Egypt, or later of Greece, which are now in the Acropolis Museum at Athens. Even Herodotus admits that the Hellenes always remained a minority in the country of their invasion; racially they were almost immediately assimilated. None the less, this combination, of which, in our everyday speech, the adjective is " Greek," was a successful one. It laid one of the three foundations of that European civilisation which has now engulfed the globe. Its cultural influence was felt from Gibraltar to Peking, from the wall of Hadrian to the roots of the

Nile, even in the centuries of its inauguration. Where its people was predominant, there also was prosperity. With the submersion of the Greeks, poverty and misgovernment fastened on their home, the shores of the eastern Mediterranean.

Meanwhile, during the intervening years, the whole Brown Race, particularly in Italy and Spain, has become diluted with foreign stock. This process was the work of the barbarian invasions that followed the fall of the West Roman Empire, from which the Byzantine sphere, but for occasional and impermanent incursions, was immune. Thus, of the four families into which the Brown Race was originally divided, that in which the physical characteristics correspond most markedly with those exhibited by the anatomical remains of the original stock, is the Greek. The theory of Slavic origin, derived from a superficial observation of village names in the neighbourhood of Athens, is as plausible as a deduction from the place-terminations of -wick and -by, that all Englishmen are descended from Danes. The popularity of Fallmerayer's opinions has been heightened by the illusion of blond giants which the familiar white marble statues of Greece present. It is simultaneously forgotten that chiselled noses, proud lips and rounded chins are still Greek features, though seldom found in coincidence, and not always easy to distinguish beneath straw hats and tooth-brush moustaches.

Thus, in so far as anthropology is better qualified to offer decision than any branch of scholarship, the defini-

tion of the Greek remains in the twentieth century
what it always was: a unit of the old Mediterranean
stock possessing an Aryan culture, akin to that of the
Scythians and Sarmatians, engrafted on its own. But
beyond the identity of bones and skulls, there exists,
for the man in the street, more convincing proof.
Since the moment of history's earliest acquaintance
with the Greeks, the essential qualities of their character have descended through the greatness of the
Byzantine, and the degradation of the Ottoman,
Empires, unchanged. The travelling pedagogue, who
admits the existence of the native population only to
lament the absence of that vacuous perfection which
he conceives to have been the Hellenic physiognomy,
will maintain an opposite opinion. But it is doubtful
whether, amid his texts and annotations, he has ever
acquired sufficient acquaintance with human character
to divest his heroes of their heroics and discover the
men beneath. Those, however, who have drunk the
humanities as a medicine rather than an intoxicant, will
recognise in the modern Greek mentality and temperament, the counterpart of the ancient. The history of
a people is not possible until the degree of constancy
in its character is determined.

Fundamentally, the salient and most permanent
impulse of the race, is an avid curiosity. The zeal
for knowledge, which inspired the first philosophers
and the first scientists, differed in no way from that to
which St Paul, in an age of new necessity, cast the

bait of the Unknown God. To-day the "men of Athens" still greet one another with the words "τί νέον—what news?" and await an answer. In the country a regular formula of personal interrogation is the preliminary to all hospitality. There results from this insatiable attitude of enquiry, a universal, and to the Briton, extraordinary, respect for learning, for books as books, and for any aspect of cultural ability. From the highest to the lowest, even to the illiterate, this national trait has endured through the ages. And, as might be expected from an acquaintance with either the Ancients or the Byzantines, history is regarded as a recreation rather than a study, the leading newspapers exhibiting daily columns from the pens of its foremost professors.

The perpetual dissatisfaction with the outward semblance of things also engenders, as it always did, a depreciatory clarity of vision. The Greeks, in contrast with the English, are lacking in that quality of self-deception which so assists a moral people in its dubious enterprises. Though capable of untruth in pursuance of an aim, with themselves they are honest. They employ fact in both speech and literature, to the detriment of those decencies which Anglo-Saxons prize above truth. And it is to this exercise of semi-cynical, semi-satirical insight into the weakness of human motive, that they owe the genuine, passionate spirit of democracy which they translated into political science, which was the foundation of the Byzantine monarchy, and with which they are still imbued. Through 3000 years Greek history exhibits no vestige of a caste system. The pedestals of popular esteem are, and always have been, reserved for men of learning, servants and private benefactors of the state, and occasional families who have enjoyed a record of public service through two or three generations.

It is not, however, to be supposed that the Greek is inquisitive only in the manner of the savage. He is gifted, in addition, with a uniform standard of intelligent ability, such as characterises, for instance, the Jew. In this " quick-wittedness " the contrast is especially marked between himself and the other Balkan races, Rumanian, Bulgar, Serb and Albanian. In addition he is spurred, as a rule, by ambition. As trader and financier, it is said that " though second to the Armenian, he can surpass the Jew." In this respect one fact is certain: throughout history, the prosperity of the Levant, an area where important trade-routes and natural riches coincide in astonishing profusion, has varied and will continue to vary with his political fortune.

Save when an opportunity for actual participation in the affairs of the state presents itself, their discussion constitutes, without rival, his national recreation. Those who have moved among the English working classes testify unanimously that their interest in politics is aroused only during the transitory excitement of elections. In Greece, so alive among the obscurest grades of society is the tradition of every man's partnership in the conduct of the country, that parliamentary government is rendered almoſt impossible, unless supported by the ſteadying loyalty that attaches to a throne. This latter the Byzantines possessed ; while the popular vice, argument, was diverted to the less deſtructive province of theology. To-day the political recrudescence of this vice is focused in countless newspapers, whose acrid party columns vividly recall the petty ſtates and infantile wars of the classical era. But, beneath the surface currents of recrimination, there flows a deep religious patriotism, a myſtical faith in the Hellenic deſtiny, which is fundamentally different from the chauviniſt imperialism of the Weſt. Corollary of this is an insane party loyalty, which can agitate the domeſtic life of the country to an inconceivable degree. In both national and party causes, the Greeks are indefatigable propagandiſts. Hence, in these spheres, truth is often elusive. Similar taſtics in business dealings lead them to excesses, which those whom they outwit term dishoneſty and double-dealing. In this conneſtion, however, it is impossible to discount the effeſt of four centuries' misrule and insecurity, from which a large proportion of the population has been not twenty years delivered. And it may be noticed, in passing, that the corruption of public servants and members of the Government is not praſtised with the open complacency that prevails among the other Balkan countries and in the United States of America.

The people are devoutly religious and devoutly superſtitious ; though their aspirations of soul have never been systematically diverted to the purposes of an institution by the exploitation of superstition, as in Latin countries. Towards nature, flowers, trees and birds, they feel a romantic, almost spiritual love. This, owing to its having attained widest expression in the writings of antiquity, is often termed pagan, as though it were in contradiction to Christianity.

Finally, and most essential clue to their character through the ages, the Greeks are imbued with the same conceit as they ever were—a conceit so cosmic, deified, part of the order of existence, that outward expression of it is superfluous and its ultimate discovery leaves the stranger with a sense of shock. European neither in fact nor feeling, they talk of " Europe " as somewhere else, and regard foreigners, though with tolerance and sometimes affection, as lacking in those essential qualities which have always constituted the Hellenic superiority over " the barbarians." This conceit renders them impulsive and, therefore, physically brave ; it also deprives them of sound judgment in moments of crisis. Since the War of Independence they appear to have been inspired with a singular devotion towards Great Britain, which originated in gratitude, and has been maintained by the Greek appreciation of the element of justice in British character. If proof of their constancy in friendship be desired, it is forthcoming in the fact that, despite the events between 1914 and 1923, this feeling has remained.

Such in retrospect and present fact, is the Greek

charaĉter. A clever, conceited and enquiring race, intensely political and intensely democratic, reserved in its friendships, conservative in its beliefs, commercially gifted, responsive to the emotions of nature and religion, the Greek people has endured, poised between Eaſt and Weſt, child of neither, yet receptive to both. Originally an alloy, it ſtood like a new metal, bridge from Africa and later Asia, to carry north-weſt the foundations of a world-civilisation. This work accomplished, it has preserved the identity of which that world then ſtrove to rob it. But how is it that the world, the barbarians, contemptuous as they are contemptible, are ſtill concerned with the exiſtence of the Greeks at all? Whence has the flood of their misrepresentation been unloosed? The source is found in that curious mixture of sincere and artificial enthusiasm, Philhellenism.

The moſt frequent manifeſtations of this peculiar mental ſtate, both in print and life, are the outcome of that jejune philosophy of living, which is the laſt heritage of the classical scholar. Student, ultimately interpreter, of Greek texts; endowed with a kindred love of exaĉt reasoning and exaĉt representation, together with a kindred absence of hiſtorical perspeĉtive and emotional outlet; he has fabricated from literature and ſtones an ideal of humanity, which he and his following have pronounced applicable to eternity. It is the singular odium of this eternal comparison, for centuries the bane of European culture, which necessi-

17

tates, once and for all, the relegation of classicism to its juſt place in the tale of human development.

In hiſtory alone, the paper Philhellenes may be held responsible for as great a volume of calculated misrepresentation as the prieſtly editors of the Old Teſtament. Fanatically jealous for their idols' preſtige, they visit the virtues of the fathers upon the twentieth-century children with a malignity so familiar that further mention of it is unnecessary. Flouting the rudiments of anthropology, dating a quarter of a century back, they continue to propagate the thesis that the ancient Greek was a Nordic giant, and that the modern is a Slav dwarf. In face of common-sense euphony, they persiſt in maintaining a pronunciation invented by the ignorant English scholars of the sixteenth-century, which utters " bazilews " for βασιλεύς inſtead of " vassilefs," " kilioy " for χίλιοι inſtead of " hilii "—thus rendering moribund a language which, after two millenniums, differs from Euripides considerably less than modern English from Chaucer. Though aware, if pretending to culture (which they possibly do not) that a cursive Greek hand has exiſted for more than a thousand years, they ſtill compel submissive pupils to perform their conjugations in a disjointed and hideous script, thus dissipating the short hours of youth, and the ſtraitened incomes of its progenitors, in useless effort. Finally, they range themselves in support of a cynical world's opinion that the twentieth century Hellene is no more than a negligible assemblage of human vices. Only the Byzantine era, being past, and in any case beyond their understanding, is spared the aggregate of their vituperation. But even those familiar with the eternal dotage of our Universities, will scarcely believe that at Oxford, until as late as 1924, Gibbon's *Decline and Fall* was still presented as a set book to candidates about to embark on two years' study, not of literature, but history.

Apart, however, from the perversion of truth, an art which is necessarily unbecoming in the paid instructors of youth, there is about the textual Philhellene a negative vacuity which betrays him. Artistically, his appreciations are those of an unsuccessful photographer. That " art translates inward meaning into visible form " is a principle as alien to his understanding as the paintings of El Greco which illustrate it. Amid the mysterious glory of St Sophia, or the pungent energy of modern industrial creation, he aches for the neat refinements of the Parthenon. In short, he is complacent. He seeks, as life progresses, not the exquisite acutening of his aspirations and their infinite expansion, but plain, unrippled attainment. Whether a participant in the age-old conspiracy of pedagogues to sacrifice the intellect of the universe to the retention of their incomes, or simply dilettante offspring of their misguidance, he is liable to succeed in his ambition. Let us leave him content, a dog with his bone. Let us regulate, also, the proportion of his importance.

Less subterraneously destructive than cultural Philhellenism, is its political counterpart, which has served, nevertheless, to sustain a mirror of equal distortion. First exposed to ridicule by the unruly dissensions between the brigand and the educated contrivers of Greek Independence at the time of Byron's death, it has since degenerated into that negative and unprofitable emotion, the abstract hatred of the Turk. Always a minor tenet of English Liberalism, this sentiment was first given prominence by its inclusion in Gladstone's mission to mankind during the Midlothian election of 1876. Echoed by the same sonorous lips twenty years later, and with such violence that Lord Rosebery, then leader of the Liberal party, was obliged to resign ; and espoused since by succeeding disciples ; it has not only wearied the general public with repetition ; but has provoked an inevitable reaction in favour of a race possessing aristocratic manners and a fondness for the horse. During the late wars and conferences, the intemperance of propagandist pamphlets, filled with such arguments as that, in the absence of brothels in Athens, Greeks deserved an empire in Asia, added to the scepticism with which political Philhellenism was viewed. In 1919, while Venizelos was being hailed in the West as the one living " undegenerate descendant of Pericles," the fate of Constantinople was under discussion among the colossi. The theory that the city was Roman in origin and had remained Roman until 1453, was accepted both by those who had been taught its history, and those who had not. Was not Justinian, who built St Sophia, the great codifier of Roman Law? And why, asked the Vatican, publicly at odds with the

"rival pope on the Bosporus," upset the balance of
the world "for the sake of a Church?" The months
dragged on; the world wanted peace and the Greeks
were causing war. At length came the disaster,
acclaimed by the English press to overthrow the states-
man whose policy had engendered it. Political Philhellenism was finally discredited.

What then is real Philhellenism? What has inspired
and still inspires strangers from northern lands and
other continents, to fight, or die, or give the remainder
of their lives to Greece? Is it hexameters and lifeless
stone? Is it the abstract of freedom, or the hatred of
infidel misgovernment? Is there, in fact, explanation?
When a man is drawn to a woman, he may want her
body; there is explanation in that. But when he falls
in love, motive defies analysis. The Greek sea-board
is also of two elements. In the brown mountains, the
rosy air and the sapphire sea; in the golden temples
and classic sites; in the broken churches and luminous
mosaics, sad residue of the Empire; in the temperament of the people itself; in these lies the body. And
the other? It is the essence which defines the *Romiosyni*,
the Greek world, and eludes the comprehension of man.
Byron knew it. When he set sail the second time for
Greece, invested with all the paraphernalia of mock-
romance, he alone, of all his contemporaries, harboured
no illusions of "a race of heroes." He said once, to a
friend, who had suggested visiting Homeric sites in
Thrace : "Do I look like one of those emasculated

fogies? Let's have a swim. I detest antiquarian twaddle." For Greeks, the epitaph of the greatest Philhellene is written in those words: " Let's have a swim."

Exactly a century ago, the road of practical Philhellenism was plain. The Greeks were fighting, before Italy or Germany or any of the Balkans had fought, to regain national existence. Philhellenes fought with them. To-day that existence is assured. Practical Philhellenism must be the Philhellenism of reconstruction.

The last fifty years have witnessed the expansion of European civilisation over the whole of the globe. In the process, European ideals, if they have gained new impetus, have suffered dilution. There is not, as it were, sufficient of the original force to maintain the quality of the whole output. As the central dynamo, Europe must continue, a century and more yet, to play her part. All available resources must be brought into action. And in the rehabilitation of our continent, of primary importance is the Levant. Endowed with a profusion of agricultural, mineral and oleous wealth; the cross-roads of trade between Russia and Egypt, between Europe and the East; heritage of a race industrious, commercial and uncloyed by empty dreams of political grandiosity; the littoral of the eastern Mediterranean, whither formerly flowed riches unknown even to the Incas, lies unhappy and penurious, lacking a circulating force to stir the potentialities of soil, sea and people: potentialities, in which may lie the future of Europe and then the future of the earth. That circulating force has arisen, and will only arise, in the political well-being of the Greeks. The twentieth century is likely to witness a bitter intensification of that covetous regard for the Near East, which was formerly the monopoly of Russia. The Levant is the concern of all. And it is to illustrate how the potentialities of the Levant once flowered, and can flower again, that this volume is written.

Let those in whose common sense this appeal finds response, go and see for themselves. They will find, after all, a higher form than the Philhellenism of reconstruction; a Philhellenism not of the mind, but of the soul. Let us, also, they will say, have a swim.

CHAPTER III

FROM sifting the numerous implications of meaning attaching to the word " civilisation," there emerges a definition, which presumes it to consist in the vitality of three elements in man's corporate mode of living. These are: the Stable; the Transcendental; and the Cultural. Vitality in each simultaneously is seldom found, save in large cities whence they radiate their combined influence throughout their city's dominion. And the rarity of even this coincidence constitutes the rarity of civilisations. Failure in the vitality of any one of them denotes a lapse from true civilisation to conditions of life comparable with those of fifteenth century Italy or the present Middle West of the United States.

First essential to the definition of civilisation is the stable element, the universal confidence in the social organism to maintain itself and its government, and to modify itself to external and internal necessity. This confidence, when it exists, pervades people unconsciously. Security of property, the standards of living, the countless services of local government—all go for granted without thought or investigation, like the sun and the stars, symbolised in those outward features, dinner-jackets, bathrooms and asphalt roads, which evoke the awe and envy of less advanced peoples.

Second is that composite element in human activity, the quest of transcendental values and their collateral ethics. To every race, in infancy and succeeding childhoods, is vouchsafed the concept of a God. This, ultimately, may lose identity in that of a gentleman. But underneath social demeanour, there remains to man his soul proper, his own greatness, his unquiet spirit seeking cosmic direction, ever striving to soar above the mental gravities of earth. It is contended that civilisations such as that upon which we are entering, retard the divine quest in humanity by the very security with which they encushion it against the fundamental workings between man and earth, man and man, man and God. But it remains to be seen whether those relationships do not, as the scientific revolution approaches its climax, attain a depth and precision of definition hitherto undreamed. And the soul, mathematically propelled, may redouble the exploration of its Affinity in space, dictating, with historical experience as its partner, successive codes and morals for the earth.

Third and final element in civilisation is the cultural, product of the scientific and artistic impulse generated by a corporate intellectual activity. It is in this province that the inspired individual souls of an age become accessible to the majority, whose diversity of intelligence and occupation will not permit their investigation of the mysteries with which they are communicant, but not, beyond the one-sided peep-hole of religion, conversant.

The stable, the transcendental, the cultural: genii of civilisation. Each has existed without the others. Hellas had Culture, Judah a Soul, Renascence Europe both. The United States of America now enjoy the blessings of Stability. But it is the fusion of the three that constitutes a civilisation, the vitality of which will vary inversely with the deficiency in any one of them. We in Europe, sponsors of a civilisation which posterity will term the most momentous phenomenon in history, are conscious of the necessity to hold the balance between them, if less certain of the ability. And it is at this point that the relevance of civilisation's analysis in connection with the eastern Mediterranean becomes clear. Only once, during the whole history of our continent and all the peoples that have contributed to our present, has this balance been discovered; and once discovered maintained for nine centuries; to contend against the agony of dissolution for another two. This was behind the walls, and within the sphere, of Constantinople.

Thus, in considering the rôle of the Levant during the convulsions of the early twentieth century, it is to be remembered that not only may the population of the Ægean coasts contribute a larger share to the maintenance of our present vital civilisation than is popularly supposed; but that it, Greek, alone of European races, has experienced such a phenomenon in the past. Culture it had. Out of the East rose a soul. From the West marched stability. The soul transformed the culture, the culture the soul. And the Byzantine civilisation, the joyous life that once crowded on the Golden Horn and flourished in woods and gardens by the sweet waters of Asia, has left a heritage to the world and its imprint uneffaced upon the Levant. Its interest in the present derives partly from the state of its people to-day; and partly from its share in the formation of, and in its affinity with, its universal successor of the West.

In considering the stability of the social edifice, the affinity between Western and Byzantine civilisation is both external and internal.

In the external relations of its political units, the chief hope of the modern world lies in the elimination of the armed and insular state, and the aggressive racial consciousness of its inhabitants. It was this spirit, though confined within the smaller units of municipalities, which reduced ancient Greece to the point of extinction. Hellenic culture, art, science, literature and philosophy, were saved only through the medium of the Roman Empire; and at long last through the creation, culminating in the transference of the capital to Constantinople, of an international spirit that was, in fact, an all-pervasive Hellenism. More influential, still, in this process of transcending racial barriers, was Christianity, newly adopted as the state religion. For it was in this process that lay the strength and cohesion of the Byzantine Empire. The world of the present

27

day offers a comparison almost exactly similar. The European countries correspond to the city states of Greece ; the range of Anglo-Saxon institutions to that of Roman; Europeanism to Hellenism; and the intellectual effect of the scientific revolution to Christianity. It may be argued that, far from creating an international spirit, the British Empire has done no more than propagate an evil nationalism. During the last half-century, the charge may hold good. But by its work of Europeanisation, of which, indeed, it is only the foremost exponent, it has laid a common ground on which the peoples of the world may find the basis of international concord. This also, on a lesser territorial scale, did Constantinople accomplish. Within her walls mingled all the races of Eurasia, and all their products, commercial, cultural, philosophical. And even now, after all her centuries of misfortune, the same races jostle in Constantinople and the ghost of the old cosmopolitan ideal pervades the city. For the Greeks she has no name : she is " ἡ πόλις—the capital." And her present Greek inhabitants, should the traveller ask their nationality, are still " Ρωμηοί —Romans." To them, a precarious 400,000, has the Byzantine identity descended.

It is widely believed that the Anglo-Saxon political ideal, lately swallowed undigested by the world, affords the greatest promise to any people of internal strength. In so far as generalisation is possible, this ideal may be termed a perpetual seeking to readjust the equilibrium which enables the state to care for the interests of the individual without prejudice to its own. Failure to maintain this equilibrium must result either in disruption, as in the case of the Roman Empire, or in the forging of hard, aggressive political units, such as Europe has endured ever since. In the light of this ideal, the internal structure of the Byzantine state bears, if not a physiognomic likeness, a singular affinity to that of ourselves: the same equilibrium, if by different means, is held; the difference in means arising from the fact that instead of, as with us, developing compactly as a manifestation of national life, this equilibrium was the result of two diverse and opposite forces. For the internal strength of the Byzantine Empire was attained by the imposition of a supremely practical machinery of government upon the most individualistic people on earth.

The previous chapter has attempted to analyse that satirical element in Greek character which must always ensure democracy wherever there are communities of Greeks, and has always prevented the arising of those aristocratic and priestly caste systems, which have only, during the last twenty years, ceased to be the inevitable outcome of the search for Stability in the older continents. The Byzantine state does not, it must be admitted, present at first sight a democratic complexion. But it may be borne in mind that the Greeks, while able to discern in all men the failings that make all men equal, are capable of an almost superstitious veneration for traditions and institutions. It was this faculty, already permeated, in the fourth and

29

fifth centuries A.D., with the deeper and more austere mysticism of the Aramean peoples, which enabled them to accept and consolidate the Eastern conception of sovereignty that beat like a strong man's heart for eleven centuries within the walls of Constantinople. The Emperor, ruling or fighting, was the viceregent and vicegerent of God; to God he was responsible. But he was also a man, and as such, bound by the laws of his other self's making. The support of the people was given not to his person, but his office, to his crown, his sceptre, and the mystical procession of his days. In their eyes, the partition or even usurpation of his functions was justified by the subsequent success of the usurper. Further, the Emperor was in theory, and frequently in fact, chosen by election, by the Senate, the Army, and the People in the Hippodrome. Equally might this triple ratification be revoked. The balance between individualism and political efficiency in the Byzantine state was maintained by an Oriental autocracy fettered by a Roman bureaucracy and supported by a Greek democracy. And it may be doubted whether the Mediterranean peoples will ever evolve a better system of government. Contemporary events seem to show that it is only the non-political temperament of the Northern races, which can withstand the dissensions of parties and parliaments.

Thus, in its relations both with subjects and tributaries, was the stability of the Empire based on principles such as our own. In the transcendental sphere the affinity is harder of definition. It may perhaps be expressed in the quality of discontent with the material aspect of things, which is common to both. In the mind of mediæval West, man existed only in terms of theology, in his relation to God. Though the Byzantines were the parents of that mind, they themselves, in constant communion with the classics, never wholly lost sight of man's rational dignity. In the West, after the Renascence and the Reformation, such was the reaction, that only the rational remained—to bring, ultimately, the scientific revolution. But it is science, in its revelation of the irrational, that has again revived for us the compromise enjoyed by the Byzantines. Certainly our determination of man has not reverted to the theological. But it recognises and fosters man's aspirations to discover the Spirit and Reality of his world. What the Byzantine sought through Christ, we may through a mathematical rationalisation of the intuitions. The goal is the same. Had Christianity remained as the Byzantines perfected it, and not been distorted by the common sense of the Latin peoples and the romantics of the Northern, it might have merged harmoniously with the present mode of thought. That now is not possible. But if the errant soul of the twentieth century is to gauge the extent of its predecessors' achievement, the ungrudging recognition of Christianity's service in rescuing man from the earthen fetters of classicism is essential. The Byzantines and all their works were consecrated to the dominion of soul over mind. We and ours too. But the mind was to them, and should be for us, the inﬆrument of its own subordination. This precept Weﬆern Europe has never, hitherto, accepted.

More plainly, however, than in the ﬆable and transcendental elements of a civilisation, it is in its culture that is reﬂeﬄed with greateﬆ prospeﬄ of endurance for poﬆerity, its charaﬄer and the personality of its people. And nowhere is the affinity between Conﬆantinople and the early induﬆrial era of the twentieth century more easily visible than in the provinces of art and architeﬄure. Againﬆ the ponderous complacence of classicism, the ﬆationed symmetry, the reasoned representation; againﬆ the whole implied negation of the beyond and the before ; there rises in the two parallel ages a queﬆ of movement and emotional expression, which burﬆs the confinement of capital and cornice, and spurns the suave contours of rotund boys and bolﬆered urns. This vigour derives in one case from Chriﬆianity, in the other from science, each the new force of its time, carrying Reason to the service of the irrational. Form and technique, moreover, both the Byzantine and the modern have sought, not locally, but universally, not from set canons of proportion and preconceived ideas of grace, but from the whole multitude of methods of artiﬆic expression with which the scope of their influence has brought them in contaﬄ.

It is a far cry from the squat bulk of St Sophia to the windows of a modern block of offices. Yet the breath of both carries the eye away to a suggestion of something beyond the material substances of brick and stone and the fashioning of human hands. In a classical building the vision of the beholder, moving up the pillars, is brought gradually to rest by the projecting encrustations of the capital, to be finally deflected to earth by the sharp edge of the cornice. In a Byzantine, though superficially many of the forms are inherited, the capital is expressly carved to carry the eye on upward, and there is no cornice. Inside and out, in all the buildings of the Empire, from the great domed mass of St Sophia to the fortified monasteries of Athos, the hint of perpendicular activity persists. Only in Tibet, which shares with the latter the distinction of political theocracy in the twentieth century, is analogy forthcoming. The cardinal importance of the subordination of all external ornament to the passage of the eye is exemplified, for contemporaries, in the town hall at Stockholm or, on a lesser scale, in the Cenotaph in Whitehall.

From the East also arrived, in the train of Christianity, the art of interpreting form; which not only rendered Byzantines the most perfect artificers of pattern that have ever been; but enabled them, in relief, mosaic and painting, to substitute an expressed insight into the symbolism of the object portrayed for the prevalent surface-representation of the Hellenistic era. The apotheosis of this method was reached in the paintings of Domenicos Theotocopoulos, commonly known as El Greco. And by him, alone favoured to

33

carry the thousand year old artistic tradition of Constantinople to fruition, has been expressed more absolutely than by any other artist, that elusive constancy of things which the twentieth century has set itself to recapture. All art and all science seeks ultimately what cannot be attained. If Greco, the Byzantine, has reached further than his fellows, let the present age congratulate itself that, in contrast to its predecessors, it does at least hold the goal in sight.

Thus, in terms of the three elements of civilisation, is the Byzantine affinity with ourselves revealed. The sympathies of a new era, in which nationalism, dogmatism and classicism have ceased to hold all the field, reveal a forgotten light in the past. But it is not merely that the light has lain hid in gentle obscurity, that the memory of the old Greek Empire had lapsed, after 1453, into beneficent oblivion. In the whole annals of the world's history there has survived the record of no civilisation which has been subject to such conscious misinterpretation as the Byzantine. The gall of that jealous and illiberal culture, which fastened on Europe as the backwash of the Renascence, has been loosed upon that which it cannot comprehend.

This attitude of prejudice in the Western mind dates originally from mediæval times, product of that fortress of rational outlook, the Roman Church. In 1054, the papal legates laid their anathema on the altar of St Sophia. Thenceforth, in the eyes of the West, the followers of the Orthodox Church were heretics who had disrupted the spiritual lordship of the Pope in Rome. Forty years later, in the guise of the first crusade, the Eastern Empire was invaded by the vast host of beggars, dotards, prostitutes and children, that had flocked to the call of Peter the Hermit. At their head rode the freebooting chivalry of Europe, to implant a retrograde feudalism and hostile Church in the ancient territories of the Byzantine dominion. Throughout the twelfth century the armies of Western Europe appeared and reappeared, ravaging where they trod. The cultured and civilised Greeks, contemptuous and resentful, remained aloof. And such cross-bedizened champions as survived the disasters of Asia Minor, jealous of the prosperous life of the Empire, returned to fill Western Europe with tales of the perfidy and treachery of the schismatics of Constantinople. " Those who were not for us were against us," was the cry. Thenceforth an odium has attached to the Byzantines which has augmented rather than diminished with time.

With the close of the Middle Ages, intellectual progress was diverted to the channels prescribed by the classical model. While the lamps of Hellas glowed once more, and provincial Athens, conveniently inaccessible, assumed an unfamiliar eminence as the former nursery of human perfection, Greek civilisation and its capital had disappeared from the horizon. But not for always. In 1734 the sluice-gates were opened by Montesquieu's *Causes de la Grandeur des Romains et leur Décadence.* And in 1776 there appeared the

35

first volume of Gibbon's *History of the Decline and Fall of the Roman Empire*.

As a master of historical technique, Gibbon is without equal. By means of his torrential style, his restrained impropriety, and the incomparable sarcasm of his attacks upon the bore of his own and others' adolescence, Christianity, he has made history an entertainment to more people than any single man. Simultaneously he has achieved another superlative distinction. Accurate in every statement of his work, there has lived no individual writer responsible for a greater volume of inferential falsehood than he. Since his advent, successive generations have sincerely subscribed to his view that the most important civilisation previously evolved in Europe was no more than a Decline and a Fall. Of all histories, that of Constantinople is least capable of biographical treatment. Following his method, there might be compiled with equal regard for fact and disdain of truth, a chronicle of the American continent from the sexual shortcomings of transatlantic presidents, fortified by an implicit belief in the veracity of the Hearst press.

The achievement, apart from the affinity with the present, of Byzantine civilisation, may be summarised in two relations : to its people, and to us.

To its people, politically, the Empire stood, a valid organism for all but nine centuries; and a courageous organism still for two more. Not once during that time did the form of government change. Of the 88 occupants of the imperial throne, 66 ascended by regular procedure. And of the 22 usurpers, the majority followed one another over small periods of years, which comprised only temporary interludes in the peaceful working of the whole.

Spiritually, it is doubtful whether there has ever existed, over so long a period of time, so large a proportion of men and women, under one government, deeply and sincerely anxious to maintain communion with their God at all moments of their lives. Ethically, public opinion did not necessarily, as in Northern countries, ostracise those who did not conform to its standards.

Culturally Byzantine intellect evolved, in painting and mosaic, a technique of colour and delineation, which envisaged the experiences of the soul as none has done before or since. An essential austerity developed, which a lavish profusion of splendid materials could never deflect ; and which, combined with largeness of general conception, produced, in St Sophia, one of the supreme pinnacles of architecture.

For ourselves, ushers of a universal civilisation, the Empire also stood for 1123 years, a solitary bulwark against the peoples of Asia which threatened, if they broke through, to extinguish that civilisation. How nearly, indeed, they might have succeeded was illustrated afterwards by the two sieges of Vienna and by the two centuries of warfare which stunted the development of central Europe and were the direct result of the disaster of 1453. While Western Europe was assimilating the negative, nomadic forces that broke upon the West Roman Empire, Constantinople was combating the positively destructive impetus unloosed by Mohammed in the seventh century. Throughout, she retained intact the great codifications of Roman law, to the revived study of which at Bologna in the eleventh century, the majority of European legal systems owe their existence.

As spiritual legacy, the Byzantine intellect has left the world the definitions of the seven Œcumenical Councils, which at present form the basis of almost every variation of Christian belief. How far Orthodox dogma may have influenced Hus and Wyclif, is impossible of determination. But it is certain that no sooner did the original texts of the scriptures, preserved by the Greeks in their tongue and developed by the Greek Fathers, pass from the dilettanti of Italy to the ardent commentators of Germany, than the whole monstrous fabric of the mediæval papacy was overthrown. Meanwhile, by the Greek Church, entrusted, since the fall of Constantinople, with the *imperium in imperio* of its people, has been preserved, to be a factor in our present era, the character of the Greek race.

Culturally, to the Byzantines' preference for the classic authors rather than original creation, to their care and infinite copyings, the modern world owes the safe descent of the wisdom of the ancient. In painting, the culminating Byzantine, El Greco, communicated his colour to Velasquez and a fount of inspiration to the twentieth century. Finally, to the Slavs in the tenth and eleventh centuries were imparted those rudiments of literacy which enabled the Balkan races to preserve their identity under the Turk ; and which, in Russia and Czecho-Slovakia, have blossomed into the vanguard of modern intellectual potentiality.

Civilisation, product of the eternal distillation and fusion of human experiment, is conceived mainly in great cities. As the great city of the Middle Ages, Constantinople stands unchallenged. For all but five centuries posterity has passed by, till civilisation has again appeared on posterity's horizon. This new vision gives access, through analogy, to the past. From it rises, as a picture through old varnish, the achievement of the mediæval Greeks.

PART II
THE ANATOMY

CHAPTER IV

THE TRIPLE FUSION

THERE is in man an innate tendency to accentuate his consciousness of the particular units of society to which he may belong. In schools and universities, where the darkeſt elements of human nature are at large, rigid groups of ſtudents look askance at those who go their way untrammelled with the conventions of others. From the earlieſt times, promoters of vice for profit have been relegated to the further side of an imaginary, if salutary pale. Until recently, Chriſtians of one belief could scarcely endure contaĉt with those of another. Associations of employers and employees continue to ereĉt canons of behaviour as exclusive as those of the mediæval guilds.

The ultimate and commoneſt expression of this inſtinĉt has been racial; and its fate, in this respeĉt, political exploitation. In the mind of the Weſt European and his transoceanic offspring—even, lately, of his transoceanic subjeĉt—separate nationality demands separate political exiſtence. It was this creed to which the arbiters of poſt-war reformation at the beginning of the twentieth century were pledged. The occasion to co-ordinate racial with political individuality over vaſt territories where such a theory had been

43

formerly unknown, was hailed with rejoicing. Britain in particular, throned on her strawberry empire, could survey with a tingle of virtuous triumph the kaleidoscope of less favoured *terra firma*. So it has happened that, towards the proper understanding of those areas where unfortunate peoples have been obliged, in self-defence, to adopt the hypotheses of Western nationalism and endure the sufferings that inevitably attend its expansion, the way, which was dark to nineteenth-century statesmen, and black to twentieth, threatens to lapse from human comprehension altogether.

The process in question first took effect as an off-shoot of the French Revolution, as a bastard sister of Liberty. Its immediate field was the Levant; its action, that of a spark to the gunpowder of economic fodder which the Turks called subject races. As the nineteenth century progressed, Serbs, Bulgars and Rumanians, encouraged by the achievements of Bismarck and Garibaldi, emerged in emulation of the Greeks. Eventually came the Great War and the disintegration of the Ottoman Empire. For the Greek world there remained one final separation of races. This was in Thrace and Anatolia. Accomplished, with unrecorded suffering, it was. Yet however complete the execution of that hellish experiment borrowed at Lausanne from the political stock-in-trade of Tamerlane, the exchange of populations, the old forces, if momentarily in abeyance, can never have been extinguished. Trade routes flow. The city stands. There is wealth in the earth. One people dies while another lives. But the cipher of past and future

44

lies far back, in one of those rare occasions when the currents of history have been quickened by the sagacity of a moment. In that moment, the Levant assumed more concrete shape than its own romance; Byzantine civilisation arose; and there came into being a latent force which, four centuries after that civilisation's extinction, could still enable the most inept of human races to uphold the skeleton of its political idea. The Ottoman Empire was the Byzantine Empire; Constantinople the heart of each. On that site to-day, in the midst of high pressure, the balance of jealousy creates a void.

During the three centuries that followed its inauguration by Augustus, the Roman Empire had displayed but small vitality in two out of the three cardinal elements of civilisation. Heaped within the vast embrace of a single law, the countries of the Mediterranean, and those adjacent, and yet again adjacent to them, lay passive beneath the heterogeneous vapour of ideas, arts and cults which swirled from Chester to Bagdad, dropping here, gathering there, but ponderous, derivative, and fruitless as a herd of mules. Culture had turned already to the past, gloating on the Attic model, and for art boasting the advance of copyists. Stability there was; indeed, it has been said that until the advent of trains, European travel was easier in that age than ever before or since. Then that, too, waned. Now the walls of the container threatened to burst : first from within, then without. Legions mutinied, Goths and Parthians rumbled. But towards the end of the third century, movements in the new chaos bespoke the birth of new order. Eaſt and Weſt had fought. They had mingled. Now they were to fuse. The hard ſteel of vital civilisation was imminent. But the base of the alloy was neither Eaſt nor Weſt. It was upon a foundation of Hellenic culture and Hellenic sense, that the well-being of soul and body, genius of Semite and Roman, found union. Thus the three spheres, Weſtern, Oriental and Hellenic, were respectively identified with the ſtable, the transcendental and the cultural elements of the new civilisation. And it was in the realisation, anticipated by Julius Cæsar, that the Greek-speaking coaſts of the Ægean were the true kernel of the Helleniſtic Roman Empire and the chief source of vitality, that the greatness of Conſtantine's change of capital lay.

To the measure of political ſtability enjoyed by the Roman Empire in the opening years of the fourth century, the Hellenic contribution, viewed in light of Conſtantine's impending orientation, had been considerable. The political experience of the Greeks was profound. From monarchy, through oligarchy and tyranny, to democracy, they had evolved the inherent national opinion that politics were every man's business. Further, to the years of this evolution, four or five centuries before Chriſt, the world owes its whole terminology of political thought and science. But it was precisely in these, when translated from word to fact, that the Greeks had failed. The eternal search for a rule of thumb, so successfully pursued in ethics, geometry and art, fell short in the practical struggle with everyday affairs. It needed Alexander and the formation of an empire overseas to test the real vitality of the city-state as a political organism. The centre lapsed. But the great cities of Egypt and Asia Minor maintained an independent existence, flourishing municipalities resembling in character the industrial towns of to-day; till we read, as of New York or New Delhi, that they were better planned, with broad, straight streets, than the old towns of the parent country. It was upon this foundation of Greek municipal life, that the conquests of Pompey and Lucullus were built into the Roman Empire. While the inhabitants of Hellas proper, repelled by the uniform vulgarity of the Roman world, had long relapsed into lethargic though gentlemanly contemplation of the past; while Athens was already provincial and tourist-ridden; Greek life, as the West Roman Empire drew to its close, still retained its vigour in the further cities—a vigour generated by the ceaseless flow of fresh conceptions from the East. With the tread of Goth and Visigoth already in the ear, did not Byzantium promise to become the nucleus, not only of art, intellect and spirit, but of trade and security as well?

This was the Greek foundation of the stable element. The superstructure was Roman, and the cupola Asiatic.

Upon the victory of Augustus at Actium in 31 B.C., the first phase of Roman imperialism, that of expansion, was over. With Cæsar now at the centre, removed above parties and factions, a new system of centralisation came into being. Governors and officials in the provinces were made more fully responsible to Rome. Taxation was revised on the basis of a land- and population-census. Even the senate of the capital was reduced to no more than a constitutional ornament. In every department, the reins were annexed to the Emperor and his household. From this date, and mainly as an outcome of the latter institution, evolved the marvel of Roman bureaucracy, the engine which never faltered till its destruction by the crusaders in 1204. And immediately the career open to talent, which it offered, became largely the prize of a Greek personnel.

But from the reign of Marcus Aurelius (161-180), the Empire found itself on the defensive. Centralisation, now excessive, had rendered the machinery more unwieldy than two and sometimes three Cæsars could administer. The extinction of local patriotism left the burdens of local government to fall wholly on the centre. The pseudo-Robot-like civilisation had flowered and was blown. Education was expensive, yet unproductive of intellectual development; there were philosophies and cults, but no exercise for the soul. Already in the second century A.D., a culture as arid and derivative as that of the eighteenth, was universal. Contemporary with this desiccation, civil wars within and frontier wars without were placing insupportable strain upon an administration designed for consolidation

rather than defence. Collapse was averted by Diocletian, who ascended the throne in 248 A.D.

The half century that followed was momentous. It
witnessed the close of the classical era, and prefaced,
by its reorganisation, the opening of another. As an
age of transition it was an age of suffering. The
spiritual ferment of the East, the infusion of life into
the withering veins of the Empire, were as blood
circulating in a frost-bitten limb. Fortunately for the
course of man's progression, the physicians proved
equal to their patient.

Diocletian's work took the form of decentralisation
and stabilisation. Rome, which had already lost its
capital and economic importance, was abandoned as
the home of the administration; and the Empire was
divided into four great compartments, the officials of
which were now interposed between the provincial
governors and the Emperor. Taxation was redistributed with a view to complete uniformity, assess-
ments being computed not on the acreage, but the
productive value, of land. As a kind of permanent
guarantee of the state revenues, all ranks of society
were made compulsorily hereditary. Children of free
labourers were wedded to the soil, thus rendering
possible the semi-feudal Byzantine land-tenure of the
future. Similarly, membership of the trade- and craft-
guilds passed henceforth from father to son. Even the
burden of unpaid local government was forced on the
shoulders of unwilling descendants. But these reforms
took effect mainly in the East Mediterranean lands, at

the centre of gravity. And thus it was that, during the whole labour of mental and political rebirth which shook the ensuing century, those lands, in contrast with the West, stood firm. Finally, and, in the light of succeeding events, most far-reaching of all, was achieved the hitherto inconceivable separation of the civil and military authorities. Stationary frontier troops were retained. But the main army was now transformed into a mobile force, no longer local in its sympathies, which could be hurried from one end of the Empire to the other as necessity demanded. In this central fighting weapon, even after the first Mohammedan incursions had compelled the Isaurian Emperors to the reorganisation of the themes under military governors, was to lie the infinite superiority of Byzantine arms over all others. Here also was an example that every state in the world was sooner or later to copy.

Above, however, the mere sequence of edicts that led the stark structure of Roman government to its last reformation, there stands that salient gift to posterity, the Roman law. Growth already of many centuries, though not finally perfected till between the years 450 and 564, this supreme outcome of the practical Roman mind was destined to prove the one continuous link between the ancient world and the modern. Its genius had arisen, in the beginning, from the ability to distinguish between Roman national custom and the general principles of justice applicable to all mankind. Put under way by the *Jus Gentium*, its scope had expanded with the Empire; and its cosmopolitanism with the increasing clarification of the general principles on which it was based. Here, of all others, was a quantity calculated to evoke the admiration of ſtrangers and the reſpeēt of subjeēts, especially when the latter were invited to reap its benefits. In conjunētion with the bureaucracy, it conſtituted the whole keyſtone of Byzantine political ſtability.

Thus, upon the municipal remnant of Alexander's Helleniſtic Empire, Roman organisation and Roman law created ſtability, firſt essential of civilisation. As the new forces, Chriſtianity from the Eaſt, the tightened hierarchies of society from the Weſt, marched to their long embrace, one space at the peak remained for the political contribution of the Eaſt. This was the definition of imperial sovereignty. A God above, though nebulous quantity enough to Diocletian, was in the air. The Emperor muſt ſtrengthen his position here below. Accordingly, the title of " Lord," the diadem, and the salutation by proſtration were borrowed from Persia, as Alexander had borrowed them before. And court ritual, the whole of that divinity, to-day rendered doubly subtle by democracy, that hedges a king, was perpetuated for the future entertainment of Europe. Conſtantine, proclaiming himself viceregent and vicegerent of an individual God, carried the idea to its logical conclusion. And it was not long before the Patriarch of Conſtantinople, in imitation of the Magian high-prieſt, cuſtomarily performed the coronation ceremony.

In estimating human achievement, alike in thought and science, politics and the arts, there applies one infallible test of greatness, which invites comparison between the most distant extremes of creation and research. This test, relevant year by year, century by century, so long as the race endures, demands simply, now of yesterday, now across vast interims of time: in what proportion has this or that advanced man towards a further comprehension of Reality, of that " likeness amid diversity " which transcends the world of touch and see, and the conscious quest of which constitutes man's distinction from the ape and gives plausible argument to the theory of progress. In no matter which province of human activity, from each step in the comprehension of the soul's affinities, must result a further expression of them; from each step in expression, a further accessibility to lesser intellects, an advance in the general comprehension of them. Thus the ultimate, like gravity a glacier, draws us slowly down the ages.

But for those lesser intellects, for the great majority of humanity, whose preoccupation with mundane affairs demands the presentation of a ready-made and intelligible abstract, the approach to the eternal problem lies not through the pan-psychology of all things and all times, but through the isolated medium of religion. Religion, if restricted in horizon, is not blind ; it pursues simply the perpetual search through the single most straightforward channel. Whether it advance in the van or the rear of contemporary thought, science, politics or art, they are infused with the extent of its progress as it with theirs. And it has, in fact, happened that the most formidable power ever generated to assist man in his quest, the power vital over the longest succession of years and in the greatest number of hearts, has been a religion. Though it may seem in the present that its course is run, subtract Christianity from the past, and what remains?—the dry sediment of classicism, insensible to the before and the beyond, conscious only of its protracted minute on the clock of perpetuity. Towards perpetuity's end, towards that station where the rails meet and the attainment of the unattainable sifts the abiding from the transient, the acceptance of Christianity by the classical world was the furthest step humanity ever took. The coincidence of the Edict of Milan with the foundation of Con-stantinople, due to the sagacity, rather than inspiration, of one man, produced both modern and Byzantine civilisations. It is therefore of interest to discover what flux of intellectual phenomena could have con-firmed the validity of so momentous a decision; and whence were spun the multitude of threads that Christianity wove to itself, and whereby it found passage to the hearts of its new and unresisting adherents.

The frame upon which the profuse metaphysical speculations of the Roman Mediterranean spluttered to extinction, was the Hellenic subscription to the wholesale efficacy of Reason. With the products of that Reason a primary education in the humanities has rendered us familiar. But of its limitations, of the vacua into which the theology of Eastern mystics rushed like cold air when the hot has lifted, it has hitherto been customary to profess ignorance.

The essence, the fundamental mood of all Greek thought, lay in the problem of the immediate present, in the quest of an *ars vivendi*. Upon this confined, unteleological aspect of existence, the idea of man's spiritual purpose seldom intruded. God was merely a convenient focus for the inexplicable, to be plotted and defined as this or that brand of philosophy demanded. Further, the whole pursuit of " well-being " was based on a short-sighted rationalism which assumed that once man was aware of his true interests, he must be incapable of action contradictory to them. Hence the grotesque slogan " Virtue is knowledge "; the implicit belief in the panacea of truth; and the consequent distrust of all instinct and all compromise, the major conditionals of any *ars vivendi*. This elevation of the mind to supreme control will inevitably find supporters in that class of persons who are more concerned with intellectual processes than the goals to which they lead. But in the majority of human beings, the speculative faculty is either absent or subordinate. Among the masses of the Roman Empire, Greek thought, the kingdom of the mind, had never wholly conquered.

There flourished, however, during the three centuries that separated Christ's birth from his acceptance by Constantine, two schools of philosophers whose doctrines, each of Greek origin, held paramount import-

54

ance in the ancient world. These were the Stoics and the Neoplatonists. Each contributed, both in concrete idea and in psychological preparation of the ground, to the eventual triumph of Christianity.

The Stoics, though still obsessed with the theory that man could not act contrary to his reason, did at length succeed, as Socrates had foreshadowed, in investing ethics with a definition independent of mere service to the state. For them, moreover, "God" assumed concrete meaning in abstract terminology, as a species of universal force, of which the soul was but a spark at exercise within the human clay, and the vehicle of homage to the whole. This insistence on the ubiquity of God was reflected in their conception of the human race as one cosmopolitan brotherhood. Through this, combined with the enunciation of a practical morality and an almost Rotarian doctrine of service to others, they forcibly appealed to the mental state disseminated by Roman rule, in which efficiency stood foremost among the virtues. It is clear, from the most cursory examination of their tenets, that the practical principles which Christianity was to popularise among the masses, were largely of their determining.

It was to the other and mystical side of the new religion that Neoplatonism, last, and as an evolutionary link, most significant, in the cycles of Greek thought, contributed. This philosophy, originating in Roman Alexandria was born of a definite contact with the East, in the form of advanced Judaism and early Christianity, which enabled it to develop the germ of Plato's un-

Greek and perhaps involuntary mystical experience. Its portentous feat, and one which stands alone in the classical world, was the renunciation of the supremacy of the rational for that of the suprarational. The very existence, implicit in the process of reasoning, of divergent opinion, seemed to demand an Absolute removed from the infinity of human disagreement. To this Absolute, invested by Plotinus with a more compact, individual quality than Plato's common factor to all material phenomena, approach was possible by experience rather than thought, by a process of contemplation that should ultimately lead the soul to escape from the shame of its imprisonment and to self-identification with Reality. This was the first clear denial of the fallacy, which formerly excused suicide, that balm to an aching heart must be sought from the intellect. But in common with all Greek thought, Neoplatonism lacked means to attract the masses, the personality of a founder or the offer of celestial reward. And eventually lapsing, despite their affinity, into conflict with Christianity, it fell back upon the tradition that it had itself discredited and developed a kind of bastard rationalism, which flourished amid the provincial conservatism of Athens till the closing of the pagan academy in the sixth century. But the affinity in the beginning was real enough. In the Neoplatonic appreciation of the suprarational one of the landmarks in the general advance in human vision wrought by Christianity was already erect. But for Neoplatonism, and in a lesser degree Stoicism, it is doubtful whether the new religion would ever have gained force to transform the ancient world into the modern.

Meanwhile, the material platform on which Hellenic mind and Eastern soul were to find espousal, the stability of Roman institutions and the consequent cosmopolitanism of mental intercourse, was playing a part, if a somewhat negative one, in the universal crystallisation of new idea. Originally, in the unimaginative mind of the early Roman, religion and law sprang from the same source, the former being no more than a series of contracts between man and his not very august divinities. But the outstanding quality of the religious element in Roman mentality was its receptivity. Just as, in the legal sphere, there was never a custom containing a germ of right principle that the Romans did not assimilate, so in the religious, there was no worship which they were not willing to incorporate in their own system of civic observance, provided it did not run counter to the interests of the state, as Christianity at first seemed liable to do. Hence, not only were the later philosophies so widely popularised, that wealthy families were in the habit of maintaining Greek dialecticians in their households as private "chaplains"; but the cults of North Africa and the East, with their strange gods and strange rites, were publicly acknowledged. Foremost and typical among them was the worship of Mithras, of which memorials have been found even in Scotland. When it is remembered that this ubiquitous cult, besides preaching morality and fraternity, incorporated in its

57

legend the flood, the ark, the adoration and the shepherds; in its teaching, Heaven and Hell, the atoning
sacrifice, the laſt judgment, and the resurrection; and
in its observance, the use of holy water, the ceremony
of adminiſtering communion, and the sanctification of
Sunday and 25th December; it is reasonable to suppose
that, juſt as the laſt manifeſtations of classical philosophy had prepared the way for Chriſtianity among
the educated, so had the religions of Persia and Egypt
among the masses. This was the result not only of
indirect infiltration, but of official Roman acquiescence
in the transportation of cults from one part of the
Empire to another. And it was largely by this means
that there evolved a further important condition of
Chriſtianity's acceptance: the universal desire in high
and low, educated and illiterate alike, for the promise,
in definite terms, of resurrection and after-life.

Having considered, therefore, the trend of both
thought and desire during the Helleniſtic age, it
remains to discover which exactly were those rare and
diſtinctive aspects of approach to the eternal problem,
that enabled a small and oppressed Semitic people to
change the face of the earth. Chriſt can have known
little of Neoplatonism or Mithras; he was a Jew,
product of Jews, and laſt of their prophets. But in
the tradition of his people and his own words, there
was disclosed a bridge to the Absolute, plain of entrance and plain of traverse, which could guide the
least of intellects, and inspire the higheſt, to its path.
Thus, where ancient Europe had failed, where the

masses had been left to superstition, and the educated to speculation, the East stepped in to demand allegiance to a faith that was neither cult nor sense, and to preach, in return, the first principles of loving democracy.

Yet in essence the new revelation was already old— old as Abraham and Ur of the Chaldees, older by a thousand years than the first Greek reflection on earth's components. While Plato and Aristotle were groping the ladder of logic towards an impersonal God conceived on the lines of a clandestine broadcasting-station, the Jews, voiced by their prophet-chroniclers, were building from their religious experience a permanent distinction between the motives and conceptions of man, and those of the parental, if terrible, Force of his restraint. Their God, single and undistorted by artistic reproduction, was the chiefest inheritance of the race. Let the race walk, then, by this, its own light. "But take heed," replied the Hellene and the Latin, to whom St Paul's explanations were consecrated, "that the light within thee is not darkness." In each individual temperament, it is the same battle fought from the beginning: soul against mind. In so far as the two joined forces, there lay the scope without limit of Christianity's appeal. But once the mind became again predominant, as happened after the schism of the Churches, the revival of Aristotle, and the shifting of religious gravity to Italy, the decline of Christianity, which the Reformation could only retard, had begun.

The main theme of Judaism, which Chriſt in the end perfected and advertised, was the emanation from God of a divine code of ethics to which man, in token of his faith in God, muſt subscribe. It was this demand for the allegiance of the soul, rather than the intelligence, which characterised all Eaſtern thought and was, centuries later, to give Mohammedanism its force. This faith of the Eaſt was translated to the Weſt by Chriſt. But the transformation wrought by him alone, apart from his tradition, lay in his inveſtiture of the Absolute with the qualities of love and bounty. The conception of the great Affinity as emanating conscious, indeed personal, beneficence towards the mortal prisons of the lesser, beckoned to its focus all the kindred ideas and symbols scattered through the philosophies and cults of the Empire. " High-mindedness," so persiſtently advocated by ancient philosophers, found itself in contact with humility, the sense of human guilt, hitherto a fourth dimension to the Greek world. The humanitarianism which was to form so contraſting a feature of Byzantine life beside the barbarism of the mediæval Weſt was already in the air. And it was here that danger seemed to threaten. What effect might love exercise on the ſtability of the ſtate?

From time to time throughout the classical era, thinkers such as the Stoics had attempted to place ethics on the level of an independent science. But this idea of guiding the course of life by an abſtract ſtudy of conduct took little hold on the catholic mentality of the average man. For the inhabitant of the classical world, the ideal of conduct remained, first and foremost, the ideal of service to society. And of all the immediate revolutions brought about by the general acceptance of Christianity, the most absolutely radical was the substitution of service, not to society, but to God. Hitherto, the vision of a personal Absolute had implied theocracy or nothing. The words "*Render therefore unto Cæsar, the things which are Cæsar's : and unto God the things which are God's*," lit the supreme compromise out of all the many compromises that were now fusing East and West for the conquest of the world. And it was Constantine, seeing everywhere the love of God replacing that of Cæsar, who took the motto and acted upon it. Under this auspice, Constantinople was created. While politics endure and the goal of man eludes, such is sacramental import of that city, of all it did, and of all it has left. Under this diarchy of Cæsar and God, the Greeks and those within their sphere, obtained a content never vouchsafed to the West. Other than the Byzantines, there was never a people who, during a thousand years of unaltered political existence, consecrated their lives with a like conscience to the joint rendering to Cæsar and God of each his things.

At the first halt beneath the prodigious, misty hemisphere of St Sophia; at the first glitter of sapphire in Galla Placidia's mausoleum; at the sparse sophistication of an imperial sarcophagus; at the golden haze of

St Mark's; at any first encounter with Byzantine art, there forms in the beholder a conviction of profound novelty, a novelty born not of its foreign qualities, but of the vast complexity, wrought into order and restraint, of its emotional and intellectual mould. While in literature, save for such scattered exceptions as the hunting epic of Digenis Akritas, the creative powers of the Byzantine were negatived by an excessive appreciation of the past; while in thought, the access to both Hellenic philosophy and Aramean theology, a combination unknown to contemporary Europe, seemed for the most part so amply sufficient as to render superfluous any additions to the beliefs of successive last generations; and while in science the wisdom of the ancient world was conserved and utilised for everyday purposes, rather than increased; in art and architecture, the Byzantines, for those who measure the value of human activity in terms of a divine quest, took strides of incalculable importance, not only in the light of their actual productions, but in their relationship to the whole cultural advance of Europe. Having now, in an age of vigorous movement, discarded the spectacles of classicism for the telescope of historical perspective, it is possible to determine, first the sources whence the essential novelty of Byzantine art arose; and once again, in what proportion did Hellas, Rome, and that nebulous quantity, " the East," contribute to this last and most pleasurable element in Byzantine civilisation.

The basic structure, such as grammar is to language,

of the art of New Rome, was Hellenic. The Hellenic
genius lay in two qualities: a capacity for material
representation; and a sense of composition. Of these
provinces in art, the monuments of Ancient Greece
have remained the unchallenged masterpieces. But
essential place as representation and composition occupy
in the whole of art, and their Greek manifestations in
Western art, there is nevertheless a major quality. This
lies in the expression, not of the recorded image, but
of the emotion provoked by it, in the communication
to the beholder of some spark of the inspiration which
is every man's creed and birthright, but which the
artist alone by his trade can bring to light. This aim,
in the archaic period, the Greeks may have held in
mind. Subsequently, confused by the wealth of their
own technical ability, they failed either to pursue or to
retain it.

Intent as always on the world around them, the
Greeks had evolved a skill in the reproduction of the
human form which even this age of scientific triumph
has not equalled. The influence of their achievement,
hitherto only faintly foreshadowed in Egypt, became
manifest in the art of every race between the Atlantic
and the Pacific. Its significance can compare only
with such inventions as bronze alloy or Edward I's
Parliament, destined to inaugurate fresh epochs in the
world's history. But the Greeks were obsessed,
atrophied, by their own overwhelming sense of balance
and proportion. It was this, with the development of
naturalistic ability, that degenerated into an irresistible

desire to please, to idealise the material with a shallow beauty more fleshy, more earthen than earth itself. All were sacrificed—strength, character, emotion, soul— to the blasting formulæ of grace, twist of neck and crick of knee, vacuous lip and bridgeless nose. In architecture, despite the patent crudity of pillar, cornice, pillar, cornice, the fault was less, the lines might be stronger, the refinements of some subtlety, as the sun-gilt trunks of the Parthenon bear witness, and the tenuous white guts of Sunium equally deny. None the less, for the benefit of future generations, the essentials remained: the ability of representation, awaiting its infusion with the suprarational; and the sense of composition, awaiting rescue from the morass of superficial convention into which the Periclean sculptors had plunged it eight centuries before. Furthermore, the intuitive simplicity hitherto so ruthlessly exploited, was now to prove half the genius of the Byzantine craftsman. It enabled him, reducing to its lowest terms the wealth of Oriental and Iranian design at his disposal, to produce the most meaning, the most restrained, and at the same time the richest decorative ornament that the world has enjoyed.

If, in the Roman, the instinct towards artistic creation was restricted by the material aspects of existence, his character has left none the less a definite impress on Byzantine architecture. St Sophia, perennial inspiration to the builders of the Near East, exhibits a magnitude of conception, a determination to enlarge the tricks of Eastern building to a grandeur in keeping with the dignity of the Empire, and a practical firmness of design, all of which were the direct outcome of the Roman tradition. In smaller spheres, this practicality is still apparent; there is nothing irrelevant in Byzantine art. Each detail claims relation to the whole. The huddled, narrative profusion of the East, the suave and irrelevant artifice of Greece, were fostered into union at the muscular breast of efficiency. In the process, all but fundamentals were cast aside.

While classical art was pursuing its impeccable and unimaginative path, forces in the darkness beyond the Eastern boundaries were taking shape for their part in the development of the modern world. Just as the Hellenic pictorial ability, carried centuries before into the heart of Asia by Alexander, had breached the prejudice of Buddhism and Mazdaism against representational art by reason of its proselytising efficacy, so now it was to fulfil the same function for Christianity, moving Westward. But Christianity, however wide its use of this assistance, represented a cultural force which was not only psychological, but backed by the concrete technical traditions of the Near East. In that fecund welter of peoples enclosed between India, Russia and the Mediterranean, it is possible to distinguish in this context two main elements, the Iranian and the Semitic.

Furthest removed from the ultimate scene of fusion was the Iranian sphere, seated between the Caspian and the Altai Mountains, and expressing a concurrence, presumed to have happened about 200 A.D., of two nomadic races, the Scythians and the Mongolian Turks. Hence, it is thought, sprang the rudiments of all Eurasian geometric design, which were from there distributed in two divergent streams; one through South Russia to Northern and Western Europe; the other to the Semitic peoples of Asia Minor, Syria and Arabia. It was this latter, hitched to the train of Christianity, that ultimately reached Constantinople and the Mediterranean. And thus it is that, to the untrained eye, Celtic manuscript illuminations are scarcely distinguishable from their Byzantine and Armenian contemporaries. The most significant, however, of the Iranian bequests was architectural. It was from this source that the Armenians, who had already adopted Christianity as a state religion some three decades in advance of the Empire, derived their method of constructing a round dome over a square bay, which, during the course of its Westward migration, created St Sophia, and ultimately displaced the box-of-bricks construction of classical temples surviving in the basilica. At length, in the ninth century, the Armenian architect of the Emperor Basil II Bulgaroctonos, combined the two in a domed and cruciform church, which became the prototype of all future Orthodox ecclesiastical building, and eventually of such pretentious temples of later Christianity as St Peter's in Rome and St Paul's in London.

Although the Jews, in all their wanderings and captivities, had, after the manner of nomads, confined their art to the geometric, this was not the case with the Semitic races of the interior. For them an art almoſt wholly free of Hellenic mannerisms already portrayed the human form of gods, prieſts and kings. And it seems plain that the representational element in Byzantine art was not derived from the Greeks alone. In the firſt century frescoes at Dura on the middle Euphrates,[1] the flatness of treatment and emotional use of colour, wholly divorced from the portrait-paintings of the Helleniſtic Empire, bespeak a fair claim to share in the anceſtry of Byzantine painting. From Mesopotamia, also, came the new medium, glass mosaic. And it muſt be remembered that, with one or two very rare exceptions, the representations of Chriſt, from the earlieſt monuments of his era on, were invariably of the Syrian type, with black beard and parted hair. Finally, the frown of thunderous agony and majeſty with which the Pantocrator, in the tall domes of Greek monaſtery churches, ſtill to this day sets fire to the innermoſt crevices of the being, has only perpetuated that approximation of earthly and divine royalty which was the ſtrongeſt motive in Semitic imagination.

Thus, juſt as mentally the Eaſt supplied new means to seek Reality, in art she did the same. In the symbolism of the geometric and in the formalisation of the represented, even when both were diverted to the

[1] The world's present knowledge of these is confined to the investigations of a single day during military operations. An expedition was despatched thither in 1928 which, it is hoped, will disclose further information.

didactic purpose of a centralising church, there lurked the germ of a great advance, which has in time affected the whole earth. That " art translates inward meaning into visible form " was unknown to the classical world, as it is unknown to the classicists of to-day. From the East came the discovery of it.

When Constantine, on the defeat and death of Licinius in 323 A.D., found himself at last the triumphant survivor of the numerous Cæsars called into being by the decentralising experiment of Diocletian, he must have been, at the age of 49, as widely travelled as any man in the Empire. Born in Moesia, province of the modern Serbs and Bulgars, and reared at the court of Nicomedia on the eastern side of the Marmora, for which city Diocletian had already forsaken the over-conservative and economically deserted capital of Italy, it was Constantine's peculiar fortune, after seeing active service in Persia and Egypt, to be acclaimed Cæsar at York, where his father, Constantine Chlorus, had died while on a punitive expedition against the Scots. The next six years Constantine spent in Gaul and Italy; in 312 he captured Rome from his colleague Maxentius; and in 313, as sole Emperor of the West, he issued jointly with Licinius of the East, the Edict of Milan, granting toleration to Christians. The following year saw the cession to him, by Licinius, of Greece, Illyria and Pannonia. But this remaining rival was not finally eliminated till 323, when each side threw its whole weight into the struggle. The campaign in

question included a naval battle for the passage of the
Hellespont and a siege of Byzantium.

In 326, therefore, if a new capital was to be built,
no man was better qualified than Constantine to choose
the site. Rome was thick with conspiracies; North
and West were barbarous or provincial; primarily it
must be in the East: a headquarters against the Parthians and the ceaseless Westward migrations from
the Steppes; and a focus of trade, of the embryo
Christianity generating in the East, of culture, magnificence, and the amenities of life. For these, with
natural security thrown in, what spot on Constantine's
earth could compare with Byzantium?

As the ship drives over the grey billows of the Black
Sea straight for the long horizon, Asia to the left,
Europe to the right, an opening, distinguishing the
two, beckons the way to the South, to the older, joyous
existence, where the hot sun has hatched man free from
the mere struggle to subsist. Seventeen miles long, in
places no wider than 600 yards, this magic creek winds
through a double range of hills, which make the
leviathans of ocean seem as toy boats in a dike and
reveal their every detail to the watchers on their decks.
Sometimes downland, sometimes rocky humps, break
the undulating line of trees. At the water's edge,
grassy valleys arrive with streams, which trickle to
the sea through groves of rustling bamboo. The hills
are thick with dwarf oaks, junipers and bay-trees,
crowned occasionally with gaunt pines, and mingled
with bracken, giant heath and yellow flowering broom.

The air grows soft with a distant smell of pinks. There are signs of habitation, boats and gardens, then the villas and palaces themselves. Upon a promontory appears the nucleus of a town; in its foreground an island lighthouse; and beyond, a blue line of open sea, the Marmora, still enclosed between Europe and Asia, with the Dardanelles half a day's journey on, leading to the Ægean. The ship swings to the right, rounds a corner, and comes to anchor in the Golden Horn, another creek as wide as the Bosporus, but narrowing quickly and curving back North again as its name implies. On a triangular peninsula, rising no more than 250 feet from the Marmora and Golden Horn, with its blunted apex craning northward as though for a view up the Bosporus, lies Byzantium; at the water's edge her wharves; at them, the ships fetching and delivering as bees at their flowers. Natural distributing house of merchandise from India and China, from Egypt and from Russia; cool, healthy, and so beautiful as to render life a perpetual holiday; guarded by narrow approaches, the difficulty of forcing which was fresh in his memory; such was the position that Constantine had chosen, as he marched out from the old Greek city already in existence, to mark, with his own hands, the confines of the new.

Materials for building were forthcoming in the marble of the Proconnesus, a group of islands in the Marmora, and the wood of forests bordering the Black Sea. A fever of construction, as though he were some eighteenth century grandee, devoured the Emperor.

PLATE II

Column of
Constantine

—St Irene

Hippodrome

Sea of Marmora—

W

N

S

E

Entrance to the
Bosporus

Sultan Ahmet Mosque

St Sophia

THE CITY OF CONSTANTINE

Throughout his dominions, magistrates were bidden found schools and professorships of architecture. No one residing in Asia Minor might enter the imperial service unless he possessed a house in the imperial capital. For the ambitious, the seekers of wealth, nobility or martial glory, this henceforth was the world's metropolis. On 11th May 330, a solemn ceremony of dedication was held. From that day to this, the plan of the city and its essential points of importance have remained unaltered.

Upon the spacious platform of the headland, with its protracted slopes stretching on one side to the silver blue of the Marmora, and, on the other, to the deeper, hill-reflected water of the Golden Horn, the principal buildings stood in proximity. To the east was the Senate House; to the south, the Great Palace, a huge cluster of erections reaching amid gardens to the sea-shore, where the porphyry pavilion, built for the Empresses to seclude and empurple the birth of their children, survived for many centuries as contemporary with the great founder. On the west lay the elliptical Forum of Constantine. Between it and the sea was the Hippodrome.

This gigantic theatre, capable of seating 80,000 people and overlooking both Europe and Asia, was 128 yards wide, 1000 in circumference, and over a quarter of a mile in length; its arched walls, of marble filled with brick, rose tier upon tier 40 feet from the ground, supporting a colonnade of gigantic marble pillars, from whose bases the seats sloped down to the arena. The curve of the western end, overreaching the slope of the land, was supported on massive vaults, which still survive, and have since been converted into cisterns. At the other extremity, stood the stables, and above them the imperial box, connected by a private staircase with the Great Palace. This was adorned with the four horses of Lysippus, those familiar prancing beasts which miraculously escaped conversion by the crusaders into specie and were ultimately removed to the façade of St Mark's in Venice; where, with the exception of a Napoleonic interlude on the Arc de Triomphe, they have since remained. The backbone of the course,[1] round which the chariots raced, was marked with other works of art, for which Constantine had stripped the whole world naked : poisoned bull and brazen ass; angry elephant with trunk that moved; Hercules of Lysippus, six feet from knee to foot; Caledonian boar; bronze eagle, through holes in whose outstretched wings the sun shone to mark the hours on a dial beneath; a giant woman bearing in her hand a life-size horse and rider. It was Theodosius (375-395) who mounted the incised obelisk of Thothmes III upon its sculptured base and four copper cubes, which rise to-day from amid the insufferable harmonies of Turkish municipal gardeners.

---

[1] The existence of an actual *spina*, though disputed by the evidence of the recent excavations, is not in doubt. Robert de Clary (1204) describes it in terms of personal observation, and gives its height and breadth as fifteen feet and ten respectively. It certainly bore the monuments enumerated above ; but whether the two obelisks and the serpent column, is unknown.

Originally a bronze pineapple graced the top, to look across to the Forum Tauri where the same Emperor's silver lady turned in the wind upon a pillar plated with pastoral reliefs. Another obelisk that once was similarly plated still stands near by, having been restored in that form by the Emperor Constantine VII Porphyrogenitus. And between the two, removed by Constantine from the oracle at Delphi and ultimately to be cleared of the accruing levels by British soldiers on their way to the Crimea, is a triple, twisted pillar of bronze, 22 feet high, and formerly surmounted by three spouting, long-necked heads, on which may still be read the names of the thirty-one Greek states responsible for the victory of Platæa over the army of Xerxes, 479 years before the birth of Christ. The two obelisks and the serpent column are in alignment. Upon the same axis, history is completed with the canopied fountain of a later Cæsar, presented in the opening years of the twentieth century. The donor was William II of Germany, he who brought to ruin the Emperors Nicholas and Charles, last inheritors of the East and West Roman thrones.

To the north-east of the Hippodrome, on the point most prominent to sailors approaching from the south, Constantine built the church of St Irene, and laid the foundations of the great church of St Sophia, afterwards completed and consecrated by his son, Constantius. In these two temples, erected to the glory of a personal Absolute and dedicated to the rational abstractions of Wisdom and Peace, the Emperor gave symbolic expression to the alliance of Greek and Semite in pursuit of a common goal which he had brought about, and which was to render Christianity both intelligible and acceptable to the most divergent temperaments. He further built for himself a smaller church, that of the Holy Apostles, which, though reconstructed by Justinian, long survived the destruction of the other two and, till its pillage by the crusaders, served as the royal mausoleum. Also he set up a column, eight drums of porphyry, bound in metal and rising from a white marble plinth. On top of this, a bronze Apollo from ancient Greece, newly furnished with the Emperor's head encircled with the rays of the sun, proclaimed the earthly majesty of Cæsar and the city's founder. Within the plinth, as though to justify the prostrations of passers-by, were sealed the twelve baskets that once held the crumbs of the five thousand ; the alabaster-box of ointment of spikenard; the adze with which Noah fashioned the ark ; the Palladium of old Rome; and the crosses of the two thieves, lately retrieved from Jerusalem by the octogenarian St Helena of York, the Emperor's mother. "O CHRIST, RULER AND MASTER OF THE WORLD, TO THEE HAVE I NOW CONSECRATED THIS OBEDIENT CITY . . . AND THE POWER OF ROME." Thus ran the inscription. To-day, as the trams rattle past, pious souls may study the announcements of important football matches on the plinth instead. The statue fell in 1106. But the relics themselves await the spade. Meanwhile, Constantine, while prone to deliver tedious sermons on monotheism to the court, retained the title of Pontifex Maximus, minted the Sol Invictus, his family deity, on his coins, and permitted the erection of pagan temples within the city. He was baptised only on his death-bed at Nicomedia in 337.

Constantine was the first grand tolerant. If, with the majority of his subjects still pagans, his attitude was born of expediency, it was not of opportunism. He condemned paganism only for the debauches which its rites sometimes occasioned. But he saw that for a world in search of a God, Christianity offered the best, and one, moreover, that he was not ashamed to represent on earth. His achievement in history was the discernment and utilisation of the vital elements in a world of extreme physical and mental chaos. In Constantinople he coalesced, with conscious purpose, the political machinery of Rome and the spiritual galvanism of the East, with the great cohesive sub-structure of Hellenic culture.

Byzantine civilisation was inaugurated. Roman in title, as it always remained, its custodians in fact were Greek. In the still visible list of those who contributed to the expenses of the great cistern which Philoxenus built for Constantine, there is no Italian name. Even the churches were dedicated in Greek. But the Byzantines were descendants of more than Hellas. The triple fusion of the stable, the transcendental and the cultural, was one of character as well. To the classical humanism, the scientific reason, and the tolerance and understanding of human nature that were essentially Greek, there was added the practical broad vision of the Roman, able always to see the wood for the trees; and the mystical distrust of the material world as the instrument of present or ultimate happiness, that is common to all Asiatic peoples. " Byzantine," whether applied to man, spirit, institution or work of art, denotes nor East nor West. It is an adjective apart, exclusive yet cosmopolitan, austere yet delectable. But in its whole composite significance, two elements predominate: the Christian and the Greek. Without this alliance, the universal civilisation of the West could never have evolved. And it is this alliance whose personality, tested to the depths of human suffering, has survived in the twentieth century.

CHAPTER V

FROM Eusebius, contemporary of the firft Emperor of Conftantinople, to Phrantzes, friend and chronicler of the laft, the long sequence of Greek hiftorians, the torch of Thucydides, has not failed. For 1123 years the Empire in the Eaft is portrayed unchanging, as a national and political organism. Its 88 effective rulers, who, with the exception of the four following the Latin Conqueft, were resident in Conftantinople, succeeded one another without intermission: 39 dynaftically; 20 by the regular process of delegation; 7 by civil or military election; and 22 by usurpation. Of the latter a few were juftified by success; while the remainder oufted one another in spasmodic groups. Thus, from the foundation of the city to its firft capture by the crusaders nearly 900 years later, those periods of difturbed succession which are popularly supposed to have rendered Byzantine government no more than a farce, numbered exactly five, lasting respectively 8, 22, 23, 10, and 19 years (A.D. 602-610, 695-717, 797-820, 1071-1081, 1185-1204).[1] Isolated revolts were more

---

[1] It is frequently asserted that "of 107 Byzantine Emperors, 65 abdicated or met with violent deaths." This calculation conveys a false impression, the phrase "Byzantine Emperors" being stretched

frequent; but successful or not, with the exception of the Nika they exercised little effect on the administrative machinery of the Empire, disturbing still less the avocations of the ordinary citizen.

The first of the eight periods into which the life of the Empire is usually divided, lasted from 330 to 518, from the foundation of the city by Constantine the Great to the death of the Emperor Anastasius. The new city, the imperial whim, was proved. Sheltered by the Black Sea, as though beneath an umbrella, from the full torrent of the Asiatic migrations to the south-west, she escaped the disasters that overtook the West, as the great leaders, Alaric, Attila and Theodoric allowed themselves to be diverted by the seductions of Italy and Spain. One complete rout the Goths imposed on the armies of the Eastern Empire, at Adrianople in 378; and the danger that threatened was not finally eliminated till a decade later than the fall of Rome in 476. Nevertheless a single century had seen the population of Constantinople overflow the boundary of her founder by a mile. In 439 Cyrus, prefect of Theodosius II, had constructed the gigantic triple line of walls, which still survive, across the five-mile base of the elsewhere sea-girt promontory, in order to defend the new suburbs.

Meanwhile the nature of Christ was reflecting the

to include the latter rulers of Trebizond, Epirus and Cyprus, besides numerous young Porphyrogeniti, who though crowned as their fathers' successors, never took actual part in government.

A WOODCUT OF CONSTANTINOPLE
Printed at Nuremberg in 1493, presumably from an older panorama

THE LAND WALLS TO-DAY

political vicissitudes of the nation most determined on its final definition. Against the ghostly preferences of the East, and the Greek concentration upon God as a celestial focus for philosophic values, the West was resolved to maintain the co-preponderance of Christ's entry into Mary's womb. The situation was complicated by the identification of spiritual with national aspirations. At the Council of Ephesus in 431, the condemnation of Nestorius' matter-of-fact analysis of Christ's elements, at the instance of the Alexandrine mystics, produced the separate Nestorian church and a distinctive Syrian nationality. And twenty years later, the condemnation at Chalcedon, in their turn, of the Alexandrine mystics, produced the separate Monophysite churches, Coptic and Abyssinian, and the final stultification of the African patriarchate's temporal ambitions. The Church of Constantinople, thanks to the assistance of Rome, was now supreme in the East. None the less, from 482 to 518, relations with Rome, where Leo the Great had already inaugurated papal pretension to universal dominion, were suspended, owing to Constantinople's acceptance of Christ's preponderating divinity to the discount of his humanity. The strength of the Empire lay in the Levant; and the interests of the state demanded this recognition for the conciliation of its fanatic populations.

Thus amid convulsions, abstract and material, the Byzantine Empire was formed and tempered. From the barbarian migrations it emerged intact when Europe lay inundated. Under its auspices the kernel of

79

Christian orthodoxy was promulgated, a permanent monument to the sincerity of Greek thinking.

During the second period, from 518 to 610, Justin I to Phocas, the phase of premature expansion instituted by Justinian was not maintained. The latter Emperor was imbued with a practical and ambitious conception of imperial government which linked his sympathies with the West and with all of the past that Rome still represented. The religious policy was reversed; the papacy was reconciled; and a persecution brought to bear on the Monophysites of Africa and Asia. The championship of Orthodox dogma was assumed, and engrained henceforth for thirteen centuries, as the foundation of Greek national consciousness. But Justinian, thus in harmony with the West, betrayed the resources and position of his capital in a grand attempt to re-capture the dominion of the whole Mediterranean. During twenty years (533-554), northern Africa, Italy, Southern Spain, and the islands of Sicily, Corsica, Sardinia and the Balearics, fell successively to the Byzantine rule. Theodora, the Cypriot Empress, would have retained, in preference, the support of Syria and Egypt by religious tolerance. With the incessant Persian invasions of Asia Minor, the Slavs and Huns penetrating even the Morea, and the Italian Lombards still unsubdued, the Empire, impoverished by excessive enterprise, was temporarily crippled at Justinian's death in 565. Leaving the outlying Exarchates of Africa (including Spain) and Ravenna, in the form of armed

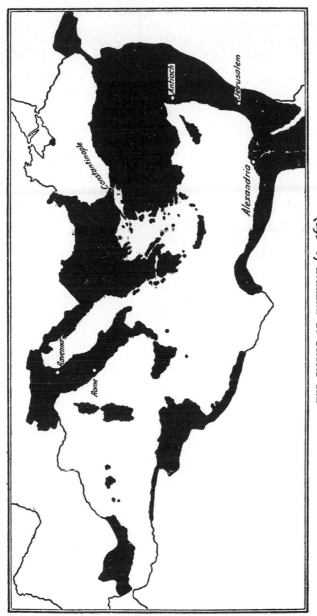

THE EMPIRE OF JUSTINIAN (c. 560)

dependencies, to shift for themselves, his successors applied themselves to the deliverance of the Balkan and Armenian borders from the respective incursions of savage hordes and Persian armies. This work was interrupted by a palace revolution in 602; and the Empire was only preserved from total anarchy by the advent of Heraclius three years later.

Ephemeral, however, as was Justinian's attempt to reconstitute the Roman Empire, the importance of his reign in the evolution of Byzantine and European civilisation is not to be exaggerated. Despite the wealth that poured by land and sea into Constantinople, it was plain to the Emperor that every branch of the administration was in need of reform. The general discontent against a corrupt and exacting officialdom came to a head in the riot of the circus factions in 532, which was only suppressed after half the original city of Constantine had been burnt to the ground, and 40,000 of the insurgents were lying dead among the seats of the Hippodrome. Justinian, whom only the courage of Theodora had prevented from flight, set himself forthwith to the centralisation of the bureaucracy, the abolition of the sale of offices, and the union of the civil and military authority in each province. But his greatest work, already begun in the earliest year of his reign, was the recodification of Roman law and the summarisation, in accessible form, of Roman legal precedent. In the volumes that he planned and caused to be compiled, the primary rules of social existence, redistributed in accordance with the Christian ethic, were registered in perpetuity for the benefit of a Byzantine, a European and a world-wide posterity. For the moment, abridged editions diffused from Beyrut to Rome, opened the knowledge of justice to all the officials and subjects of the Empire.

There remained, after the Nika riot, to rebuild the main quarters of the city. And in Justinian's ultimate version of the church of St Sophia; together with all the contemporary churches and mosaics at Rome, Salonica and Ravenna; in these, more plainly than any document can show, is visible the first-flowering of the Byzantine genius. The grammatical elements of art, symmetry, technique and racial consciousness, are absorbed, if not yet wholly, in an expression of cosmopolitan, mystical emotion so overwhelmingly coherent as to stir almost to the surface the tears of the beholder.

Such were the first products of the fused civilisation. Culturally and socially the achievement was permanent. But the imagination of Justinian proved politically too great a burden. His life had been devoted to a castle in the West. And the East was awaiting revenge.

The third period begins with the reign of Heraclius in 610 and ends with that of Theodosius III in 717. From 602, following the usurpation of Phocas, confusion had surrounded the Byzantine throne. The assassination of Maurice, his predecessor, who had formerly aided the Persian king, Chosroës II, to regain his own throne, was made the excuse for a Persian onslaught of such magnitude that the existence of the whole Empire was imperilled. As Antioch, Damascus, Jerusalem, Chalcedon and even Egypt succumbed, Heraclius, who had sailed from his father's Exarchate of Carthage to assume the leadership of the Empire, despaired even of preserving the capital. Despite the attacks of the Avars on the west, the incursions of the Lombards into Italy, and the final loss of Spain, the Emperor concentrated on the repulse of the Persians. In 628 he entered Ctesiphon in triumph, retrieving thence the Holy Cross which had been carried off from Jerusalem thirteen years before. But this very success raised two dangerous issues. The cost of the war, to which even the church had contributed, could only be defrayed by taxation so heavy as to render Byzantine government odious to its non-Greek subjects. And it was essential that Egypt and Syria, alienated by the Monophysite persecutions, should be consolidated. Political consolidation implied, as in the England of Elizabeth, religious uniformity. Orthodoxy was firmly established at Constantinople; but a compromise with the adherence to Christ's unadulterated divinity, prevalent in Egypt and Syria, was sought by the postulation of a single, and that divine, will, at work within the conventional dual nature, carnate and incarnate. Monotheletism, as this gallant expedient was termed, found favour with neither of the two parties whom it was designed to unite in a common political framework. In the West, it resulted, eight years after Heraclius' death, in the kidnapping of a pope. And in Egypt, it was enforced only at the point of a patriarchal sword. Meanwhile, as the Emperor, overcome by the theological and financial complications of his situation, only deepened the discussions which he sought to heal, a new race had achieved national consciousness by means of a religion which demanded no such acute refinements in its definition of the Almighty. In 634, within three years of Mohammed's death, the Arab Moslems of Medina won their first skirmish against the Byzantine garrisons of Palestine.

To the Semite, the Syrian and the Egyptian, the early hosts of Islam, tolerant in religion, and rendered odious by no greedy bureaucracy, appeared in the light of deliverers from the material and spiritual oppression of the Byzantines. Unsupported by the native populations, the Greek forces were forced into retreat. By 640 Palestine was lost and Egypt invaded. The death of Heraclius in the following year resulted in the evacuation of Alexandria. Persia and Armenia were overrun. Eventually the struggle shifted to the sea. Cyprus fell; and in 655 the Greek fleet, under the Emperor Constans II, was defeated off the coast of Lycia. But with the accession of Constantine IV and the discovery of Greek fire, the situation changed. For five years in succession the recurring naval assaults on Constantinople were repulsed ; and in 678 the Arabs, brought to their first standstill on land and sea alike, were glad to conclude a peace. Three years later, the Monothelite doctrine, having now, with the rape of Egypt and Syria, lost its *raison d'être*, was formally condemned at the sixth Œcumenical Council, held at Constantinople in 681.

Thus there was peace; and the Empire received a breathing-space before being called upon to repulse the last and greatest of the Saracen attempts to burst the confines of Asia at the Hellespont. Unfortunately, from 695 to 717 a period of internal anarchy lessened the advantage gained and hastened the inevitable loss of North Africa. Simultaneously, on the north-west frontier, the encroachments of the newly formed state of the Bulgars gave cause for alarm.

From the seventh century forward, the main currents of Byzantine history may be traced. The Balkan and Mohammedan questions were now incarnate in the Bulgars and Arabs. Administratively, the exigencies of the period had crystallised the civil and military organisation of the provinces into the system of themes and marches. In religion, the territorial conquest by the Moslems of the patriarchates of Antioch, Jerusalem and Alexandria, had enhanced proportionately the prestige of Constantinople as a central authority. The Empire was now centred more wholly on the Greek seaboard. And the last vestiges of Latin, even as an antiquarian adjunct of court ritual, lapsed from use.

The fourth period, from 717 to 867, opens in the former year with the march on the capital, and acclamation by Patriarch and people, of Leo the Isaurian, governor of the Anatolic theme. Within a few months of his assumption of imperial dignity, the tide of Arab

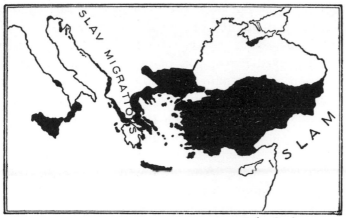

THE EMPIRE OF THE ICONOCLASTS (*c.* 800)

expansion reached its high-water mark; and for a whole year the Mohammedan fleet and army invested the capital. But while the Greeks were living in comparative comfort behind their walls, the besiegers were reduced by famine and frost to a condition which resulted, even at their own computation, in the loss of 150,000 men. This defeat marked a decisive check to the blast of Islam, compared to which the marauding expedition that won Charles Martel immortality fifteen years later was but the fortuitous puff of a movement already spent. The prestige of Byzantine arms was carried by Leo's son, Constantine V Copronymus, to Armenia and the Euphrates. With the capital of the Abbassid Caliphs transferred to the distant city of Bagdad, and the Bulgars on the West reduced by a series of campaigns between the years 755 and 780, the Isaurian Emperors inaugurated a new era of

87

security which not even the extinction of their line by
an unnatural mother or the devotion of Michael III
the Drunkard to horses could disturb. Internally,
they displayed perception of essentials and directness
of action. The administration of the themes was
systematised, and the army redisciplined. A series of
enactments sought to check the unceasing absorption
of agricultural freeholders, the yeoman defenders of
Eastern Christendom, by the increasingly independent
landed aristocracy. And in a simplification of Justinian's code, known as the *Ecloga*, a more definitely
Christian conception of family life was introduced;
the death penalty was largely replaced by mutilation;
and class distinctions in sight of the law were abolished.

It is, however, in the emergence of what has since
become known as Protestantism, in the first great
attempt to defend the new appreciation of transcendental values, that had come from the East, against
the golden calves of the South, that the true importance of the period lies. Accompanying the new
dynasty from the hinterland of Asia Minor, where
precisely the same battle was being fought among
the followers of the Prophet, the iconoclast aversion
to sacred representational art was launched on the
Empire in 726 by Leo's edict against ecclesiastical
pictures. Extraordinary repercussions ensued: riots
in the capital were echoed by a rebellion in the Peloponnese; while in Italy Byzantine authority was so
weakened that, within thirty years, the Exarchate of
Ravenna was under the control of the Lombards, and

the Pope, detaching himself from the Empire, had sought the patronage of Pepin, king of the Franks. Such provinces as remained to the Greeks in the south were placed, in retaliation, under the spiritual juris-diction of the Patriarch. Meanwhile, upon the suc-cession of Constantine V, the whole fabric of popular religion was threatened by a legislative attack on relics, the cult of the Virgin, and the intercession of the saints. The depth of the Emperor's convictions produced a series of persecutions which were chiefly directed against the icon-loving monks. But in 787, the Empress Irene, in order to bolster her venture on the throne, restored the pictures.

The defeat, however, of the Eastern zealots was only temporary. In 815, on the advent of a new Armenian Emperor, the pictures were again proscribed, and the intransigence of the monks, combined with their continued absorption of national wealth and energy, led once more to their persecution and dis-persal. But a transformation was being wrought in the religious life of the Empire: the monastic reforms of Theodore of Studium, which, as foreshadowing those of Cluny, were destined to exercise a profound effect on the whole of Europe, had produced not only a more ordered and active asceticism than formerly, but had infused the church with the ideal of complete emanci-pation from the authority of the state. Thus inspired, the monastic party sought aid from Rome, whose theoretical primacy in matters spiritual had not yet been disputed. As a result, the violence of the icon-

89

oclaſt reaction againſt them was only enhanced. At length, however, in 843, "veneration" of the icons was permitted. Finally, the breach with Rome which the controversy had provoked, and which had been accentuated in 800 by the Pope's coronation of Charlemagne as rival Emperor of the Weſt, was consummated in 867 by a formal though temporary schism.

Thus, in letter, the firſt of the ſtruggles to defend the spiritual inheritance of Chriſtianity from the insidious materialism of the Mediterranean failed. But in compensation, Byzantine art and the germ of European painting were saved. Furthermore, the iconoclaſt movement had purged and reawakened the Greek intelligence. Without it the world might never have witnessed the supreme junction of pictorial representation with emotional formalism that Byzantine art achieved. Contemporarily, the conversion and cultural habilitation of the Slavs by Salonican missionaries, and the refoundation of the university of Conſtantinople by the Cæsar Bardas, already foreshadowed that Renascence of taſte and learning which was to illumine the crowning centuries of the Empire's good fortune.

The fifth period, from 867 to 1057, is marked by the limits of a single dynaſty, that founded by Basil I the Macedonian, favourite of Michael III the Drunkard, and his murderer. European hiſtory, save perhaps in the house of Vasa, offers no parallel to the uniform success with which this line of hereditary rulers and their military coadjutors pursued the welfare

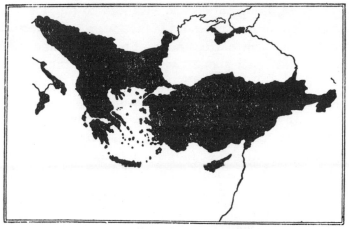

THE EMPIRE AND ITS DEPENDENCIES AFTER THE CAMPAIGNS OF
BASIL II BULGAROCTONOS (*c.* 1015)

of a single dominion over so long a course of time as
two centuries. Territorially the Empire was expanded
to its fullest extent; and for more than a hundred years
the invincible armies of Constantinople, consciously
inspired champions of Christianity and civilisation,
thrust the forces of Islam back into the deserts of
Arabia and the fastnesses of Kurdistan. Four new
Asiatic themes were reclaimed; and, to the north,
Armenia and Georgia were forced to exchange Moslem
for Byzantine suzerainty, the former State eventually
submitting to complete annexation at the beginning of
the eleventh century—though the unwisdom of thus
robbing the frontier of its buffers was immediately to
be proved. In the seventies of the ninth century, Silicia
and Cappadocia were regained by Basil I. As the tenth

91

progressed, the frontier was advanced to the Tigris in the north and the Euphrates in the south. Thenceforth the fighting centred for the most part round the right-angle in the coast above Cyprus. Under the generalship of Nicephorus II Phocas, and John I Tzimisces, Aleppo, Antioch, Edessa, Damascus and Beyrut were taken. In 961 the capture of Crete had restored to the Greeks the control of the Ægean. Byzantine arms seemed destined almost to the deliverance of Jerusalem.

In the west the successes were the same. From 889 to 924, the Tsar Symeon of the Bulgars had carried war to the very walls of Constantinople in his attempt to assert a supremacy of the Balkans. After his death in 927, Slav ambition remained passive until aroused by Svatioslav, an emigrant Prince of Kiev. This new combination was defeated in 970 by the Emperor John I Tzimisces, and the whole country annexed up to the Danube; only, however, to be reconquered in the next decade by the Tsar Samuel. In 986, therefore, the Emperor Basil II Bulgaroctonos embarked on the first of those famous campaigns which closed with the defeat and practical annihilation of the entire Bulgarian male population in 1014. The whole Balkan peninsular now admitted the imperial rule; and the Emperor proceeded on a tour of inspection which ultimately led him, admiring, to the great golden-pillared church of Athens, the Christianised, though yet unmutilated, Parthenon. In Italy, also, the incursions of the Arabs furnished excuse for Byzantine intervention; and from 915 to 1025, the south of the peninsula, up to the borders of the Papal States, acknowledged the imperial sovereignty.

Relations between the Orthodox and Catholic Churches were at firſt diſturbed. The frailties of the Cæsar Bardas, regent of Michael III, having drawn upon him the reproaches of the Patriarch Ignatius, the latter was deposed, and Photius, a savant, whose profound knowledge of classical philosophy and the exiſting literature on all subjeċts from medicine to agriculture,[1] ensured his influence with the upper classes of the capital, and seemed to excuse his hurried inveſtiture with the orders of prieſthood, was elevated in his ſtead. The Pope's refusal to recognise him, combined with a series of subterranean intrigues on the part of Rome with the objeċt of winning the Bulgars from allegiance to the Church which had converted them, resulted in a schism. The theological basis of the quarrel, which was formulated by Photius, denounced the Roman insertion of the *Filioque* in the creed as heretical, since it implied the emanation of the Holy Spirit not only from God but from his human son and thereby offended Greek susceptibilities concerning the purity of the individual's abſtraċt communing. On the accession of Basil I, Photius was deposed, but recalled five years later. Not until 898 was peace reſtored, which was ratified in 920 and maintained until the laſt years of the dynaſty.

At home, in the vaſt embattled medley of shops,

[1] The analysis of his library, which has survived, reveals important works which have not.

93

slums, baths, palaces, gardens, churches and monasteries that comprised the Κωνσταντίνου Πόλις, city
of Constantine, guarded of God, days of extraordinary prosperity were coinciding with the military
glory won by the soldier-emperors abroad. All the
wealth of three continents seemed to pour down the
trade-routes of the Levant and the Black Sea, down
the great Russian rivers, overland from India and
Cathay by Trebizond, to that which was in truth the
safest spot on earth; and from the riches of the city
materialised an architectural and artistic splendour
which was rendered doubly magnificent by the mystical
disquiet, the celestial fixation, of the Byzantine temperament. Without, the Russians were converted to Christianity; and at Kiev, on the commercial highway of the
Dnieper, the deliberate adoption of Byzantine civilisation brought a new nation into existence and a new
genius to its own awakening.

But while the radiance of the queen of cities was
borne in traveller's tale, and refracted in legend, from
the Atlantic to the Pacific, contact with the immediate
and barbarous West had been almost wholly ruptured
by the difficulty of language and the increasing divergence of sympathies. Within the Empire, moreover,
new forces were afoot, the independence of patriarchs
and feudatories already an embarrassment. Without,
the Seljuk Turks were converging from the north-east.
And in central Italy, the Normans, shadow of insatiable
rapacity, were about to emulate the success of their
cousins at Hastings.

With the death, in 1053, of the Empress Theodora, sole remaining descendant of Basil I, there opens the sixth and most complex period in the imperial history, which culminates in the capture of Constantinople by the crusaders in 1204, and the removal of the Greek monarchy to Nicæa. Already the essential strength of the Byzantine state had been shaken. The attempts of the Macedonian emperors to continue the work of the Isaurian in limiting the power of the Asiatic magnates had produced insurrections on a vast scale, which had only been finally suppressed by Basil II Bulgaroctonos. Upon the extinction of the Macedonian house, a struggle for the throne ensued among the great feudal families. It was not until thirty years later that the accession of Alexius I Comnenus, in 1081, and after him, of his son and grandson, brought new strength to a state still the strongest in Europe and possessing almost a monopoly of civilised life, but nevertheless on the ebb of its glory. Meanwhile, the bureaucracy was faltering between the devil of feudal civil war and the deep, though seemingly more distant, sea of external invasion. A revival in classical culture was reflected in an unpractical trend of politics. An anti-militarist movement, directed against the semi-independent leaders of the Asiatic regiments, resulted in the neglect of the border fortresses and the reduction of native troops in favour of mercenaries, who themselves revolted. On the sea, the disastrous policy of purchasing defence was to bring ruin to the Empire's trade and the transport against it of the crusaders in those very ships from which the Byzantines were wont to draw their navy. Already, at the beginning of the period, feudal dissensions, combined with the maladministration of an intellectual clique headed by Psellos the Platonist, were the cause of the disaster of Manzikert in 1071, the loss of almost all Asia Minor, and the advent on the Ægean coasts of the first Turk.

It had seemed, as the eleventh century progressed, that the corporate force of Islam, sapped by the Shi'ite heresy and the ineffectuality of the Caliphs of Bagdad, was on the point of dissolution. But the last heirs of the Prophet were yet to come. In 1055, Toghril Beg, leader of a new race from the lands beyond the Oxus, was proclaimed Sultan by the Caliph. From 1063 to 1091, the Seljuk Turks continued to expand. Ani, the capital of Armenia, fell to them, together with Konia in the south. The Byzantine armies, marching to oppose them, were utterly routed at Manzikert between Erzerum and Lake Van, and the Emperor Romanus IV Diogenes made prisoner. Ten years later, Greek possessions in Asia Minor were temporarily confined to thin littorals on the Black Sea and the Ægean. The wealthiest provinces of the Empire were desolate, towns ruined, fields forsaken. Worst of all, the chief recruiting-grounds of the army were lost for ever.

In the same year as Manzikert, the Turks had occupied Jerusalem, and Christian pilgrims, hitherto peaceably received by the Arabs, were now molested. The mystic chivalry and urgent land-hunger of the West were thus beckoned to a new outlet. And the

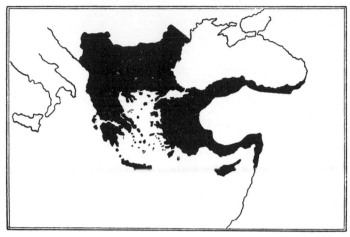

THE EMPIRE UNDER MANUEL I COMNENUS (*c.* 1180)

Emperor Alexius I Comnenus was able, with the help of the crusaders, to regain possession of Nicæa, Smyrna, and all the west and south coast of Anatolia as far as Antioch. Against the Seljuk Empire, now divided by internal factions, John II Comnenus, Alexius' son, continued the re-orientation of the Byzantine frontiers. But Manuel I, his successor, despite the earlier victories of his reign, was decisively beaten at Myriocephalon in 1176. With the establishment of Saladin in Syria and the fall of the Latin kingdom of Jerusalem eleven years later, the momentary ebb in the Moslem tide was turned.

Such was the initial advance of a force destined to extinguish the half of European civilisation and to reach its limit only before the walls of Vienna. Simultane-

97

ously a more immediate fate was moving on Constantinople from the West.

Throughout the Macedonian era, the arrogant success of Byzantine material enterprise had been reflected in the ghostly province of the Church. Proportionately as the Patriarch's power increased, that of the Pope diminished; till, but for the resurrection, through the reforms of Cluny, of Papal self-assertiveness, the autocephaly of the Orthodox Church, in fact a reality, might have been granted in theory as well, for the mere asking. But in 1049, the election of the reformer Leo IX to the Holy See having coincided with the Patriarchate of Michael Cerularius, there resulted a dispute over the south Italian bishoprics, which was deliberately provoked by the latter in contradiction to the wishes of the Emperor Constantine IX Monomach. Legates were despatched to the Eastern capital. The manuscript of a profound curse was laid on the altar of St Sophia. And the Patriarch, inspired by a frenzy of popular acclamation, ratified the breach that he had engineered, in full council—and, as it proved, in perpetuity. The moment was one of incalculable significance. Henceforth, in the teaching of popular Catholicism, the Greek was neither Christian nor brother. And in that age, popular Catholicism and the eastward expansion of feudalism were on the point of identification.

The Council of Clermont launched the first crusade in 1095; and in the summer of the following year Peter the Hermit arrived in Constantinople. Already, in the middle of the century, the Byzantines had come in contaЄ with the Normans in south Italy, whence the latter had finally ouЄed them by the taking of Bari in 1071. A decade later Robert Guiscard had crossed the Adriatic to Epirus, and penetrated inland as far as Macedonia and Thessaly. Thus it was not unnatural that, in the eyes of Alexius I Comnenus and his subjeЄs, the religious and myЄical ideals of a hoЄ composed of those same Normans, ill-mannered, illiterate, and boaЄing of upЄart pedigrees; and of a rank and file whose devotion to the sepulchre could scarcely compensate the pillaged householders on whom, as they marched, they lived; the ideals of the firЄ and subsequent crusades should have been obscured beneath the political import of a movement which threatened to, and ultimately did, implant an alien feudalism in the Ægean lands. The forces of the Empire were diverted from the EaЄ where its Јrength might Јill have lain. And with this firЄ attraЄing of the WeЄ, this firЄ protruding of those million tentacles with which the other half of Europe was deЄined to envelop the globe, the " EaЄern QueЄion " was begun.

Unable to avert the invaders, the Emperor Alexius I decided to use them. In return for money and provisions, the leaders of the hoЄ agreed that any towns formerly contained in the Empire and captured from the Moslems, should be returned to it. But the surrender of Nicæa to the Greeks was followed by the retention of Antioch, Jerusalem and many lesser towns in the hands of the Norman princes. In retaliation for

99

the Emperor's opposition to this violation of agreement, Bohemond of Antioch organised a " crusade " against the Greek capital itself. He was outwitted by Alexius and retired to Italy, humiliated.

The second crusade, of 1147, was led by the Emperor Conrad III Hohenstaufen and King Louis VII of France. Their respective followings raped and plundered their passage through the Greek dominions, to be ultimately defeated by the Turks and left to perish by their leaders on the south coast of Asia Minor. In both camps an attack on Constantinople had been mooted during the transit, but abandoned.

Some years later, the Emperor Manuel I Comnenus, encouraged by a temporary reclamation of part of southern Italy, planned, as he thought, to restore the Empire of Justinian. The Latin principalities of the East were forced to acknowledge his suzerainty. And the diplomatic bribes, which he alone was rich enough to dispense, focused in Constantinople the wires of half the states of Europe. Though it may have seemed, during this analysis of the long-gathering cyclone of adversity that was to burst on the capital in 1204, that the twelfth century was for the Greeks one of depression, in fact never was life in Constantinople more radiant, never the amenities of existence more luxuriant. In art, architecture and even in literature, in the multitude of charitable foundations, in the vast wealth, and in the new ideas generated by revived contact with the West, the vitality of the mediæval Greek Empire was still un-disputed. It was the death of Manuel I, in 1180, and the turmoil which followed the overthrow of the Comnenus dynasty, that eventually set in motion the last diabolic machinery of events.

Throughout the century, the hatred of Greek for Latin had accumulated. In 1182, the unpopularity of the Norman Empress-Regent, Mary of Antioch, led to a massacre of the foreign residents in Constantinople. And seven years later, the third crusading army, under the Emperor Frederick Barbarossa, was openly attacked by Byzantine troops. Meanwhile a Norman-Sicilian fleet had sacked Salonica with extreme brutality. And, in 1198, the Emperor Henry VI was on the point of starting in person against the capital itself, when he died. The whole might of the West was inflamed against the people who resisted its encroachment and denied its Pope. And the advent of a fugitive pretender from Constantinople, begging help for a dethroned and imprisoned father, was sufficient to divert the now preparing fourth crusade from Egypt, whither it was destined, to Constantinople.

The movers of this orientation, neither of whom returned from it alive, were Boniface of Montferrat and Henry Dandolo, the blind Doge of Venice. Transport was supplied by the latter town. In July 1203, the expedition was peaceably received in the Greek capital, though the previous restoration of the monarch whom it had come to succour, robbed its presence of the last vestiges of plausibility. But the champions of the Cross, once arrived, remained, demanding payment for services never rendered. In 1204, the people of the city, exasperated by the subservience of the reigning dynasty to the Latins, overthrew them and raised Alexius V Mourtzouphlos in their stead. The Latins determined on a second assault. On 12th April the virgin city fell; and the treasures of nearly nine centuries, together with the works of art collected by Constantine the Great from every quarter of the classical world, were delivered to destruction. Of this disaster, the Turkish capture in 1453 was but a corollary. For humanity in general, history reveals no greater misfortune. A European civilisation was to all intents and purposes extinguished. Its successor of the twentieth century was left to emerge stifled by aristocratic, national and pseudo-classical prejudices. And the races and lands within its care entered now upon seven centuries of poverty, illiteracy and slavery.

The seventh period of Byzantine history, marked by the transference of the capital to Nicæa while the Latin Emperors ruled within the walls of Constantinople, lasted from 1204 to 1261. In the first confusion, feudalism, commercialism, and Hellenism vied with each other in the process of disruption. In vassalage to Baldwin of Flanders, Emperor-elect of the barons, a multitude of dependencies arose, of which the most important were the kingdom of Salonica under Boniface of Montferrat, the barony of Athens, not for six centuries to return to Greek rule, and the principality of Achaia. The acquisitions of Venice were intended to consolidate her trade. As long ago as the reign of

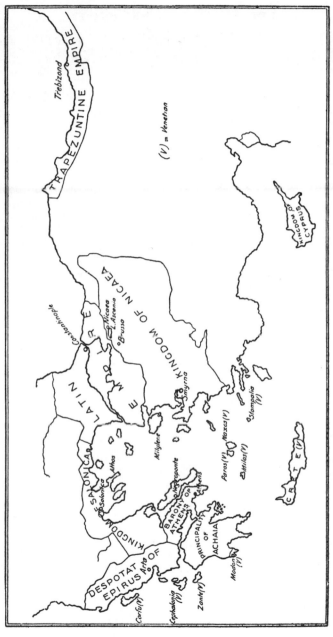

THE PRINCIPAL STATES OF THE LEVANT AFTER THE FOURTH CRUSADE (1204)

the Emperor Alexius I Comnenus (1081-1118) she had manœuvred, in return for naval assistance and political services in Italy, a grant of immunity from the heavy duties imposed on all the merchandise of the Empire; a privilege which had seriously hampered the native Greek merchants, not themselves exempt, and had seriously diminished the imperial revenues. Her rule was now installed at Durazzo on the Dalmatian coast; at Modon and Coron in the Peloponnese; in Crete, Eubœa and Gallipoli; at Heraclea on the Black Sea; throughout most of the Ægean Archipelago; and in a large quarter of Constantinople herself. The rallying points of Greek independence were three: at Nicæa, where Theodore I Lascaris, son-in-law of Alexius III Angelus, had gathered round him the remnant of the Byzantine aristocracy and bureaucracy and established the Patriarchate; at Trebizond, also now an Empire, supporting the rule of a grandson of Andronicus I Comnenus, from Heraclea to the Caucasus; and finally in Epirus, a Despotat governed by an illegitimate Angelus, stretching from Lepanto on the Gulf of Corinth to Durazzo.

The attempt of Western chivalry to evolve a working political organism from the ashes of its conquest, that " miracle wrought by God " as Pope Innocent III termed it, was not successful. The new feudatories were insubordinate; the Venetians and their monopoly of trade absorbed the revenues; the latent nationalism of the Balkan Slavs, varying, as always, inversely with the power of Constantinople, was reawakened; and the

Greeks, despite efforts made to win their friendship, remained implacable in their enmity. Before 1204 was out, Boniface and Baldwin were already at war with one another; and within three years both had perished fighting the Bulgars. Henry of Flanders, Baldwin's brother, was an able ruler, but survived him only till 1216. He was followed by the children of his sister, Yolande, the younger of whom, Baldwin II, was crowned in 1228 at the age of eleven, and reigned as long as the city remained in Latin hands. Meanwhile the Despots of Epirus had retaken Durazzo, Corfu, and even, in 1222, Salonica. Gradually all hold on Asia was also lost. And the Emperor Baldwin, having pawned the Crown of Thorns to a merchant of Venice, and delivered the lead off his own roof to the mint, departed, on a circular tour of the courts of Europe to beg assistance.

At Nicæa, Theodore I Lascaris had been succeeded in 1222 by his son-in-law, John III Vatatzes. During the latter's reign of thirty-two years, all Asia Minor in possession of the Greeks immediately before the conquest was recovered; the eastern frontier successfully maintained against Turks and Mongols; and Salonica recovered from the Despot of Epirus. In the delectable shady city on the shores of the Lake of Askania, Byzantine life flourished still: schools and hospitals were built; histories written; the bureaucracy, un broken heritage of Rome, restored. Finally, the Emperor, united with his Holy Roman counterpart in a common loathing of the Papacy, set the seal to his prestige by his marriage with the latter's daughter, Constance of Hohenstaufen. He was succeeded in 1254 by his son, Theodore II Lascaris, who died four years later, leaving a son of eight years old, John IV. The power thus rendered vacant by a minority was assumed by Michael VIII Palæologus, an able man of noted family and imperial descent. Crossing to Europe, he annexed the greater part of the Despotat of Epirus; in 1261 he concluded a treaty with the Genoese, granting them, in return for naval reinforcements, the former privileges of the Venetians; and on the 25th July of the same year, Constantinople was recaptured by a Greek reconnoitring expedition which found entrance through a disused aqueduct. Baldwin II, the Latin Patriarch, and the Venetian colonists fled. And the Byzantine Empire, diminished, but fortified with a new patriotism, entered on its last fight with adversity under the leadership of the founder of its last dynasty.

It is customary to regard this eighth and final period of Byzantine history as a kind of irrelevant epilogue, attached only by the courtesy of the historian to the company of its resplendent predecessors. Let it, however, be remembered that for half a century yet the Ottoman Turks, who, four hundred years later, were still on their way to Vienna, were debarred from Europe; and that for another century and a half after that, the impregnable walls in their rear delayed their movements and wasted their strength; that it was not until the fourteenth century that the Balkan races, on the eve of submersion, had fully assimilated those elements of Byzantine civilisation which were to stand them in stead of nationality until the day of the crescent was over; that it was only now that the seed of painting sown by the Greeks in Italy gave forth its inaugural bud in Giotto; that the parallel Renascence of Byzantine painting was yet to come; that the whole body of Hellenic culture, the secret of that attitude which the world has since called humanism, was still sealed in Constantinople; and finally that the Greek faith in the Greek destiny had still to be tempered in the last misfortunes of the Empire against the greater misfortunes of the future; let these facts be remembered; and it is plain that Byzantine civilisation died, not at the fourth crusade, but with the city that gave it birth.

The dominions of Michael VIII Palæologus consisted of Nicæa and the north-west corner of Asia Minor, Constantinople and Thrace, Salonica and part of Macedonia, together with a few islands. The capital itself was ruined and depopulated; the administration had lost its working traditions; trade was in the hands of the Italians; and Bulgars, Serbs and Turks continued to menace every frontier. Meanwhile, Charles of Anjou, inheritor of the claims of Baldwin II, was planning a crusade against the still heretic Greeks, from which the support of the Papacy was averted by a forced union of the Churches in 1274. But patriotism and anti-Latinism in Constantinople were henceforth to be one. Neither the nobility, the priests nor the people would acknowledge the Pope. In 1281, the

Emperor and all the Orthodox Church were again made excommunicate. Byzantine diplomacy resorted to its old weapon. The despatch of 30,000 ounces of gold to Peter of Aragon engineered the Sicilian Vespers, in which 7000 Normans perished. Thus the long-threatened and now imminent scheme to support the Angevin pretensions to the Empire, was frustrated.

Michael VIII died in 1282. In his successors conspicuous ability was absent. And the long civil wars in the reigns of Andronicus II Palæologus and John V Palæologus, a feature hitherto almost unknown in Byzantine history, during which each side called to its aid the enemies of the Empire, weakened the Greeks in face of the converging forces. In the Balkans, beside the Bulgarian state, the Serbian kingdom of Stephen Dushan, in the middle of the fourteenth century, stretched from the Gulf of Corinth to the Danube and from the Adriatic to the walls of Salonica. It remained only to take the imperial capital. Thrace was conquered. But Dushan died within sight of the walls, and his empire dissolved after him in face of the Turks.

This latter people, perpetually impelled from behind by the Mongol migrations that had begun with Jenghis Khan in 1242, lay scattered in nomadic confusion over the length and breadth of Asia Minor. Under the leadership of Othman, a national nucleus, later to assume his name, was formed. During the rule of Murad, Othman's grandson, the Turks became infected with that religious fanaticism which was to lend the fire of more than earthly ambition to their subsequent enterprises. In 1306, they had crossed to Europe. The whole Balkan peninsula was gradually overrun; Sofia capitulated in 1385; and two years later the Serbs were utterly defeated at the battle of Kossovo-Pol. The West was now alarmed. A new crusade preached by Pope Boniface IX only resulted in the crushing of a pan-European army at Nicopolis on the Danube in 1396. In 1399, the Emperor Manuel II Palæologus toured the West, even to London, in search of reinforcements. In his absence Constantinople was invested; and the end seemed imminent, when the sudden defeat of the Turks by the Tartar army of Tamerlane at Angora, in 1402, caused a diversion.

The respite lasted twenty years. Under Murad II the Turks continued their advance into Bosnia, Albania and the Peloponnese. And in 1430, Salonica was captured. The Emperor John VIII Palæologus determined on one final effort to gain the sympathy of the West. After long discussions conducted by Emperor, Pope and the leading theologians of the Orthodox and Latin Churches, the union of those institutions was solemnly celebrated at Florence in 1439. The effort was of little avail; in Constantinople once again the people refused to acquiesce; the resultant crusade came to disaster at Varna on the Black Sea in 1444; and in 1448, another Western army was almost annihilated at the second battle of Kossovo-Pol. Yet still, where the might of Europe failed, the Greeks behind their walls held out. In 1451, Mohammed II succeeded to the leadership of the Ottoman Turks. Immediately pre-

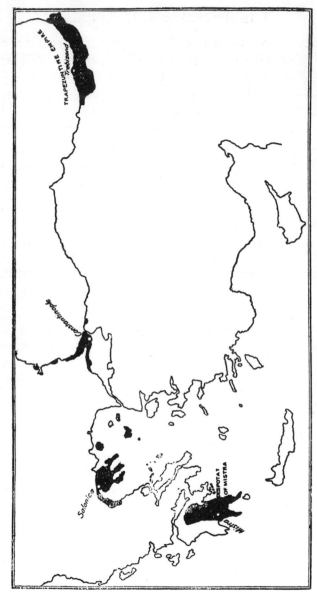

THE OUTPOSTS OF GREEK INDEPENDENCE AT THE OPENING OF THE FIFTEENTH CENTURY

parations were set on foot for a grand assault on the city that inflamed the Sultan's dreams. Gigantic cannon were conſtruƈted. Men were assembled from the furtheſt corners of the Ottoman dominions. Within the walls, the Emperor Conſtantine XI Dragases could call on only 8000 men to defend by sea and land fourteen miles of battlements. The siege laſted fifty-three days. Early in the morning of 29th April 1453 the Turks entered the city. And the laſt of the Eaſt Roman Emperors died in battle for his own and his people's good name.

Still, however, in the separate Empire of Trebizond on the Black Sea and the Despotat of Miſtra in the Peloponnese, Greek independence held out. The former was reduced in 1461. In the frescoed churches of the latter, the Renascence of painting that might have been, that was in faƈt to find its flowering in El Greco, was already visible. But this outpoſt of Hellenism had capitulated in 1460. The Middle Ages were over. And the Byzantine era, the bridge between the modern world and antiquity, was at an end.

CHAPTER VI

THE SUBSTANCE OF THE STATE

THE political needs of every people have certain elements in common; and the analysis of any long-lived political organism, if only for the rarity of such a phenomenon, muſt always evoke intereſt in a world where the search for the perfeƈt ſtate is without end. As Europeans, we have been taught to look with peculiar respeƈt upon the political aspirations of a single and immutable temperament: the Greek. That those aspirations, disappointed in the classical era, eventually found satisfaƈtion; and, having found, retained it through the numerous centuries of the Dark and Middle Ages by means of one single political form in which no change was ever contemplated; is often forgotten. Not only was the achievement unique both in date and duration. But the example remains to-day: primarily for the Greeks; especially for the Mediterranean peoples; and ultimately for the world. It remains not to be copied; but to illuſtrate, by its endurance, which of the eternal demands of peoples it succeeded in satisfying.

Contraſted with the contemporary ſtates of Weſtern Europe, born, mutilated, ſtifled at the caprice of each mediæval Napoleon, the Greek Empire preserved always as its prime interest the welfare of the community as a whole. Its policy might be influenced, but the entire resources of the state were never as in the West absorbed, by the private ambitions of princes and prelates and a lesser nobility always aspiring to be greater. Whatever the changes in authority, the usurpations or partitions of the imperial office, or the personal predilection of its occupants, the administration continued unaffected; the provinces were governed; the revenues arrived. The rule of favourites and foreigners, dictated by the whims and amours of the sovereign, was unknown. The structure of the Byzantine state was one that neither monarch, nobility nor people could sunder. Simultaneously its cohesion was not dependent, as to-day we are accustomed to think essential, on an aggressive racial consciousness. Its patriotism was of a religious, mystical nature, linked with the infallibility of the Hellenic destiny and the championship of Christianity. In this latter province, moreover, in the daily, hourly exercise of the mystic faculty, the Greek passion for speculative argument, natural as the leaves to the tree, was diverted from the tortuous, political channels where it will always find wreck, to the infinite and immaterial oceans of personal imagination.

The absolute sovereignty of the Byzantine Emperor " ὁ πιστὸς ἐν Χριστῷ αὐτοκράτωρ τῶν Ῥωμαίων — the faithful in Christ Emperor of the Romans," was derived ultimately, often immediately, from the

113

Senate, the Army and the People of Constantinople. The monarchy was elective; and though it frequently happened that the real initiative lay with the tumultuous popular opinion of the capital, only the proclamation of an aspirant's claim by the senate or some section of the army could validate the assumption of imperial power. Of these bodies, each had to ratify the nomination of the other; the people followed suit; the election was registered by the Senate; and the process was completed by coronation. In the event of disagreement on the side of one of these parties, the issue was apt to be decided by force, and these occasions have been termed, with often questionable justification, usurpations. But once in his hands, the power was the Emperor's to share with an imperial partner in his lifetime, or bequeath after his death to his sons, daughters, relatives, or anyone he might think suitable. Among the occupants of the throne, a phenomenal level of ability was thus maintained. Empresses in their own right, or Emperors more concerned with their subjects' mental than bodily welfare, were provided with military colleagues. While, simultaneously, dynastic attachment, most comprehensive of political bonds, was engrained in the people at no risk of political inefficiency. Throughout the history of the Empire, this right of election was preserved as a remedy against such emergencies as a sudden minority or the extinction of a dynasty.

But despite this nice equilibrium of practical considerations, nothing could impair the conception of

PLATE IV

ROMANUS II AND HIS FIRST WIFE EUDOXIA.

Associated in the Imperial office with the former's father, Constantine VII Porphyrogenitus, in 945

absolute majesty, of divine power on earth, which clothed the Emperor and caught the emotions of his subjects and neighbours, till even the adjacent rulers were fain to reflect what glory they might of it by studied imitation or actual investiture in their seats at the hands of the Byzantine monarch. The world was Christ's and the Emperor his living representative, ἰσαπόστολος, equal of the apostles, who might even enter the sanctuary with the priests. Like the Liturgy, the ritual of his days paraphrased the life of his Patron. Twelve guests ate at his table. Each apartment of the palace was furnished with a vestry for the changing of his vestments. At Easter he donned a garb of resurrection. The splendour of his surroundings dumbfounded the senses. The plenitude of his power seemed to know no bounds. Such was the visual prospect, designed mainly for the impression of foreigners. For, in fact, even when the diadem was safely conferred, he was hemmed with limitations. While only he could issue and dispense the laws, he was bound also to uphold them: as the fount of justice accessible at all times to petition, the people regarded him as their protector against the aristocracy and bureaucracy. Furthermore, the bureaucracy of functionaries trained in the Roman tradition, inflexible against innovation, precluded altogether the pursual of a purely arbitrary rule. And the bureaucracy, from the Emperor's point of view, was indispensable, if only as a safeguard against potential discontent on the part of the Micrasiatic magnates.

In short, the letter of power—or, indeed, in the case of those who deserved it, the actuality—was delegated by the sources of that power to a depotism of pontifical and symbolic magnificence, sufficient to focus the scattered allegiance of races and individuals within the Empire. At the same time, the democratic instincts of the Greeks were quieted: for their ruler was no longer ordinary man. Thus, for the first and last time, their susceptible imaginations were harnessed to their political well-being.

The second, and, in the light of subsequent history, most significant factor in the stability of the Byzantine Empire, was the continued vitality, fortified by successive adaptations to the trend of public need, of the Roman law. While, in the West, from the sixth to the twelfth centuries, the intentions of equity were obscured by an inextricable turmoil of Germanic custom and feudal privilege, within the sphere of Greek rule access to a uniform machinery of justice was the privilege of all. That it should have remained so was due to Justinian. Upon his accession in 527, the collected principles, precedents and modifications of a thousand years' legislative activity were beginning, in the provinces at least, to rob the scales of their balance. Manuals of law were scarce and expensive. And it was no part of a Greek official's education to acquire the Latin in which they were written. Actuated by his vision of a new and homogeneous Mediterranean dominion, the Emperor, in the first year of his reign, entrusted to his minister, Tribonian, and nine assistants, the work of revising the existing codes, with a view to the inclusion of recent legislation and the elimination of anachronisms. This labour was completed in fourteen months; and copies of the final code were despatched to all the magistrates of the Empire. The next three years were devoted to the Pandects, wherein 3,000,000 lines of precedents and *dicta* were reduced to 150,000. Meanwhile the Institutes, an authorised legal primer, had been published for the benefit of students and the regulation of legal training. Haphazard law-schools were closed. And their functions were concentrated in the three centres of Rome, Constantinople and Beyrut. For future generations henceforth, despite the occasional subsidence of legal education, the fundamentals of Roman equity, and the happiness thereby implied, were the property of the Byzantines. As a monument to that combination of broad conception with the will to execution which, in Justinian's case, amounted to genius, his subjects erected an equestrian statue of him on a pillar at the south-west corner of St Sophia, his church and other achievement. Thus, in copper semblance four times mortal size, with " a great plume on his head the shape of the tail of a peacock," and a gold orb in his right hand, he survived for the Turkish armies to wonder at.[1] His body fell to the crusaders in 1204, who tore the vestments from

---

[1] The description is taken from Clavijo. A fourteenth-century drawing of the statue used to exist, and presumably still does, in the Library of the Serai at Constantinople.

it. But the work lived till to-day. Without the discovery of the Corpus Juris in the eleventh century, and the assistance of Azo, the Bolognese, to Bracton, the father of English law, in the thirteenth, the whole process of European justice must have emerged unaided from a sea of tenaciously held local habits.

During the succeeding centuries, two main epochs were distinguished for their constructive legislation. In Justinian's code, certain novelties had been due to the increasing influence of Christianity in everyday life. The position of wives and children had been strengthened against the lingering tyranny of the early Roman householder. The lot of slaves was ameliorated, and pagans were excluded from civil rights. Under the iconoclast Emperors, who were the first to attempt substantial modification of Justinian's original code, this Christian tendency was pushed to Puritan limits which harmonised with their severe spiritual ideals. The status of a man's mistress was no longer afforded legal recognition; and divorce was made more difficult. Simultaneously the tendency towards equality in family life was advanced: the position of women as property-owners and guardians brought level with that of men; and each child secured a share in the inheritance. Exemptions from justice in favour of rank were suspended: henceforward men were equal in the sight not only of God, but of the law. This marked the definite acceptance of one of the fundamental axioms of the modern state. In the sphere of private morals, however, the reforms were not permanent. Under the

Macedonian Emperors, with whom the second period of recodification opened, concubinage became once more a legal state, and the grounds of divorce were made large as formerly. The Basilica, as the new code was called, was essentially a reversion to Justinian's original, though further simplified. For five centuries, until the Turkish conquest, it remained the current law of the Greek lands, from Mistra to Trebizond. The Pravda, of early Russia, was simply a transcript of it. And four centuries later, upon the reconstitution of a Greek state, it was resumed as the groundwork of modern Greek law.

It is impossible, without crediting the reader with an extensive knowledge of legal technicality and terminology, to present a fuller analysis of Byzantine legislation. Let it simply be borne in mind that those principles of justice which form the basis of society in twentieth-century France or Scotland, were formerly as deeply engrained in the subjects of the Greek Empire as in the inhabitants of those countries to-day; that a sprinkling of Syrian custom was incorporated, which was mainly apparent in a safeguarding of contracts against the native ingenuity of the Levant, together with an opposition to the law's interference in family relationships; that there was also a separate canon law competent to deal with marriages, legacies and suits, where one of the parties was an ecclesiastic—though, save in the matter of royal morals, no Byzantine Thomas à Becket ever came in conflict with a state that was itself scarcely secular; and some idea may be gained

of the social security which the Empire enjoyed. In
the provinces the law was administered by particular
judges; while, in the capital, there were special municipal courts under the supervision of the Eparch of the
city. Political suits were judged by the senate, a body
like the English House of Lords, half noble, half
efficient, which, in its character of advisory council,
could initiate, though not put in force, legislation. The
final court of appeal was the Emperor, either in person,
or, more usually, through a court of judges and
great ministers known as the βασιλικὸν δικαστήριον.
Sentence in criminal cases consisted usually of mutilation or confiscation of property. The supposed cruelty
of the former punishment has been the subject of much
comment. Comparison with the American practice of
sterilisation might seem invidious. But it may be
remembered in extenuation, that as a substitute for the
death penalty, it gave the sinner time to preserve at
least his soul intact; and that to many a Byzantine, his
mangled body or the world which his blinded eyes could
no longer see, were in any case but transient unrealities
compared with the imminent and vivid glories awaiting
him on his deliverance from mortal trammels. Imprisonment, for a nation of philosophers, was considered
no hardship. But whatever the faults of the system,
whatever the characters of individual Emperors, it was
always considered the first duty of the ruler to uphold
the administration of justice, and to enable his subjects
to reap its full benefit. To this doctrine, the Emperors,
down to the lowest and the last, subscribed.

By degrees, however, the careful regulations for legal education established by Justinian, lapsed; and the science of jurisprudence fell to the care of the municipal guilds. But in law, as in all learning, the eleventh century witnessed a revival. In 1045, the Emperor Constantine IX Monomach refounded the old law-school of Constantinople. How long this institution, in its second version, survived, is not known. But the Emperor's enterprise illustrates the reawakened conception of law as a science rather than a mere set of regulations. Momentous repercussions resulted in the West. In the schools of Rome and Ravenna the Institutes and Pandects were already to some extent familiar. But it was Bologna, acting on the new impulse in the East, that sprang suddenly into international prominence from the revived study of Justinian's law in its purest form. The whole of Europe was permeated. And the last survival of the Roman Imperial cult, the doctrine of divine right, of royal absolutism symbolised in court ceremonial and legally defined and legally advocated, came now to reinforce the shifting bonds of fealty and vassalage. Hence arose that grotesque conception of monarchy, unfettered by the checks imposed on its Eastern counterpart and lacking the smallest guarantee of continued efficiency, which Louis XIV carried to its pinnacle. The immediate effect was to discount the theory of papal absolutism; and for the next two centuries all active legislation in Western Europe owed its inspiration, directly or indirectly, to Bologna. Bracton, whose introduction of

Roman law and method into his *De Legibus et Con-*
suetudinibus Angliæ, created the English legal system,
modelled his work on a treatise of Azo of Bologna.
And it was to his early studies in the same town that
Francesco Accursi, coadjutor of Edward I, owed the legal
facility which has brought that king his greatest fame.

Upholding the Byzantine conceptions of sovereignty
and law thus outlined, there stood that massive and pro-
ficient Atlas, the Byzantine bureaucracy.   In the states
of Western Europe, the methods of administration remained in a condition of perpetual flux till the nineteenth and twentieth centuries.   In Constantinople, by
contrast, though the seventh century saw a change of
titles and a certain redistribution of duties, the essential
formation was never altered.   Inherited directly from
Rome, the system preserved, until the time of Justinian,
a Latin nomenclature of office and the use of Latin as
an official language.   On these grounds, numerous
historians have maintained that, until the seventh
century, the Byzantine Empire was a purely Roman
institution; though by an analogous process of reasoning they might with equal accuracy call England
French from the Conquest to the reign of Henry III.
The main reformation, if it can be thus definitely
termed, was part of the centralising policy of the
Emperor Leo III the Isaurian, who ascended the
throne in 716.   For the few great official posts, relics
of the Augustan household, were substituted a body of
more numerous and consequently less independent

PLATE V

LATER BYZANTINE OFFICIALS

Theodore Metochites, Grand Logothete to the Emperor Andronicus II Palaeologus, about 1320

PLATE VI

LATER BYZANTINE OFFICIALS

Apocaucos, High Admiral during the minority of the Emperor John V Palaeologus, about 1340

Logothetes; while the actuality of power which they thus forfeited was transferred to the crown; Leo's hypothesis being, as was natural considering his own temperament and circumstances, that its wearer must always be inspired by a Napoleonic passion for combined civil and military activity. From this moment arose that divergence between the militarists from Asia Minor and the more purely Hellenic civil service which, in the eleventh century, was to become disastrously acute. Succeeding years proved, however, that this arrogation of power to the throne varied in validity with the efficiency of its occupant; and that, in fact, the strength of the bureaucratic tradition was little impaired. Nor was there any parliament, any fluctuating expression of popular fancies and ill-judgment, to come between the sovereignty and its officials and clog the everyday machinery of the state. (On special occasions popular opinion never lacked expression: witness the perpetual stultification of the attempted union of the Churches.) The privy council of the Emperor, assembling in the sacred precincts of the Great Palace, was at the same time his executive. Here gathered the Logothetes: the ministers of the army and navy; of communications, posts, police and foreign affairs; of finance, the public revenues and the imperial estates; each with his secretaries; and each reinforced by the multitudinous and carefully-trained personnel which comprised his Λογοθεσία—Ministry. These great functionaries were generally, though not necessarily, recruited, after passing a difficult examination, from distinguished families in which public service was a tradition. Each bore two titles: one denoting his place in the ancient, though not in theory hereditary, grades of nobility conferred by the Emperor; the other, the actual business of his office. In this way the hierarchies of rank, each with its valued privileges, were shared between the claims of birth and talent. Each official, in his labours, was spurred by the prospect of higher reward, of wealth derived from both salary and recognised perquisites, and of honour and insignias which his contemporaries might respect and envy. All ambition towards personal advancement was thus directed to the service of the machine.

In the sphere of provincial administration, the unceasing pressure on the Empire's frontiers resulted in a gradual negation of the conditions which Diocletian's reorganisation at the end of the third century had presupposed. A junction of civil and military authority became inevitable, first materialising, as a sequel to the outlying conquests of Justinian, in the Exarchates of North Africa and Spain, and Ravenna. These were ruled by governors who could make their tenure hereditary and were personally responsible to the Emperor alone. During the dangerous period of the seventh century, when the Greeks bore the brunt of the first Moslem expansion, the system thus inaugurated, though no longer open to hereditary exploitation, came into force throughout the Empire; and with its perfection by the Isaurian Emperors that followed, there came into existence the "themes," as the newly

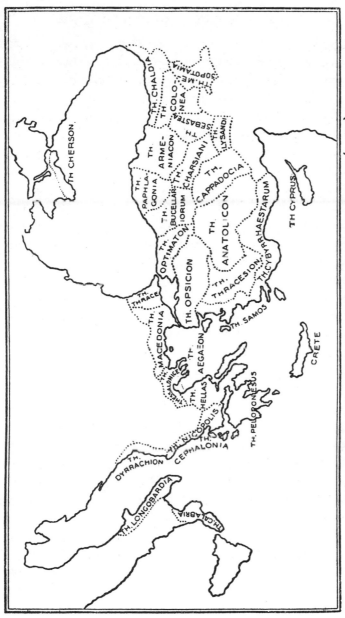

THE ORGANISATION OF THE THEMES UNDER THE MACEDONIAN DYNASTY (c. 975)

organised provinces were henceforth known. Each was under the command of a General; and these soldier-administrators ranked with the powerful officials of the state, those of the Asiatic provinces taking precedence over the others. The larger of these territorial units maintained separate forces of about 10,000 men each, which were charged to the expense of the local populations. At the same time, a central army was stationed in or near Constantinople, thus preserving that mobility of action which had been Diocletian's primary object in freeing the army from the burden of provincial administration. But though, under the Isaurian reorganisation, the whole military, financial and judicial power was concentrated in the hands of the Στρατηγός or Governor, there was also resident a civil representative, who was independent of the Governor's authority and in direct communication with the Palace at Constantinople. A limit was thus set to those provincial despotisms which were always potential, and sometimes actual, sources of insurrection and usurpation. With the coming of the crusaders in the eleventh century, and the consequent infiltration of feudal ideas, the imperial practice of granting extensive land tenures, carrying with them a large measure of *de facto* personal jurisdiction, in return for military aid and levies, threatened to disrupt the administration and interfere with the arrival of the revenues. On this point, the division between the bureaucrats and the great military landowners was widest.

The spectacle of a body of trained officials in active opposition to a virile military party is not one which history often presents. But for those familiar only with the automata of Whitehall or the peculators of Washington, the personnel of the Byzantine bureaucracy is not easily visualised. The vicissitudes and methods of its schooling may be traced in the history of the royal universities of Constantinople, which were founded mainly to that end. First province of learning in which all were to be instructed, was the humanities; even the texts considered essential to the moulding of these girders of society have been preserved in the gigantic manual of convention left by the scholar-Emperor, Constantine VII Porphyrogenitus. And it may be to the recognition of the fact that a clerk will do his work better if he is a human being as well, that the world owes the infinite copyings of which one here and one there escaped to tell the modern world of the wisdom of the ancient. In philosophy, literature, rhetoric, and all branches of mathematics including astronomy and geometry, professors were attached to the successive foundations. In 727, the already existing university of the Octagon was closed by Leo III, the Isaurian, partly, it may be supposed, on account of its monkish teachers, partly as the nursery of a class whose influence he was determined to weaken. A century later, however, the iconoclast Emperor, Theophilus, was promoting the instruction of mathematics. And twenty-five years after, the Cæsar Bardas, the Regent, opened what is commonly called the Byzantine Renascence with his reconstitution of the university of the Magnavra, in the precincts of the Great Palace. His work was continued, in the first half of the tenth century by Constantine VII Porphyrogenitus, under whom not only were the professors paid, but also the students —a clear indication of the purpose for which they were there. All were personally known to the Emperor; and from their ranks, in due time, were chosen the judges, the civil servants, and the prelates of the Church.

At length came the glorious reign of Basil II Bulgaroctonos, who held all forms of learning in open contempt. But the more prosperity, success and leisure were theirs, the more the minds of his subjects turned to their books. It needed only the accession of a pedant-Emperor in the person of Constantine IX Monomach, husband of Zoë, last but her sister of the Macedonian dynasty, to bring the bureaucracy, reinforced in popular opinion by its recent discovery of Plato, into its own again. The military magnates were ousted from power, and their places taken by vain academicians, in whose selection birth and tradition were considered superfluous. In Asia Minor, a system of scutage was introduced, whereby the obligation on the part of the landowners to maintain levies for the service of the state was converted into money, thus weakening both their power and the Empire's borders. Finally, 1071 saw the disaster which this cleavage had rendered inevitable. The Byzantine army was almost annihilated on the Armenian border; the Emperor Romanus IV Diogenes taken prisoner; and the richest provinces of Asia Minor were lost for ever. Before its reorganisation by Alexius I Comnenus on his accession in 1081, the Byzantine

army had almost ceased to exist. But if the fault is to
be laid at the door of the anti-military party, it must be
remembered, in mitigation, that even so strong a
monarch as Basil II had been seriously threatened by
insurrections of the magnates.

The conditions that led to the defeat of Manzikert
have been recounted at some length, because they illustrate the curiously balanced elements of the Byzantine
administration: a liberally educated civil service working in conjunction with a military aristocracy. With
the loss of the inland themes, the power of the latter
was gone. And though the throne became now the
perquisite of the great families, the backbone of the
state was still, as formerly, the bureaucracy. Not until
the middle of the fourteenth century was the system
officially interrupted. It then became necessary, owing
to the perpetual incursions of Turks, Normans, Italians
and Spaniards, and the consequent isolation of the
capital from the provinces, to create minor autonomies
known as Despotats, under royal governors. Thus the
disintegrating Empire assumed an almost federal character. And Constantinople was shorn of the few
revenues that still remained to her.

An important, though wholly distinct, function of
the central authority in the capital was the treatment of
peoples newly conquered or subdued. In this the
Byzantines sought not only conciliation, but also to
evoke for their civilisation and institutions such a degree
of admiration on the part of savage races that the latter

were fain to reflect all they could of the glory of the
queen of cities. In the writings of Constantine VII
Porphyrogenitus, it was laid down as an established
principle that each subject nationality should retain, as
far as possible, the laws and customs peculiar to it. It
was also the policy of the Greeks to make use of the
native nobility in the work of local government. Thus
the early Ventian Doges received their pictorially
familiar robes at the hands of the Emperors of Constantinople. And even after the savage campaigns of
Basil II Bulgaroctonos, the Bulgar nobles were received
at Constantinople and invested with the insignias of
Byzantine rank. Some of them, like the Venetians
before them, obtained wives of noble Greek family.
The latter was a common means of securing the good-
will of adjacent potentates, there existing in the capital
no prejudice against the marriage of even royal princesses to Tartar chieftains and Moslem Emirs. The
far-flung monasteries of the Orthodox Church, together
with travelling missionaries and merchants, helped also
to implant the seeds of a uniform faith and culture. It
was, in fact, the aim of the Byzantine Empire to win
the adherence of its subjects and the submission of its
neighbours, not by the imposition of a spurious
nationalism, but by the attraction which the brilliance
of a great civilisation must always exercise upon the
moth-like tribes within its sphere of light.

For the Byzantines, therefore, in three elements lay
the political stability which was the first condition of

their civilisation: in sovereignty; in law; and in a trained executive. The absence of any vestige of parliamentary institution may not accord with the political ideals of the twentieth century. But nowhere since its introduction to the Mediterranean countries has the unhappy fetish of constitutionalism produced efficient government. And the Greek, above all, with his whole temperament saturated in political emotion, may well ask himself the question: How did a seeming autocracy maintain the efficacy of the Byzantine state without offence to his democratic susceptibilities? The secret lies in that uncommon adjustment of forces which the Mediterranean peoples have yet to rediscover.

CHAPTER VII

IT is the habit of contemporaries, when their attention
is diverted to the glories of the past, to recall with
critical distaste the uncouth conditions of living that
accompanied them. The radiance of the *Roi Soleil* is
dimmed at recollection of the uses to which the stairs
of Versailles were habitually put. The English Renascence is more sullied by the prospect of Henry
VIII's single cambric shirt than by all the executions
of Bloody Mary. And to what purpose Parthenon and
Colosseum, when prosperous citizens beneath them
lived in mud huts and stone cubicles? Through all the
history of Europe, it is only in the case of Constantinople
that these nervous queries do not arise. The amenities
of life were proportionate to the Empire's wealth. And
there is no more remarkable proof of the unique position occupied in history by mediæval Greek civilisation than the size of the Byzantine budgets, which
have remained, computed on the bullion value of their
gold alone, without precedent until the present age.
This wealth was the great auxiliary condition of the
Empire's stability. It remains to discover whence it
was derived; what its amount; and of what nature its
international consequence.

PLATE VII

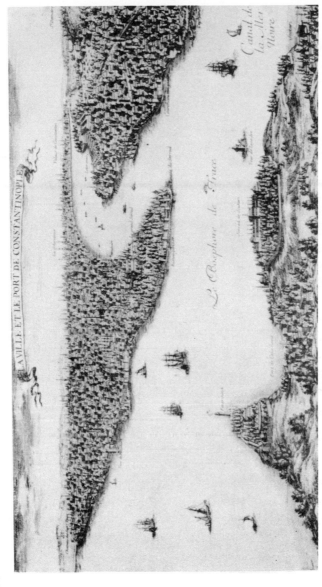

CONSTANTINOPLE, THE GOLDEN HORN AND GALATA

Taken from Asia

It has been said that the transference of the Roman capital to Conſtantinople opened up the Eaſt as the discovery of Columbus did America. Whatever the exaggeration of this ſtatement, it was here, henceforth, at this thwarted kiss of two continents, that the trade between the richeſt extremities of Europe, Asia and Africa, was sucked and spewed at the lips of the Golden Horn. Through Antioch and Alexandria, till their conqueſt by the Moslems, through Salonica, Trebizond and Cherson, the ſtreams of commerce flowed. From Hungary, Germany and Central Europe; from the Adriatic by the road from Durazzo; from Kiev and the early Russian ſtates, down the Dnieper and the Don, to the Black Sea; and from Samarcand, Bokhara, and the Caspian; from Persia, India and China; from Ceylon, from Abyssinia and the heart of Africa up the Red Sea; from every degree of the compass came the caravans and fleets, to pour their dues into the imperial cuſtoms, and dump their goods in the clearing-house of Conſtantinople, the " middleman " of three continents. Furthermore, in the eyes of three continents, or rather their adjacent territories comprised in the Levant, the city ſtood as a symbol of security in a discordant and unſtable world. Not once in nine centuries was the Byzantine government bankrupt; and for nine centuries the walls remained impregnable by land and sea againſt the ebb and flow of Islam and the barbarous contaƈts with the North. The European, the Levantine, horizon, offered no comparable safety. Countless sums were inveſted from without in this universal truſt.

133

And for the Moslem, here was a depository where he could obtain the interest on his money that his faith forbade. Under every impulse, from every quarter, wealth converged. Good position and good reputation are familiar slogans. For Constantinople, as with other institutions, they formed the basis of commercial prosperity. The Greeks themselves were wont to say that two-thirds of all the world's riches were concentrated within the city's walls.

Of the merchandise that arrived in the capital, the greater part was raw material; and even of this much was redistributed in the West. All the hackneyed refinements of our mediæval life, those treasured spices and medicaments, were introduced, prior to the thirteenth century, from the Byzantine mart. From India came pepper and musk, cloves, nutmeg, cinnamon, and camphor; from Persia, sugar; from China, ginger and rhubarb. Aloes and balsam, preserved fruits, curative nuts, and Arabian incense accompanied them. For the manufacture of those *objets d'art*, of which book-covers and reliquaries filtered through to the West, and some still survive in such sanctuaries as Athos, the traders brought ivory and amber, pearls and precious stones; for the colouring of enamels, mosaic cubes, and manuscript illuminations, saffron, indigo, alum and gum. In the heyday of commerce, before the eruption of the Mongol races beyond the Oxus, porcelain from China and glass from Mesopotamia were imported ready-made. Byzantine looms received their flax from Egypt, their cotton from Syria and Armenia; while the names Muslin, Taffeta, and Damask bespeak the large trade in the finished textiles of the East. Coasting round the shores of the Black Sea in their river-built boats, the Russians contributed gold and silver, honey, wax, furs, corn, fruit and slaves. Every foreign merchant arriving in Constantinople was obliged to report to the State authorities. He was permitted to remain three months; and if by that time his wares were not sold, the State undertook to dispose of them on his behalf.

Within the city, the various craftsmen were organised in guilds, which were under the supervision of the Eparch. Consumer and producer alike were protected from the middleman; wages and hours were fixed; and any form of trade-competition or possibility of the concentration of trade-control in the hands of an oligarchy of capitalists, was out of the question. Each guild purchased the raw material for its members at prices fixed by the State. Its wares were exposed for sale only in specified places, the more precious trades, such as the goldsmiths and silversmiths, enamellers and glassmakers, being grouped together near the entrance to the Great Palace under semi-royal patronage. Artists also were protected, particularly by such Emperors as Theodosius II or Constantine VII Porphyrogenitus, who were themselves painters. But the most jealously guarded of all the industries was the manufacture of the magnificent silken stuffs, which the Byzantines prized above jewels, and of which the export was absolutely prohibited. The story is famous of how the Holy Roman Ambassador of the tenth century, Liutprand, on his second mission to Conftantinople, was deprived by zealous officials of the very ftuffs with which he had been officially presented in the capital.

Until the time of Juftinian, all raw silk necessary for the produćtion of these ftuffs was sent from China to Ceylon, whence it was eventually fetched by sea to the Persian Gulf and transported thence overland. The Persians had thus a monopoly of the carrying trade, from which they did not hesitate to profit at the expense of the Byzantines. About 550, however, so the ftory runs, some Neftorian missionaries succeeded in smuggling eggs of the silkworm over the Chinese border. And it is certain that within a decade the silk induftry was fully eftablished round Conftantinople. Thenceforth it was the moft foftered business of the Empire; the prosperity of old Greece and the Morea was reconftituted by it; and the European monopoly thus inaugurated was maintained intaćt till the eleventh century, when Roger Guiscard transported the secret and the insećts from Thebes and Corinth to Palermo. After the fourth crusade, the Nicæan Emperors continued to protećt it, John III Vatatzes even forcing his subjećts to wear materials of Greek manufaćture rather than those imported from the Weft. And its vitality may be eftimated by the magnificence of the ftuffs which Greek workmen, adhering to the traditional patterns, continued to produce after the Turkish conqueft. But the almoft sacred charaćter that attached

to the moſt precious fabrics was due to more than their
artiſtic value or intrinsic worth, large as both were.
From the royal purple, or scarlet as it was in faɕt, with
its woven golden pattern of encircled eagles, through
the numerous shades, lemon, rose and apple-green, and
the numerous devices, ivy-leaves, roses, arabesques,
each variety conſtituted an insignia of rank or office.
When the Emperor travelled, cheſts of them accompanied him for diſtribution to local governors and
envoys; and visiting monarchs, such as Amaury I of
Jerusalem in 1171, were loaded with similar presents.
Half the majeſty of the imperial court was enshrined
in these uniforms. And was the fount of honour to be
smirchcd by thc casual bartcr of its veſtmcnts for any
barbarous chieftain or Norman upſtart to assume?
Only the nondescript might be exported. And the
demand from within the Empire was large enough.
Visitors to Conſtantinople teſtify to the splendour of
the inhabitants; each man, says Benjamin of Tudela,
in the second half of the twelfth century, was clothed
like a prince.

Thus, as is the fortune also of a world linked by rapid
transport, commerce brought to the mediæval Greeks
all those amenities of life which were the particular
discoveries of other races. Hence derived the profusion and universality of that financial phenomenon,
the Byzantine gold coinage. Even to-day, in England,
the " bezant " is ſtill familiar as a heraldic synonym for

137

a gold piece. Prior to the fourth crusade it conſtituted the greater part of the portable wealth of Europe. And in the nineteenth century, treasuries of conquered Indian princes were found by British soldiers filled with coins bearing the pontifical impress of the Greek Emperors of the Eaſt.

The Byzantine budgets, after the manner of modern, were calculated every year. Of subsidiary income, the chief sources were patents and monopolies, mines and arsenals, and the extensive crown-lands. Such expedients as the debasement of the coinage or the sale of titles were adopted only in the laſt desperate years, the Emperor Alexius I Comnenus' trial of the former at the close of the eleventh century having been only temporary. The main revenue, however, was derived from the cuſtoms' dues and the land-tax. The former were collected in enormous profusion in the capital, and also at all frontiers. The latter, which, since land was the staple inveſtment, corresponded to the present-day income tax, was assessed on a detailed scale of values. House property remained in one category. Agriculturally, the theoretical unit of taxation con-siſted in the natural resources capable of maintaining a single man: five acres in the case of vineyard, twenty in that of plough, and in an olive grove, 225 trees. The syſtem had faults: monaſtic and military landlords were often exempt; the nobles might manage to avoid the tax; and in such cases an added onus was consequently borne by the small cultivator. To remedy this condition, and to ensure the identity of eſtimate and revenue received, districts were made collectively responsible for the production of the sums for which they were assessed. Nevertheless, though the rich could not then so easily escape, the smaller independent proprietors, obliged in bad years to sell their freeholds in return for assistance in paying their share, tended to become absorbed by the larger. This process was to some extent checked by the legislation of the Isaurian and Macedonian Emperors. The everlasting and most urgent problem before the central administration was to ensure the honesty of the tax-collectors. Measures to this end were generally among the first reforms of an able ruler.

While it is impossible, owing to lack of evidence, to arrive at any exact analysis of Byzantine finance, certain isolated statistics[1] are available to corroborate the travellers' fables and the encrusted splendour of such few *objets d'art* as have survived into the present. Where large sums were concerned, the general monetary unit seems to have been the pound of gold: worth, as pure bullion, slightly less than £43. It has been computed that the purchasing power of precious metal in the Middle Age was five times greater than it is in our own. And though this comparison is open to dispute, the fact that the Byzantine Emperor Theophilus was paying £85 in bullion (two pounds of gold) for a horse, while his contemporary, Egbert, could get

---

[1] The following figures are only calculated approximately. For more detailed analysis, see Andréadès' *Le montant du budget de l'Empire byzantin*.

one for two-thirds of a pound of silver, illustrates the enormous purchasing power of Byzantine gold at least outside the capital. £85 for a horse may seem on the other hand to denote exceedingly high prices inside it; but the Byzantine nobles were enthusiastic breeders of horses, especially for polo; and £425 (£85 × 5) would not to-day be considered an unreasonable price for a first-class pony. There seems, in fact, justification for ascribing to the intrinsic metal of the bezant a quintuple value in modern terms. The history of Western Europe before the discovery of America teems with problems arising from the shortage of currency. And if it is open to doubt whether a pound of gold was always worth £215 (£43 × 5) in Constantinople, it seems probable that, outside, its power of purchase was even greater.

It is recorded by both Benjamin of Tudela and the Venetians that the Comneni Emperors drew yearly between four and five million pounds sterling in specie from Constantinople alone: an income which, in modern parlance as defined above, benefited the government to the extent of £20,000,000 annually. The island of Corfu, at the same period, contributed a yearly 1500 pounds of gold, £64,000 in metal and £320,000 in purchasing power. Following the sack of the capital in 1204, the crusading barons, after consulting the existing accounts, guaranteed the Emperor Baldwin I an annual income of approximately £6,300,000 in specie. This was from but a quarter of the Empire; and it has, therefore, been deduced that under the Comneni, the whole annual revenue, already, be it remembered, considerably shrunk since the days of the Macedonians, amounted in terms of purchasing capacity to £126,000,000. However hypothetical this figure, it is interesting to compare it with those received by the British Exchequer in 1883-1884 and 1913-1914, which totalled £86,999,564 and £195,640,000 respectively. Proportionately, reserves in bullion of £5,500,000 and £10,000,000 (£27,500,000 and £50,000,000 in purchasing value) were left by the Emperors Theophilus and Basil II Bulgaroctonos in the imperial treasury. The two millions laboriously hoarded by King Henry VII of England five hundred years later, to the grateful astonishment of his subjects, fade into insignificance. And an idea of the diffusion of wealth in humbler places may be gathered from the fact that in 935 two thousand male inhabitants of the Peloponnese paid £4280 in specie as commutation for military service: an average, in terms of purchasing value, of £10, 14s. apiece.

The part played by this wealth in maintaining the stability of the Byzantine Empire is apparent by contrast with the states of Western Europe, where permanent services, such as a standing army, fleet, or bureaucracy, were almost entirely precluded, owing to the difficulty of raising sufficient coin for their wages. As a rule, the only rewards that a king could offer his adherents were land and hereditary privilege. Hence the perpetual expansion of feudalism and the perpetual scourge of civil war that accompanied it. In the

East, on the other hand, the political organism rested on its money, and in the end failed with it. At the centre, the expenses of concentrating the whole of Byzantine majesty in the imperial office were enormous. Vast public works at royal charge, fortresses, walls and aqueducts; intimate and bewilderingly splendid private edifices; a daily ceremonial involving the employment of thousands; an interminable ritual of present-giving and largess-throwing; bounties, hospitals and religious foundations; altogether a prodigality as lavish and beneficial as it has generally been called purposeless and vulgar, was prescribed by custom and expediency. Focused round the palace, the Logothetes and their ministries of trained officials demanded enormous upkeep, particularly that of Foreign Affairs, or of the Barbarians, as it was Hellenically designated. In the archives of this, were records of the characteristics of every people with which the Empire was in contact, their strengths and weaknesses, their leading families, and the particular presents that they most appreciated. The bulk of the latter was doubtless bullion, and whole nations were kept in fief by subsidies which historians persist in terming tributes. The cost of rebuilding Milan during the struggle with Barbarossa was defrayed by the gold of the Emperor Manuel I Comnenus; the massacre of Normans in 1282, known as the Sicilian Vespers, by that of Michael VIII Palæologus. And four and a half centuries earlier, when John the Grammarian was despatched on embassy to Bagdad by the Emperor Theophilus, he took with him a sum of nearly £90,000 in purchasing value, which he distributed "like the sand of the sea."

The chief responsibilities of the treasury, after the support of the court and central ministries, were the army and navy and the provincial administrations. Salaries, even of private soldiers, would seem to have been high. In 809, King Kroum of Bulgaria captured 11,000 pounds of gold, equal to £470,000 in specie, and in reality worth some £2,350,000, which was being transported with the army for its payment. And in 949 the Emperor Constantine VII Porphyrogenitus notes that an expedition to Crete of 14,459 men cost 3706 pounds of gold, in other words £159,000 in specie and £795,000 in actual value. A comparative table of salaries recorded by that Emperor in the middle of the tenth century, and translated into purchasing value, together with those current in the British Empire immediately before the outbreak of the Great War, reveals a curious approximation:—

BYZANTINE		BRITISH	
Corporals . .	£4 a week	Sergeants (infantry, without allowance) . .	£1, 5s. a week
Lieutenants (with servants, etc., to find) . .	£440 a year	Lieutenants . .	£122 a year
Captains . .	£600 ,,	Captains . .	£210 ,,
Governors of 5th class themes (border marches)	£1070 ,,	Governor of Falkland Islands .	£1500 ,,

BYZANTINE		BRITISH	
Governors of 4th class themes (maritime)	. £2140 a year	Governors of Newfoundland, Bahamas and Tasmania between	£2000 and £2750 a year
Governors of the five 3rd class themes	. £4280 „	Governors of New South Wales, Victoria, Jamaica and Straits Settlements	. £5000 „
Governors of the three 2nd class themes	. £6420 „	Governors of New Zealand and Ceylon	. £7000 „
Governors of the three 1st class themes	. £8560 „	Governors of Madras, Bombay and Bengal	. £8000 „
		Governors-General of Canada, Australia and South Africa	£10,000 „

In the cases of New Zealand, the civil and military commands are combined, as they were in the person of the Byzantine Στρατηγὸς, or Governor. It may also be noticed in passing that the chair of philosophy in the University founded by the Emperor Constantine IX Monomach in the middle of the eleventh century, was worth £856 a year, exclusive of keep and titles. This compares favourably with the £800 a year, supplemented by rooms in college, which was received by the occupants of the three philosophic chairs in Oxford before the Great War.

Thus by means of a constant system of reward, prejudicial to no interest of the state, was the best service of officials assured.

144

Trade and the Bezant

It is remarkable to think that while the world to-day conducts its affairs almost wholly by written draft, transactions in the Byzantine sphere involved transportation of the actual gold; that in fact the mediæval Greeks conducted a finance of almost modern dimensions without the assistance of the modern credit system. Produced by the Empire's trade, the bezant was absorbed in the Empire's welfare, social and political. Yet there was more involved in the Byzantine Dives than domestic accounts. The repercussion was international. Fluttering at the golden beacon, the lazzaroni of Europe and Asia alike beseeched commercial favours of the imperial government. And just as at Constantinople there arose the first systematisation of European diplomatic procedure, it was there also that the first principles of the extra-territoriality of ambassadors and the treatment of resident foreigners were formulated. Racial and religious distinctions, save where Christological heresies were concerned, were viewed with toleration. The Jews, hounded over the face of the earth, found refuge behind the walls of Galata. And the crusaders, to their inexpressible indignation, discovered in the city a Saracen mosque of official construction, where services for the Moslem residents were conducted in the full light of day. This magnetic cosmopolitanism which stamped mediæval Greek civilisation, was definitely organised, and from the tenth century on, exercised an increasing influence on the policies of the West.

The earliest and most pertinacious of the regular

traders seem to have been the Russians. The peculiar structure of the first Russian city states, based on a commercial rather than a territorial authority over the neighbouring magnates, rendered Byzantine trade indispensable to their existence. For what reasons their intercourse with Constantinople was threatened, history does not record. But whatever the circumstances, they were prepared, if necessary, to preserve it by force; and many a fleet from the great rivers above the Black Sea was repulsed from the city walls by Greek arms and Greek fire. In 911, however, an agreement was reached which constituted the first of the famous " Capitulations," and the first enunciation of the principle of extra-territoriality. The rules were strict. The Russian merchants were allotted their own quarter; but they were forbidden to enter the town save by one gate; they were to be disarmed; their numbers might not exceed fifty; and they could remain no longer than a winter. It was with them, moreover, that there came those Scandinavian adventurers who formed the original nucleus of the Varangian Guard, which surrounded the Emperor's person, and was to prove the refuge of numerous adherents of King Harold of England, exiled after the Norman Conquest of 1066, whose descendants are mentioned by the chroniclers of the fourth crusade. Left in freedom by the government, for many years these Saxons retained their language, dress and weapons. And the tiny basilica church, dedicated to SS. Nicolas and Augustine of Canterbury, which tradition assigns to them, may still be seen among the lettuce-beds and melons of a Stambul back-garden.[1]

It was, however, with the advent of the Italians that the form in which the Capitulations have descended to the present century cryﬆallised. Aﬅual dates are obscure; but it appears that the Amalfitans, in the middle of the eleventh century, were the firﬆ to obtain a wharf on the Golden Horn. In 1082, they were followed by the Venetians, to whom, in return for the assiﬆance of their fleet againﬆ the Normans at Durazzo, the Emperor Alexius I Comnenus granted complete immunity in all the ports of the Empire from the dues which were the chief source of the ﬆate revenues, and which even the Greek merchants themselves were obliged to pay. Before the century was out, the Genoese were also eﬆablished. And in 1110, as counterbalance to the fleets of the firﬆ crusaders, the Pisans were provided with a quay, and allotted seats both in the Hippodrome and St Sophia, an illuminating sidelight on the thoroughness of Byzantine hospitality. Each colony had its own bazaars, its own courts— abolished by the Turks in 1923—and its own baily, who combined the funﬅions of magiﬆrate and captain.

[1] The church is now known as Bogdan Serai. Up till 1865, tombstones of the Varangians still existed on a tower in the vicinity. In that year, the request of the British Ambassador that they might be removed to the British cemetery at Scutari prompted the Turks to use them for building purposes. The copies of the inscriptions, which were taken, were accidentally burnt in 1870. And any record of the transactions that may have survived has been consigned by the fantastic humour of the Foreign Office to a gaol in Cambridge. Such is the valley of historical research.

147

Enormous success attended their ventures. So important did Venetian interests in the Levant become, that, during the Latin Empire, the transference to Constantinople of the Doge himself was mooted. And at the end of the twelfth century, there were said to be more than 60,000 Italians in the settlements on the Galata side of the Golden Horn. Benjamin of Tudela, writing on the careless, prosperous eve of the catastrophic fourth crusade, enumerates the diverse merchant-throng: Syrians from Babylon and Palestine, Persians and Egyptians, Russians and Hungarians, Patzinaks and Bulgars, Lombards and Spaniards, Georgians, Armenians and Turks, Christian and Mohammedan, Latin and Greek, elbowing down the narrow streets, where to-day the same and yet others with them mount the trams or glide past in limousines. For the Capitulations, like most Byzantine institutions, were borrowed by the Turks to fill the deficiency in their own nomad evolution. Those of the Genoese and Venetians were ratified in 1453, and the conquered Greeks and resident Armenians simultaneously were invested with a similar status under the control of their respective Churches. Then in 1536, the French, allied with the Sultan against Charles V, obtained the same concessions. And after them the English. The West was again arrived.

While the Italians were thus discovering the Eastern trade-routes, preparatory to diverting them from Constantinople altogether, the Greek loss was proportionate to their gain. Byzantine enterprise, already inert with

excessive prosperity, was crippled by the insensate preference granted to the Venetians under the Emperor
Alexius I Comnenus. The carrying trade of the Levant
fell into other hands. Unlike the Italians, rich Greeks
were too cautious to invest their money in the uncertain
fortunes of trading-ships. By 1150, after sixty-eight
years of the Venetian Capitulations, commerce and the
revenue resulting therefrom, were said to have decreased
by a half. Advancing in wealth as every one else de-
clined; saddled with the marauding reputation of their
fellow-Westerners, the earlier crusaders; and communi-
cants of a detested and heretical church; the Latins
of Constantinople became the object of increasing
popular hatred. Political relations with the Doge were
strained by the Byzantine successes on the Dalmatian
coast. In 1171, the Emperor Manuel I Comnenus
arrested all the Venetians in the city, confiscated their
property and deprived them of their privileges. In
1175, normal relations were restored. But seven years
later, in the tumult that followed the accession of
Andronicus I Comnenus, the Latins, who had espoused
the cause of his opponents, the Protosebastos Alexius
Comnenus and the Empress-Regent, Mary of Antioch,
fell victims to the uncontrolled mob. Priests, women,
children, and even the sick, were massacred. With the
exception of such as found refuge on board the ships in
the harbour, scarcely an Italian survived. The council-
rooms of the West, already thick with projects for an
attack on what was still the city of fabulous wealth,
quickened their preparations. In 1185, the Normans

sacked Salonica; in 1189, Barbarossa meted similar fate to Adrianople. The confusion consequent on the extinction of the Comnenus dynasty at length offered opportunity of which the champions of the Cross were not slow to take advantage. They were led by the Venetians. And the Venetians were drawn East by the lure not of land, but of trade and wealth. The astonishment of the Western host on arrival at Constantinople can scarcely find words. Not all the riches of the fifty richest cities in the world, says Robert de Clary, could surpass those of this. According to Villehardouin, "*vous pouvez savoir qu'ils regardèrent beaucoup Constantinople ceux qui jamais ne l'avaient vue; car ils ne pouvaient penser qu'il pût être en tout le monde une si riche ville, quand ils virent ces hauts murs et ces riches tours dont elle était close tout entour à la ronde, et ces riches palais et ces hautes églises dont il y avait tant que nul ne le pût croire s'il ne l'eût vu de ses yeux. . . .*" And he writes of the Great Palace after the sack: "*Du trésor qui était en ce palais il n'en faut pas parler; car il y en avait tant que c'était sans fin ni mesure.*"[1]

It is impossible to enumerate in a breath " the consequences of the fourth crusade." The social disorganisation of the Empire, the ruin of its capital, the disastrous resurgence of Slavs and Turks on either side, were all among them. But one above all was outstanding, and was destined to render the decline in Greek fortunes irrevocable. This was the absolute loss

[1] Modern French rendering.

of Levantine commerce. At the parcellation of the Byzantine territories in 1204, the Venetians had appropriated all the chief islands and ports as outposts for their wharves and warehouses; and the majority of these they retained after the reoccupation of Constantinople by the Greeks. Furthermore, the immunities that they had formerly possessed were now the property of the Genoese, to whom they had been pledged in 1261 by the Emperor Michael VIII Palæologus, in return for the assistance of their fleet. As a result, the financial predicament of the Empire during the last two centuries of its existence was piteous. There were no ships; and the annual income derived from the customs by the Genoese on the north side of the Golden Horn, was seven times as great as that of the Greeks from the same source on the south. The Emperors were at their wits' end. Writing in the middle of the fourteenth century, the Emperor John VI Cantacuzene laments: "Nowhere is there any money. The reserves are spent; the royal jewels sold; and the taxes do not materialise, the country being entirely ruined." At the marriage-feast of John V Palæologus, there was not a piece of plate, either gold or silver, on the table. And some twenty years later, the same Emperor was actually detained in Venice for debt. In 1423, Salonica, the second town of the Empire, whither formerly a fair like that of Novgorod had drawn the merchants of three continents, was sold to the Venetians for 50,000 ducats. Yet buildings, mosaics, paintings, stuffs, and silver and gold, jewelled and enamelled, have descended from the fourteenth and fifteenth centuries. Their extreme splendour indicates not necessarily exaggeration on the part of plaintive contemporaries, but rather a criterion of those vaſt riches which, productive of an even greater splendour, had been once the complement in ſtability of the Byzantine political genius.

CHAPTER VIII

THE QUEST OF REALITY

THE difference between art and religion is that, while the former seeks to express the *processes* of man's communion with Reality—in other words, the emotions—the latter seeks Reality itself, seeks to track it down, to unravel it from the illusions of the flesh with which the emotions are interwed, and to pin it to the mind for the furtherance and ultimate fulfilment of man's spiritual progression. But if religion is the hunting of Reality, what is Reality? On that rock, the voyage of all the world's thinking has been split. But one at least of its attributes, the present recognises which the immediate past has not. Reality—or rather, that vague, instinctive conception of it with which every one is born, and which a classically conceived education immediately relegates to subconscious depths—Reality provides the criterion which must determine and co-ordinate the basic significance of every object, action and theory. We may commemorate, on Whit-Sunday, the good service of Christianity. We may retain our concept of a divine fatherhood watching from above. But in the twentieth century, the unending creep of spiritual ascension has led our quest beyond the invocation of God's emissaries (their authenticity is not under discussion) and the

153

search for grace in physical sacraments physically hallowed. In the first burst of the Renascence; in the French Revolution; in the feverish dawn of mechanical discovery, others also preened themselves on arrival at this detachment. Detachment? Theirs was no detachment. They were sucking still the breasts of Reason, that portentous, Roman-nosed goddess, gay with the pallor of perpetual disinterment. Cross and classicism met; fought; fused; now perish of interaction. We in our present age, turning a point in the world's history, induct, if we can, an enlarged quest of Reality; we poise tentatively for another pace in the progression of *homo sapiens*. Every object, action, theory, shall contribute to our religion, if such we call it. With science, we have left our suckling. But what do we await?

In such case, also, during the third and fourth centuries, were the Greeks and the habitants of the Hellenised Roman Empire. Done with rationalism (see pp. 30-32 and 53-61), they, too, were awaiting. Christianity came, and was hailed to Europe by the mystic cravings of their later philosophies. And the intellects of the Greek East, Paul, Athanasius and the early Councils, forged the steel of a dogma that should withstand the insidious logical cult of the South. The new religion was adopted by the state; and the state's first action was the transfer of its centre to the Greek lands. Constantinople, the Κωνσταντίνου Πόλις, was the first Christian capital of the first Christian empire. It was then, in 330, not in the year 1 A.D., that the Christian era was begun. And the Greeks were its custodians.

This it was that conſtituted the heritage of the Byzantines, that gave them their traditions and their national pride. Every aspeƈt of their lives was implicit with the Cross. They were as saturated in the Chriſtian religion, as the modern English in the gentleman's code.

In the opinion of the Victorian rationaliſt, mediævalism, by which is meant the permeation of everyday life with the supranatural, or, conversely, the pursuit of God's personal Reality in every incident of everyday life, was a quaint joke, a phase of Gothic interiors and chivalresque romance, but fettered with illusion, superſtition and intelleƈtual impotence. Miracles, it was said, have not, and do not, happen. In Conſtantinople, among the Byzantines, where the cryſtal threads of mediævalism were spun to heaven unclouded by the materialism of Weſtern Catholicism, let it be underſtood: miracles did happen. Theirs was the commoneſt of agencies. For, in the eyes of the Byzantine, mortal life was a maze-like venture amid non-terreſtrial forces, demoniac and divine, circling around him, imminent and overwhelming. With the demons pressing on him, tempting him and bringing him misfortune, how else combat them than by miracles, how otherwise be sure of God's counsel and support? Unless it be definitely recognised that among the mediæval Greeks miraculous intervention was frequent in every grade of event, it is impossible to comprehend the Byzantine mentality. To call Byzantine society theocratic, would be exaggeration. But to call it secular, would be untruth.

In this environment of ghostly prodigy, religion assumed for the Byzantine a daily, hourly import. But the two are not to be identified. Miracles were miracles, natural phenomena of the Byzantine world, such as trees or thunder-storms. Theology, the Christian duty, and the sublimation of the body, lay apart on a higher plane, admittant of individual interpretation. For the peasant, the miracle constituted perhaps the most potent factor in spiritual belief. But for the majority, the exercise of the religious faculty was something actually creative, barren for posterity, ridiculous to historians, but to men steeped in communion with invisible Forces, sufficient to summon all their artistry to its pursual and allegiance. Orthodoxy, the analysis and definition of the Christian's triple Godhead, was essentially the prerogative of a people trained in the refinements of logic by the very *nuances* of their language. It was the prerogative of the Fathers; and in the opinion of the lesser men, from the Emperor in his court to the craftsman at his booth, it was their prerogative as well. To embrace the monastic profession in middle age was but the culmination of life's predominant hobby, the probing of God's mystery and man's destiny. This acute popular interest in religion finds some analogy in the Puritan enthusiasms of the sixteenth and seventeenth centuries. And it is possible that, had Byzantine culture and Greek intelligence survived in the fullness of the Empire's political glory to form the basis of a general East European civilisation, there must early have come about an Eastern Reforma-

tion which would have joined forces with the North and
held a successful balance againſt the withering mental
influence of the counter-reformed Roman Church.

This social and temperamental fixation on the transcendental revolved round two inſtitutions, officially
united, but diſtinct in their influence. One was
monaſticism, the other the Church. Surviving unchanged till the present time, both have exercised
profound effect on the hiſtory of the Levant. But for
them, it is doubtful whether the Hellenic nationality
would now exiſt.

To comprehend the significance of Greek monasticism—the lesser of the two, but the more immediate
in its personal contact with the people—it is necessary
to trace the Chriſtian ascetic ideal to its root. During
the firſt two centuries after Chriſt, the Chriſtian life
implied, for all its professors, an ascetic warfare, a continued and combatant service againſt the world and the
flesh. But with the gradual transformation of the new
brotherhood from an exclusive minority into a commonplace majority, the more fervent felt the call to demar-
cate still further the barrier between themselves and
average humanity. This impulse assumed, in Egypt
and Syria, an eremitic form. Wild solitaries, mouths
a-work with divine revelation, sprinkled the caves of the
desert. Amongſt them, diveſted of all his possessions,
launched St Anthony in the laſt years of the third
century, to battle through two decades of solitude with
demons whose actuality was such that the clamour of

the fight could be heard by the awe-struck listeners outside his retreat. Eventually he emerged, to form the nucleus of an anchorite community. His life, written by St Athanasius, was translated into Latin and spread to the West. The consequence was enormous. Throughout Europe, monks and miracles now entered the accepted order of things. And the Dark and Middle Ages thenceforth assumed that peculiar complexion of unreality which makes them so defiant of our understanding.

This first stage in monasticism, the ideal of solitude as historically typified by St Anthony's earlier life, never ceased to exercise its attraction on the Greeks. In the popular estimate, the pure achievement of corporeal subjection rendered the Stylite on his pillar, or the hermit vermin-eaten in his fastness, objects of heroic veneration. And the saints were in fact the fathers of the people. Let disease or misfortune come: the holy man was at hand. Let land-owner oppress or bureaucrat extort: the champion of the poor was waiting. For what could an anchorite suffer at the hands of authority? The world could lose him nothing. He stood, rather, to gain a martyr's crown.

The second stage in the development of the monastic idea was begun by St Anthony and perfected by his contemporary, St Pachomius. This was the association of hermits in loose organisations for purposes of worship and economic maintenance. But the ideal of solitary self-communion remained. And to exchange the intermittent glimpse of a fellow-recluse for unbroken isolation was considered advance to a higher life. It was St Basil, in the middle of the fourth century, who first repudiated this Oriental conception of the perfect existence, and formulated, in opposition to it, the precepts of a restricted communism. To him, St Benedict owed the inspiration, which, a century later, he implanted in the Latin West.

The achievement of St Basil in this third phase was twofold. First and foremost he brought the monastic ideal within reach of the ordinary man. In his view, the competitive and artificial mortifications of the hermit were at variance with the true pattern of Christian life. That, in reality, he held, was to be found in a cenobitic fraternity, demanding not feats of endurance, but an absolute equality of property, comfort, and worship, vested in each member of the monastery. Here could those weaker men find refuge, who lacked the fiery mysticism of the anchorite. And, secondly, monasticism was now brought into definite relation with Church and state. In the economy of the latter the monks must take their part. Charitable and educational activities for the benefit of the laity were henceforth to be part of their functions. By the time of Justinian their position was recognised and regulated in both civil and ecclesiastical law. And from a condition which threatened to reduce them to packs of fanatical dervishes, they gradually assumed a primary importance in the official hierarchy. Convents for women, of almost equal frequency, were organised on the same basis.

The precepts of St Basil could in no sense be called a rule of life. By the eighth century, the prevailing laxity and illiteracy of the monks had drawn on them the Puritan wrath of the first iconoclast Emperors, those stern realists who could not easily tolerate the useless absorption of wealth and energy which seemed to be the chief function of monastic institutions. But the situation was altered by the advent of Theodore of Studium, whose detailed regulations for the guidance of the monks of the monastery of St John of Studium, whose abbot he was, opened a new era of religious fervour, and sought, moreover, to promote such activities as the copying of books, which might benefit society as a whole. To this source, the Carlovingian revival in the Western Church, which was to culminate in the reforms of Cluny a century later, undoubtedly owed part of its inspiration. And here, also, was a precedent for the new community of St Athanasius of Athos, which was ultimately to furnish a monastic prototype for the whole Slavonic world.

This was the fourth stage. Henceforth the growth of the monasteries knew no curb. Even the mystic Emperor Nicephorus II Phocas, himself the patron who suggested and made possible the venture of St Athanasius, sought to check their acquisition of property by a law analogous to the English statute of Mortmain, *de Religiosis*. But Basil II Bulgaroctonos was obliged by public opinion to abandon the restriction a few years later. One monument of the system has survived, unique and unscathed, to illustrate by its treasures,

paintings and buildings, the idyll of a Byzantine retreat. This is Mount Athos, embowered amid flowers
and trees, in the silvery blue of the northern Ægean.
Here, from the eremite fortified among the naked crags,
with only the eagles and the sea his allies, through
the clusters of hermit-dwellings on their ledges, to the
great embattled monasteries at the shore, all the stages
of monastic development persist. Over the wooded
ravines and stony ridges a strange essence floats. Is
this the world we know? Or is it still the Byzantine
world, midway between heaven and earth, thick with
the print of unfamiliar souls?

The second institution upon which the religious life
of the Empire hinged, and of which monasticism was
but the popular adjunct, was naturally the Orthodox
Church. Its structure derived from the earliest
missionary years of Christianity. And the interest of
its history has been more than academic. During four
centuries of Turkish rule, the political and national
identity of the Greeks was merged in their ecclesiastical
organisation. The tale of each reached, not conclusion,
but the end of a decisive chapter, in the year 1923.
During the first three hundred years of its existence,
Christianity was essentially an urban religion. Only in
the Hellenised towns of the Roman Empire was there
found the imaginative intelligence capable of its reception. Its original organisation corresponded, therefore, with the political and commercial centres of
gravity of the time. Thus, at the Council of Nicæa, in

the year 325, the Patriarchates were three: Rome, Alexandria and Antioch. The city of Constantine was not yet in being; and the old Byzantium was situate in the diocese of Heraclea. But at the second Œcumenical Council in 381, it was proclaimed that " the bishop of Constantinople is to have the prerogative of honour after that of Rome, because she is new Rome." Despite the unwisdom of entering upon the most disputed issue in Christian history, it may be noted that, at the Council of Chalcedon, seventy years later, the term " equal prerogatives—τα ἴσα πρεσβεῖα " was expressly used to define the ecclesiastical relationship between new and old Rome. The Church of St Peter was to remain the first among equals; any conception of authority, if, indeed, such was threatened, was repudiated. And when, in 588, John the Faster, Patriarch of Constantinople, assumed the title of Œcumenical or Universal Archbishop, he evoked a protest from Pope Gregory the Great against the primacy of any one bishop, which contains the strongest condemnation ever penned of the later policy of Gregory's Church.

Meanwhile a parallel rivalry was arising in the East with Alexandria. In the case of Egypt, where monasticism was born, Christianity had transformed a province of the Empire into a fanatic theocracy, headed by its Patriarch. After half a century's friction following the promotion of " New Rome " to equal dignity, matters came to a head in the deposition of Nestorius, Patriarch on the Bosporus, on an imputation of heresy

engineered at the third Œcumenical Council in 431 by
Cyril of Alexandria. But Conſtantinople returned to
the charge. If Neſtorius might not separate the natures
of Chriſt, neither should Egyptian myſticism unite
them. The monk Eutyches, champion of the latter
doctrine, was attacked; and though, in 449, Flavian,
Patriarch of Conſtantinople, was deposed and so in-
jured in the packed Synod of Ephesus that he died, the
Alexandrines were finally beaten with the support of
Rome at the Council of Chalcedon, two years later.
The divergence was permanent; the native followers
of the Egyptian Church, having loſt their bid for the
supremacy of Chriſtendom, now decided to be independent of it; and the religious policy of Conſtantinople was left suspended between political intereſts in
Italy and the southern Levant (see pages 84 and 85).
Toleration for the Monophysites, advocates of the single
nature, meant schism with Rome. The embarrassment
of the situation was only resolved in the seventh
century, when Antioch, Alexandria and Jerusalem—
the latter city having been created a Patriarchate in
deference to its associations—were engulfed by Islam.
Henceforth the see of Conſtantinople occupied un-
disputed preponderance in the Eaſt, as Rome in the
Weſt. Nevertheless, in memory of his city's diocesan
parentage, the Œcumenical Patriarch continues, down
to the present day, to be handed the Patriarchal ſtaff at
his enthronement by the Metropolitan of Heraclea or
his representative.

Whatever the pretensions launched from time to

time by individual Patriarchs and Emperors, the Greek Orthodox Church has remained, throughout its history, faithful to this principle of *primus inter pares*, which was the key-note of ecclesiastical organisation under the Councils. It was fundamentally the negation of this principle on the part of the Italians, and their assumption of " authority," which provoked the ultimate schism with Rome in 1054, and rendered futile all subsequent attempts to heal it. From that date, the position of the Patriarch of Constantinople in relation to the autocephalous churches of Antioch, Alexandria, Jerusalem, Cyprus, Mount Sinai, Athens, and those which the varying fortunes and divisions of Slav nationality have called into being, may be compared with that of the Archbishop of Canterbury in the British Empire. The co-equal Churches are permitted independent growth, but are bound in unity by communion with the Œcumenical Patriarch. The executive of the whole is the Œcumenical Council, which has not assembled, and even then did so with incomplete representation, since the desperate attempt to save the Empire by a union of the Churches at Florence in 1439.

The same principles of local independence and adaptation to political necessity have governed the internal organisation of the Greek Church. Then as now, next under the Patriarch were the Metropolitans. These, of whom a certain proportion bore the title of Archbishop, were resident in the chief towns of the themes, and were superior to the Bishops of the lesser towns.

Each Metropolitan or Archbishop could convoke synods of the Bishops under him. Under the latter, again, were the parish priests. The tradition of literary and theological scholarship among the higher clergy was never interrupted. And from the sixth century, these had been usually, though not always, recruited from the monasteries. No priest might marry after ordination. Those who had already done so, could not aspire to the rank of bishop or above.

Thus constituted in the spirit of a religious commonwealth, rather than a religious absolutism, the Orthodox Church, more especially in its Byzantine phase, has suffered the accusation of Erastianism, of subservience to the political rather than the spiritual interests of its people. It is true that the initiative of summoning an Œcumenical Council lay with the Emperor; and that the election of the Patriarch was often a matter of his personal choice. But that the Church, and the chosen Patriarch, were mere creatures of his bidding, in no way followed. Byzantine history teems with illustrations of the readiness with which monks and prelates were prepared to stake life and position in support of their principles: how Theodore of Studium upheld the primacy of Rome against the iconoclast Emperor Constantine V; how the Patriarch Nicolas Mysticus forbade the Emperor Leo VI the Sage enter St Sophia on Christmas day, 906, following his fourth marriage; how the Patriarch Polyeuctes excommunicated the Emperor Nicephorus II Phocas on similar grounds; how the Emperor Alexius I Comnenus, with his mother Anna Dalassena[1] and his whole family, fasted and slept on the ground for forty days in expiation of their soldiers' pillage of church plate; how the Emperor Michael VIII Palæologus, after years of excommunication, publicly abased himself at the feet of a new Patriarch, in penance for the blinding and imprisonment of his youthful ward, John IV Lascaris; innumerable instances confirm the independence of principle to which the Church, assured of popular support, held fast. If there were no great contests such as set the Popes and Hohenstaufens by the ears or rent the England of the Stuarts, let it be remembered that the Byzantine state was in itself almost as much a religious as a political institution. When the Emperor John II Comnenus returned from a victorious campaign, it was the Virgin's icon that rode chariot-borne through the streets of Constantinople; the monarch, triumphant, walked behind, carrying a cross. Thus also, in pontifical procession on a broiling August day, entered the same Michæl VIII Palæologus after the delivery of the city from fifty-seven years of Latin domination. The case was, indeed, as Rambaud has written: "Entre l'Église et l'État, il n'y a pas lutte, mais harmonie, presque confusion. Il n'y a pas de honte pour le patriarche à être nommé par l'Empereur, ni pour l'Église à être subordinnée à l'État, car l'État est à peine laïque." Half the enigma of Byzantine history is solved in the words: à peine laïque.

[1] A masterful woman, who introduced a fixed breakfast into the Palace ritual.

The social significance of religion to the Byzantines has been described. The channels through which they pursued their quest, the contemplative life and the Church, survive. But the gratitude of posterity is not confined to the Levant and the Slavs. It was Greek intellect that shaped first the appeal, and then the formula, of Christianity for the world at large. Finally, at the back of the iconoclast movement, which assaulted the Orthodox Church in the eighth century, lay a degree of spiritual aspiration, which provides a key to the understanding not only of all future Protestantism, but of the Byzantine cultural ideal and of that of the twentieth century with it.

During Christ's life and the apostolic era, Greek was already the *lingua franca* of the Mediterranean, the tongue of commerce and the vehicle of ideas. And it was the later Greek-writing authors of the New Testament who first set themselves to the task of harmonising rational philosophy with the Christian ethic and the Jewish God. Not until the third century did a religious work appear in any language but Greek; and that only for the benefit of the patently uneducated. During its first six centuries of dogmatic systematisation, Christianity enjoyed the service of the subtlest and most precise language that humanity has evolved. And it was especially the solution of the Christological controversies of the fourth and fifth centuries, which Byzantine pride revered, and which gave the Orthodox Church its peculiar stamp, not as a creator of doctrine but rather as a champion of definition.

The necessity before the early Church, campaigning against every variety of prejudice and inherited super-stition, was to evolve a compromise in definition so comprehensive as to embrace the salutary elements in all previous ethical and theological speculation, yet so rigid so to allow no loophole through which the essential balance of the Trinity might become upset. Scarcely had Constantine, with the eye of Roman practicality, adopted Christianity for the unification of his world, when a vast cleft was threatened by Arius' abstraction of Christ from his rightful place in the Godhead, to that of a created being, a demi-god pendant between heaven and earth. The Emperor, alarmed at the re-percussions of what were to him, and, indeed, without prolonged psychological concentration on the tempera-ment of the period, are to us also, " these small and insignificant matters," convened the first Œcumenical Council at Nicæa in 325. He presided at it, paid its expenses, and fathered the promulgation of the Nicene Creed. Thus the prime article of Orthodox Christian belief, like the Empire it was to sustain, emerged the product of Roman sense and Greek intelligence. With the statement, negative in its width, that Christ possessed perfect divinity and perfect humanity, the central factor in the Christian Trinity was fixed.

But the problem remained as to the relation of these two natures. And though the preponderance of one or the other must ultimately rest with individual pre-ference, the ecclesiastical rivalries of the fifth century sharpened the scent of heresy. In Asia Minor and

Syria, the tendency of religious speculation, voiced by
Theodore of Mopsuestia, was to emphasise the historic
value of Christ's life on earth as divorced from his
divinity; and while admitting the full perfection of
that divinity, to deny that it was ever transmitted
through the womb, that, in other words, God was
born of woman. In Alexandrine Africa, on the other
hand, the divine attributes were threatened with over-
emphasis at the expense of the human. Nestorius,
Patriarch of Constantinople, having been trained at
Antioch, was a partisan of the former view; and on
championing the thesis that Christ's two natures were
contained, despite the seeming unity of one body, in
two personalities, was deposed and exiled in 428. The
Alexandrines, however, who had secured this triumph,
had united in their zeal, not only the personalities, but
the natures. The direction of the carpenter's plane
by Christ the man was held to be identical in emanation
with that of universal destiny by Christ the God. This
doctrine in its turn was condemned at the Council of
Chalcedon in 451.

These two decisions separated large bodies of Christians from communion with the central Church. That
of Chalcedon led to the formation of the Monophysite
branch, of which the Churches of the Egyptian Copts,
the Syrian Jacobites of Antioch, and the Abyssinians
still survive. While all Eurasia tells no more romantic
tale than that of the Nestorian Church, which retained
its allegiance to the deposed Patriarch of 428 and the
doctrines of Theodore of Mopsuestia that he had

defended. How this community threatened the supremacy of the Magi in Persia, entered into personal relations with Mohammed, and transmitted to the Arabs those threads of Hellenic learning which eventually, preceding the Renascence, found their way to Spain and Western Europe; how its missionary and civilising effort embraced Arabia, India, Ceylon, Tartary, Afghanistan, Siberia and Eastern China, and may have contributed the original inspiration of Tibetan Lamaism; how a Chinee, born in Peking, came to administer Holy Communion to King Edward I of England in Gascony; how the Roman Synod of Diamper tortured and burnt the Indian remnant of this once vast brotherhood in 1560; and how the Inquisition of Goa was abolished by order of the Prince Regent of Portugal from Rio de Janeiro in 1812; these histories are told elsewhere.[1] At the latter vicissitudes of the Nestorians, at their fight in the Great War, and at their reward, those who recall the inconvenience of small allies during Peace can feel no surprise.

In great schisms, but yet greater measure of consolidation, ended these earlier controversies. Viewed in the light of their enormous contemporary significance, they are isolated from the modern understanding. But with iconoclasm it is different. The root of that movement is intimately related to the mental and artistic ferment of the present day.

The problem that lay at the bottom of iconoclasm,

---

[1] See H. C. Luke, *Mosul*, and Sir E. A. Wallis Budge, *The Monks of Kublai Khan.*

this campaign for the deſtruction of representational art, of all portrayal in terms of physical actuality, was precisely that which is troubling the moderniſts of our time, and leading them to those extravagances which the intelligentsia has been educated to indulge and the colonel to regard as pathological. That the function of art is to translate the philosophic emotions evoked in the artiſt by the inner significance of material objects into visible and ultimately intelligible form, is an axiom that has not always been recognised. It was unknown to Antiquity; and it was wholly forgotten in the eighteenth and nineteenth centuries. But in the early Chriſtian and early Mohammedan eras, as in the twentieth century, its acceptance was undisputed. A diſtinction between the two epochs, the mediæval and the present, may be drawn, which in itself explains this affinity. All "inner significance"—that which it is the function of art to interpret—must exiſt for the individual in terms of his own individual reactions, which the language commonly calls emotions. And the diſtinction lies in the fact that from the fourth century to the Renascence, the whole body of human emotions was inveſted, unlike those of to-day, with the garment of religion. The problem, which is now exercising modern artiſts from the ſtandpoint of psychological Realities, of harnessing art more entirely to the expression of emotional reactions, was then attached to the single queſt of a personal Reality formulated by Christianity. But in both cases the essentials of the problem were the same: How far is representational art capable

171

of fulfilling art's function: that is, the expression of an abstract worth? From the purely æsthetic point of view (that of to-day), the answer is that the human eye and the human sensibilities are so accustomed to traffic in familiar objects that they will not react to expressed emotion, unless that emotion is expressed in terms of those objects. But from the religious point of view, when the emotions are focused in a Godhead of omnipotent sanctity, of what account are the human sensibilities and their reactions, compared with the insult offered the holy elements by portrayal? For to clothe Reality in terms of the transient, in terms of terrestrial object, is to degrade it. Modern artists, while unable to discard the language of familiar object, seek to subordinate its importance wholly to that which it is used to express; the purely representational tends to grow less and less. They, in fact, seek the mean which the Byzantines, culminating in El Greco, came nearer to finding than any people before or since. That the Byzantines so far succeeded, was due to the influence of iconoclasm. Thus the impulse behind all campaigns against idolatry, from the second commandment to the vandalism of Cromwell's Puritans, is one and the same as that which prompts John, Epstein and the fry that come after, to subordinate the physical exactitudes of their sitters to the reactions which the latter's whole beings, bodily and other, convey, through the senses, to the artist's intelligence. A painter and a sculptor of relative importance are only one example. But the example serves.

PLATE VIII

CHRIST, RULER OF THE WORLD

Now this instinct against purely representational art
came from the East. " *Thou shalt not make to thy
self any graven image, nor the likeness of any thing
that is in heaven above or in the earth beneath, or in
the water under the earth.*" Thus the Jews protected
their Reality, while the Greeks reproduced the transient.
Eventually there evolved the new religion; and in the
case of Christianity, it was mainly through the medium
of representational art, through pictured incidents in
its founder's life, together with lurid illustrations of
celestial reward and punishment, that the Levantine
and European masses received their early lessons in
religion. In the beginning it was the same with
Mohammedanism: illuminated manuscripts and mosaics
in the mosques depicted scenes from the Prophet's life.
But the seventh century witnessed a tightening of the
iconoclast prohibition. In Persia, where a representational art had been, from time immemorial, a national
heritage, it was destined to failure. Elsewhere, however,
where Islam flourished, there henceforth representational art was taboo. The soul of the artist must find
play within the limits of geometric convolution. And
though to-day, though not perhaps for ever, it is our
opinion that the emotions are best expressed in unfamiliar
transformations of familiar objects, there is something
that commands admiration in this ideal of abstract
expression through pure design.

Meanwhile spasmodic movements in Christianity
had foreshadowed the coming struggle. As early as
the fourth century, prominent clerics were inveighing

173

against representations of Christ; and in 599, a definite outbreak of iconoclasm at Marseilles was stifled by Pope Gregory the Great. Furthermore, in southern Armenia, an advanced form of Protestantism was already exemplified in the practice of the Paulicians, a Christian sect which rejected the cult of Virgin and saints, candles, crosses, incense, purgatory, infant baptism, and more than one grade of ministry. The Emperor Leo III the Isaurian, who ascended the throne of Constantinople in 716, was of Armenian origin. In 726, the first edict against the holy pictures revered in every Orthodox church was promulgated. The whole of European art, both the sculpture of the past and the painting of the future, was threatened. For, in those days, in fact if not in theory, the separation of the secular from the religious was impossible.

Apart, however, from the mystical and probably subconscious ideal which impelled the assault on representation, there existed definite abuses in the religious life of the Byzantine community, which the iconoclasts wished to reform. In process of time, the icons, or sacred pictures had become objects of actual veneration; although, as St John Damascene pointed out, this was not surprising in view of the miracles they performed. Further, the monks, their champions, while increasing in numbers and wealth, were ceasing to be distinguished for either learning or piety. The story of the movement divides into two periods, 726 to 787, and 815 to 842, in the interval between which the pictures were restored by the Empress Irene. Astonishing results attended the first edict: there were serious riots in Constantinople, an abortive rebellion in Greece, and a successful one in southern Italy. With the accession of Constantine V Copronymus in 740, a Cromwell in character and ability, relics, the cult of the Virgin, and the intercession of the saints were all attacked; monks were persecuted; works of art destroyed. But in 780, Irene, the Athenian widow of the Emperor Leo IV, assumed power; and in order to attract popular favour prior to the dethronement of her son, for whom she stood regent, had the pictures restored by the Œcumenical Council of Nicæa in 787. Simultaneously, the monks, inspired by Theodore of Studium, were in process of self-reform. It was part of the Studite programme to render the Orthodox Church independent of the Byzantine state by a fuller recognition of the authority of the Pope. But while the iconoclast sovereigns, strong in the support of an Asiatically recruited army, had added much to the glory of the Empire, their opponents, the iconodules, were weak and unsuccessful in war. In 813, the threat of Bulgarian invasion gave rise to a military revolution, which placed on the throne Leo V, another Armenian. The decision of the Council of Nicæa was revoked, and the persecution of the monks resumed. Leo's successor but one, the Emperor Theophilus, himself an artist, tried to divert their talents into secular channels. But the Studite party was too strong, and the love of the icons too deeply engrained in the average Hellene, for the spiritual purism of the East to be maintained in

175

perpetuity. Upon the accession to power in 842 of another Empress-Regent, the pictures were finally reinstated.

What, in sum, were the positive results of the controversy? European painting, already cradling in Constantinople, was saved. And from now onwards, Byzantine art assumed that peculiar austerity and economy which has rendered it one of the supreme achievements in emotional expression. The Orthodox Church was affected in a similar manner: its kinship with Protestantism past and future, was one not of doctrine, but of spiritual feeling. What part this feeling, communicated through actual relationship with the East, may have contributed to the emancipation from Rome of the Lollards and Hussites, and ultimately to the whole Reformation, it is as difficult to surmise as that of the Cathars and Bogomiles. But it may be recalled that among Wyclif's twenty-four Conclusions condemned by the Synod of Blackfriars in 1382, the ninth advocated the reconstitution of the Church " after the manner of the Greeks "; and that the first action of the Hussites (with whose doctrines Luther afterwards identified himself), following their excommunication at the Council of Florence in 1450, was to send a deputation to Constantinople, seeking admission for them to the Orthodox Church. It is here, in the light of historic consequence, that the salient outcome of iconoclasm is to be found. The monks had won the icons; but they had lost their bid for papal authority. Henceforth there was a definite divergence between Constantinople and Rome. With this emergence and fruition of a spiritual austerity beyond the comprehension of Latin materialism, the history of Christianity develops from the formative to the contrasting.

It may be supposed that when the historians of a thousand years hence come to analyse the European modes of thought and living which now dominate the world, a factor in their calculations will be the admittedly beneficial influence of Christianity in the building of European civilisation. They will disentangle the various communions of that religion; they will mark the Reformation as its turning-point; and they will then, judgment matured by thirty generations' detachment, note the upshot of new and extraordinary phenomena in that branch of it which retained its allegiance to the ancient Pope in Rome. The success with which, from the seventeenth century on, the counter-reformed Latin Church pursued its formula for the cure of souls; the devotion of its servants; and even the measure of their spiritual attainments; these they will applaud. But the manner in which the great multitude of its adherents was henceforth effectually debarred from communion with the Holy Spirit, the paramount, and for the future, only permanent element in the Christian Trinity; together with the hourly denial practised, from the Vatican to the remotest missionary, of the Christian ethic, can but evoke surprise. We as contemporaries can give the Roman Church its due: to the troubled and the wavering it brings a peace that is nowhere else to be found. But history loses sight of detail in perception of an institution's relative contribution to the furtherance of the human quest. Subsequent speculation may debate as to whether it was the Italian core or the Spanish infiltration that inaugurated these traditions. But the verdict of a posterity unbiassed, as we are, by the survival of partisan Christian sects, can be foretold. In that view, post-Reformation Catholicism must appear a bastard aberration from the main body of Christendom; a product of obsolete Mediterranean materialism which henceforth played no part with Christianity in man's discovery of Reality; which desecrated his divine soul with self-constructed specifics of salvation; which extinguished all intellectual and material progress wherever its influence was strongest; and finally, which outraged, separately and in the aggregate, every canon of behaviour which enables a human being to dwell in amity with his neighbour.

To this postulated criticism, the Greek Orthodox Church offers commentary. The latter history of its Byzantine phase reveals, in its relationship with Rome, the beginnings of those tendencies on the part of the latter which, even in the twentieth century, continue to render odious the Papal Curia and all its political works. It provides also a contrast valuable for the understanding of both institutions, and one obscured by no serious doctrinal dispute. This contrast is temperamental. And in temperament lies the key to the history. For in that must be sought the fundamental explanation of the great schism, for which, in the first instance, the Greeks were more responsible than the Romans.

The psychological difference between the two Churches lies at bottom in their temporal outlook. To the Greek, who by nature lives entirely in the present, the conception of future resurrection and future after-life is obscure. To the Roman it is clear as his own hand. The result is that while, for the latter, the whole impulse of religion is in essence eschatological, woven with the idea of post-human progression, for the Greek it is derived from the desire to seek transfiguration, not in the future, but the present. The Roman, in this life, is concentrated on the problems of sin and grace: his eyes are fixed on the below; the other world, though parent of his activity, is yet far off. For the Greek it is here. He lives in two worlds at once, and his eyes are on the upper of them; the Eucharist is not so much a means of grace as a " medicine of immortality —φάρμακον ἀθανασίας." While, in Roman opinion, God became man that man's sins might be forgiven with a view to *future* immortality, in Greek it was that his human nature might be deified, not in some future state, but *now*. Thus for the Roman the prime function of religion is an ethical one, the regulation of conduct. For the Greek it is the piercing of the sensory veil, the junction of the divine spark in man with its ex-terrestrial affinity, God.

These contrasting interpretations of religion, material and pneumatic, are exhibited in different methods of

Church organisation. To the Roman, temperamentally bereft of spiritual guidance, the juridical authority of the Church forms the basis of his religious practice. Such an idea, to the Greek, is actively repellent. Hence the Orthodox Church is sympathetic, within the limits of Orthodoxy, to a measure of individual interpretation which Catholicism cannot tolerate. The number of national autocephalous Churches, secure with vernacular Liturgy and Bible, which it contains, enable it to avoid the ceaseless political friction that Rome's jurisdiction of souls has always provoked. And even in the case of other Churches such as our own, it has always recognised definite aspects of Christian truth, to which, as such, consideration is due.

It was these opposed points of view, which iconoclasm accentuated, that validated the schism between the Orthodox and Catholic Churches. But the blame for the embitterment which followed must rest with the evolution at the Roman centre of a completely centralised authority, and the consequently amoral attitude towards all non-co-religionists in which this resulted.

The first serious divergences appeared during the iconoclast period. The Papacy, embarrassed almost to the point of extinction by the incursions of the Lombards and the absence of help from Constantinople, was obliged to seek the protection of Pepin, King of the Franks. The name of the Eastern Emperor was henceforth omitted in official documents. And another of the West was deliberately conjured into tutelary

being by the coronation, somewhat to his embarrassment, of Charlemagne, in 800. Definite estrangement
resulted; and in 843, when the icons were finally
restored by the Empress Theodora, the estates and
jurisdiction of the Pope in Southern Italy were not.
Attempts meanwhile were being made to win the
newly converted Kingdom of Bulgaria to the Latin
usage. Fruitless as they proved—for the Pope could
not grant the ecclesiastical independence tolerated by
the Patriarch—they fanned the flame of Byzantine
resentment. Finally, the forcible substitution of
Photius for the Patriarch Ignatius on account of the
latter's censure of the Cæsar Bardas' morals; the interference of the Pope on behalf of Ignatius; and the
formation by Photius of a doctrinal basis of dispute;
accomplished the first schism of 858. Normal relations
were renewed forty years later under the Macedonian
Emperors. And as the Patriarchate now reflected the
political refulgence of the Empire, so the light of the
Papacy waned in proportion. But the era of the Cluny
reforms was at hand; a present-laden embassy to Rome
demanding complete ecclesiastical autonomy was foiled,
contrary to probability, by a sudden pan-Western
agitation; and in 1049, Leo IX, child of the new
ideals, was elected Pope. Opposite him, in Constantinople, the Patriarch Michael Cerularius was
a man of equal vigour, shorn of affectation by suffering in prison, and educated in the liberal tradition
of the bureaucracy, to which he had been originally
destined.

The schism which followed was deliberately manipulated by the Patriarch as the logical means of ending
a perpetual friction,[1] and in championship of that
national exclusiveness with which the Church had
become identified under Photius. The bone of papal
jurisdiction in South Italy was repicked; the doctrinal
weapon that the Latins, by adding *filioque* to the creed,
represented the Holy Ghost as proceeding not only
from God, but also from Christ as well, instead of
through him, was refurbished from the armoury of
Photius; and the papal Legates, testifying to the recti-
tude of Emperor and people as opposed to Patriarch,
deposited the curse against schismatics with which
they had come provided, on the high altar of St Sophia.
" *Let them be Anathema, Maranatha, with Simoniacs,*
Valerians, Arians, Donatists, Nicholaitans, Severians,
Pneumatomachi, Manichees and Nazarenes and all
heretics; yea with the devil and his angels. Amen. Amen.
Amen." The breach was ratified by the enormous
popularity of the Patriarch with the people. It was
opposed to the good judgment of the Emperor Constantine IX Monomach. But though the majority of
his successors, and many enlightened people on either
side, continued through centuries to desire a reunion,
the thrust had struck too deep. The religious honour
of the Byzantines was insulted in perpetuity. While
the Latins, after the manner of their Church, were now

---

[1] Between the accession of Constantine in 330 and the Photian
schism of 858, the severance of official relations had already extended
over 203 years.

trained in a rancorous detestation of the Eastern ex-communicants.

For four centuries longer, the history of the dispute oscillates between political and spiritual considerations. There followed, immediately, the crusades. Pope Paschal II promised support to Bohemond of Antioch in a project to destroy the schismatic Empire; Roger II of Sicily received similar encouragement. In retaliation, it was an avowed ambition of the Comneni to be crowned in St Peter's. At length began the preparations for the fourth crusade. Pope Innocent III,—famous in English history for his summary excommunication of King John,—in whose opinion the papal right of pan-European domination admitted of no distinction between the spiritual and the temporal, forbade in plain terms the proposed attack on Constantinople. Nor did he scruple to vent his feelings after the event. " Ye have drawn not your sword against Saracens, but Christians . . . ," he wrote to the marauding host, " Ye have preferred earthly to heavenly riches . . . ye have spared nought that is sacred, neither age nor sex; ye have given yourselves to prostitution, adultery and debauchery in face of all the world . . . ye have glutted your guilty passions not only on married women and widows but on women and virgins dedicated to the Saviour; ye have pillaged the churches . . . ye have stolen the crosses, images and relics in such fashion that the Greek Church, though borne down by persecution, refuses obedience to the apostolical see, because it sees in the Latins only treason and the works of darkness, and loathes them like dogs." Yet the man who penned these words of righteous indignation, who disavowed the Venetian Patriarch, Morosini, himself as pretentious as a Photius, and who allowed the Greeks their own rites, was able, in the same breath, to refer to the Latin Conquest, as that " miracle wrought by God to the glory of his name, the honour and benefit of the Roman see, and the advantage of Christendom." A forced union of the Churches was proclaimed at the Lateran Council of 1215. But the intemperance of the papal Legate in the Levant obliged even the Latin Emperor to intervene. And by 1245, of the thirty bishoprics of the Latin Patriarchate, only three suffragans remained. The Vatican found it more profitable to negotiate with the displaced Greek court of Nicæa than to support the phantom wreck of the miracle wrought by God. And in 1274, thirteen years after the recapture of Constantinople by the Greeks, common fear of the Italian Angevins led Pope and Emperor to proclaim yet another " union." Like its fellows, it was abortive. The hatred of the Greeks, sincere before, was now indelible.

But the Empire was entering on its last struggle. And help from the West was conditional on religious agreement. In vain the Emperor John V Palæologus abjured his faith from the steps of St Peter's. In vain his successor Manuel toured the West, dazzled Paris with his garb, and spent Christmas at Eltham in search of aid. But at length, during the respite from Turkish attacks following Bajazet's defeat by Tamerlane in

PLATE IX

THE EMPEROR JOHN VIII PALAEOLOGUS
by Pisanello, from life

1402, harmony seemed in sight. A General Council of the Roman Church was assembled at Basle, whose first act was to quarrel with Pope Eugenius. Envoys from both Pope and Council arrived simultaneously in Constantinople, provoking a third from Sultan Murad, suggesting that, under the circumstances, his friendship might perhaps be of greater worth than that of Western Christendom. Eventually, in 1437, the Emperor and his delegation, their expenses paid by Eugenius, embarked; admired the treasures of Venice pillaged from their own capital; and arrived at Ferrara, where an outbreak of plague necessitated the Council's transference to Florence. A common basis of agreement was reached; and the union was ratified in the Duomo, the Te Deum being sung in Greek. The celebration was repeated, amid general execration, in Constantinople and Moscow, from which latter city the Russian Cardinal Isidore barely escaped with his life; while the Patriarchs of Syria and Egypt were one in their denunciation of the unholy concord. Meanwhile, the Pope despatched such assistance as he might. But his sincerity, and that of the Emperor John VIII Palæologus, were unavailing. The oft quoted and reviled remark attributed to the High Admiral Notaras, that he would rather see " the turban of the Turk in the capital than the tiara of the Latin," represented a genuine and justifiable point of view on the part of the Greek public. For three centuries the Latins, in the guise of soldiers of the Western Cross, had harried their Empire, had robbed it of prosperity, had overthrown its machinery, and desecrated its most cherished shrines and institutions. The first act of the Patriarchate, reconstituted by Mohammed II after his capture of the city in 1453, was to repeal the act of union. Since then, essays in religious fraternity have moved in other directions.

CHAPTER IX

A PECULIAR indecision attaches to the words " art " and " artistic." Whereas the latter is relevant to numerous spheres of cultural activity, the former is employed mainly to differentiate one of them from the rest. " Art " in common parlance, implies the creation of form, in two dimensions or three, as opposed to other manifestations of " artistic " expression, such as music or writing. And it was in art thus defined, in representation and design, in leviathans of architecture and microcosms of craftsmanship, that the Byzantine genius found its medium, and thereby bequeathed posterity a legacy both in concrete monument and formative affect. In relation to posterity, Byzantine art has suffered twofold misfortune: only in the present century has a revived affinity, born of escape from the trammels of classicism, trained the critical eye once more to its appreciation; and even in this age of prodigious communication, its memorials remain for the most part singularly inaccessible, either fortified against wheeled traffic by the mountainous coasts of the East Mediterranean, or, in such localities as Constantinople and Kiev, necessitating, in their inspection, an expenditure of time and money that the ordinary traveller

187

cannot afford. Italy, profuse in tourist facilities, provides an exception, but one which, by itself, can convey
only a one-sided impression of the art in question. And
a journey to Spain will reveal that which nothing else
can, the painting of the last Byzantine, El Greco.
Otherwise, the West of Europe is sparsely furnished
with material examples of mediæval Greek culture.
None the less, their significance, once understood,
goes deep. Dutch tavern and Umbrian hummock
fade like the memory of a loved but departed nurse.
The veils of prettiness, the opacity of coherence,
are pierced.

Yet still the novice, in orbit of the light, gropes.
Over a period of twelve centuries, there must be landmarks of achievement and transformations of manner
to be grasped. Manuals of Byzantine art are scarce,
expensive, and usually incomplete. An historical
summarisation of that art's three phases in development, illustrated by patently outstanding monuments
and facts, may therefore be excused.

The first period, dating from the foundation of Constantinople in 330, reached its golden age in the reign
of Justinian. The imported Oriental art of mosaic—
by which is meant the inlay of coloured glass cubes
—was now brought to a technical perfection which the
compositions on which it was employed did not justify.
At Ravenna, however, in the mausoleum of the Empress
Galla Placidia, dating from the middle of the fifth
century, the background of vaulted sapphire to the un-

convincing Romano-Hellenistic figures renders this earliest of Byzantine monuments unique in its beauty. The mosaics of this first phase, though often, as in the case of the portraits of Justinian and Theodora in St Vitale at Ravenna, historically interesting, lack the emotional significance of later Byzantine art; this, in its ultimate form, was the outcome of forces not yet discernible on the intellectual horizon. At present the compositions tended to derive either from a directly Roman source, as exemplified in the fantasies of curtained architecture which decorate the dome of St George at Salonica; or were else, as in the case of the patterned birds to be seen in the subsidiary vaults of the same church, of purely Eastern inspiration. The apse of St Apollinare-in-Classe at Ravenna reveals an attempted impregnation of Hellenistic form with the anti-naturalistic grouping of the East. But the result suffers from a lack of co-ordination in its methods, and a too obvious symbolism. Similarly the colours of the time do not exhibit those principles of interrelationship which were to govern the painting and mosaic of the future and were to give, in the end, Byzantine genius its most enduring means of expression. On the other hand, contemporary ivories and sarcophagi already display that complete mastery and economy of design which remained essentially constant through twelve centuries.

The main problem which the period resolved was that of ecclesiastical architectural form. The pure basilica, legacy of classical temples, with its square atrium or narthex, rounded apse, and long naves flanked by twin or quadruple rows of pillars, made a stand for continuity. It survives, outside Italy, in the ruined churches of St Demetrius and St Paraskevi at Salonica, and in the Syrian deserts. Simultaneously, in both Syria and Anatolia, the octagon and rotunda types of old funerary monument were undergoing surprising development, outcome of the search for a more religious and more intellectual plan than that offered by the ponderously apprehensible classical model. By the accession of Justinian, round churches such as St Constanza at Rome and St George at Salonica, were familiar; octagons, of which St Vitale at Ravenna and SS. Sergius and Bacchus at Constantinople still remain, in process of expansion. While that of the Holy Apostles at Salonica already exhibited the familiar cruciform surmounted by five cupolas. But with the arrival of the Anatolian brick pendentive, by means of which a dome could now be imposed on four square walls, themselves poised on the four central piers, there came about a fusion of basilica with octagon or rotunda, which eventually developed into the familiar and infinitely far-reaching type of the Greek cross. The destruction of the old churches of Constantinople in the Nika Riot of 532 gave Justinian his chance. In the new St Sophia that he erected, a domed basilica, all the gathering individuality of Byzantine building was crystallised. It simultaneously attained an emotional pinnacle which the materials of architecture have yet to surpass.

PLATE X

ST SOPHIA WITH TURKISH MINARETS

There followed, in the seventh century, an age of extreme unreſt; and in the eighth, and the ninth after it, the iconoclaſt Emperors, under whom the true course of artiſtic development, despite a fashion of magnificent secular decoration borrowed from the court of the Caliphs at Bagdad, was brought to a ſtandſtill.

The second period, therefore, opens with the anti-Puritan reaċtion that set in during the regency of the Cæsar Bardas in the middle of the ninth century; the revived ſtudy of science and the humanities that it engendered; and the accession in 867 of the Emperor Basil I the Macedonian, who launched the Empire on a path of material glory, from which it was only precipitated by the irruption of the crusaders at the beginning of the thirteenth century.

Byzantine art now emerged both spiritualised and humanised. Vaſt wealth was pouring on the capital; and an extreme magnificence charaċterised the build-ings of the time. If, amid this splendour of gold mosaic and precious marble, architeċture tended to lose its purity of conception—as in the no longer exiſting New Church of Basil I, from which St Mark's in Venice, begun in 106?, was copied—in piċtorial art, the fusion of cmotional symbolism with the representational was now successfully accomplished. At leaſt thus it was in the churches, where a definite iconography was henceforth prescribed for the decoration of every vacant inch of their interiors; of the secular art of the time, which flourished within the precinċts of the Great Palace, and is described in contemporary chronicles, nothing has survived. This, moreover, was the age of Byzantine culture's widest expansion. From the still extant mosaics of St Sophia at Kiev, executed by Greeks in the eleventh century, to the gigantic, Gothically enthroned Christ of Monreale, dating from the twelfth, the whole of south-eastern Europe is scattered with memorials to the Greek Empire's prosperity. The masterpieces among them are in Greece: the monastery churches of Daphni, near Athens, and of St Luke, near Livadia, in Phocis. In the latter the ensemble of marble and mosaic survives complete, unhidden and unrestored, to celebrate the gorgeous middle period of the Empire and to show how the radiance of Constantinople was carried into the lives even of poor harvesters and mountain shepherds.

At length came the crusades, and with the fourth of them, an end to Byzantine magnificence. The churches of the fourteenth and fifteenth centuries are small, sparsely marbled, and for the most part painted where formerly would have been mosaic. But simultaneously with the return of the court to Constantinople in 1261, a Renascence in pictorial art took place, which flourished right through the last century of struggle and was never, even two centuries after the Turkish Conquest, degraded wholly to the merely decorative peasant level of later Russia and the remaining Balkans.

With the continued subtilisation of represented form which had been in process since the iconoclasts had implanted their ideals in the Byzantine mind, the

192

technique of representation was in danger of becoming
lost. Its rescue was due, as subsequently in Italy, to a
recrudescence of classical humanism. As early as the
eleventh century the reconstitution of the University
of Constantinople by the Emperor Constantine IX
Monomach had seen a revival of the study of Plato
and the tentative elevation of Reason to a place in
Christian esteem. Thanks to the strength of ecclesiastical tradition, the result was not, as in Italy, a reversion
to Hellenic naturalism and superficiality; but rather a
testimony to the manner in which representational
facility, while still subordinate, may assist the artist
in his emotional aims. One of the earliest and,
with the exception of the paintings in the Pantanassa
at Mistra, certainly the most beautiful monument of
this third and last period in Byzantine art, is the
present Kahrié mosque in Constantinople. The
mosaics of the interior, erected between 1310 and 1320,
exhibit a gentle dignity and grace of composition
strongly reminiscent of the contemporary work of
Giotto; in colour they wholly surpass him. But, as in
Italy, it was painting, owing to lack of money, that
now took the field, developing, as the disintegration of
the Empire progressed, in two main centres: the city
of Mistra, capital of the isolated Greek despotat of the
Morea; and the monastic republic of Mount Athos.
So far, at least, surviving frescoes enable us to con-
jecture. Simultaneously the Greek technique was
communicated to Serbia, and gradually, in debased
form, to the whole Balkan peninsula. Two schools,

traditionally known as the Cretan and Macedonian, may be distinguished, employing as a rule separate iconographies, and dating their earliest extant productions from the thirteenth century. The latter, in coloration and light, approximated more nearly, though independently, to the Giottesque school of fresco-painters; emotionally its aim was higher; technically its ability less than theirs. The Cretan artists, on the other hand, maintained the divergence between East and West Europe to the end; the luminous interplay of their colours and their sense of form existing by virtue of its own intrinsic light, admit of no analogies in more familiar spheres of art. How, but for the Turkish Conquest, European painting might have been rescued from the slough of Italian naturalism during the seventeenth and eighteenth centuries, is apparent in the works of El Greco, foremost exponent of this school and last and greatest flower of Byzantine genius. It is instructive and painful to reflect that, in the popular trend of art, " immortal Guido " was almost exactly his contemporary.

Thus from the middle of the fourth century to that of the sixteenth, the æsthetic tradition germinated in Constantinople and oscillating between extremes of mystic incapacity and inherited Hellenic facility, was a creative force, of which the products stand to-day as landmarks in the cultural history of the world. In pure design and scenic composition; in the abstraction of sheer æsthetic splendour from intrinsically splendid materials; and in compromise between depicted object and depicted emotion, the rival of the Byzantine artist is yet to be found.

This compromise, the harnessing of familiar form to the expression of its contained significance in the mind of the artist, must continue so long as man thinks in the language of his eyes, to be the goal of art. How iconoclasm in some measure perfected this equilibrium in Byzantine painting and mosaic has been explained on pp. 170-173. But Byzantine art, in all but the representational, had emerged from the formative period of the triple fusion before the advent of the Armenian purists. Its existence, in embryo, was coincident with that of Christianity itself. And the characteristics of the religion illustrate those of the art. Christianity was born of cosmopolitanism, demanded universal acceptance and admitted of complex intellectual speculation. Similarly, Byzantine art was no product of a single national or mental temperament, but was rather the outcome of a great psychological wave, world-wide, transcending racial barriers and gathering intellectual differences to a unity. In its intellectual aspect lay its distinction from Western mediæval art, which borrowed the forms of Eastern without the mental alertness, due to perpetual contact with the ineradicable vestiges of classical humanism, which inspired them. Again, the Christian purpose is concrete, its path decided, and its pursuit of that path, unswerving. The methods of Byzantine art are alike. The expression of that Reality, which the religion seeks actually to grasp, allows of no pleasing affectations of sentiment or grace. All is economy, unerring recruitment to one aim, and vast assurance in that aim; intelligible form is reduced to its lowest possible terms (hence the danger of lapse to mere formula on the part of the inept); there is no deviation to bribe the slovenliness of optical perception. The purpose of both is to entrain man's spiritual affinities toward their greater Counterpart, the religion through the mind, the art through the eye. To the creating Byzantine, art was the expression of his quest; to the beholding, the furtherance. Christianity, product of the East, brought with it the Eastern method of emotional symbolisation. None the less, beneath all the abstractions of Byzantine art and the religious hypnotism that beset it, the Hellenic sanity, instinct for balance, arrangement and purity of form, remained perennially alive.

Of the plethoric satisfaction, fulfilment of the eye's most secret crevices of desire, which the essence and rendering of Byzantine pattern afford; of the subtlety of contour, expressed in undercutting and relief, which brought the two dimensions of stone and ivory to its service; of its impeccable proportion and openness of form, diminishing nothing of its symbolic mystery, yet combining by the utmost elaboration of detail the extremes of textural effect; verbal description can convey only the principles. But as these principles percolated from pure design to the simplification of represented form, man, beast and landscape, the uneasy symbolism of the earlier Christian art,

196

vagrant palms and discomposed sheep, was eliminated. There developed, instead, a definite cubism in drapery and in natural phenomena, such as trees and rocks; a contrasting shiny darkness for the accentuation of face and limb; and a treatment of celestial portent not in the familiar physical terms of mediæval domesticity, Renascence beatitude or baroque tornado, but geometrically, in compartments whose very simplicity of outline is alone compatible with the pent reservations of the artist's feeling. To this skeleton of representational formalism, colour gave the flesh, colour employed not merely as an adjunct to the modelling, but fired with an independent life, so that its so-called light and shade derived not from some fancied external source, but from an intrinsic virtue born of its own interplay. And there emanated, from this combination, an expression of mystical emotion to which the modern mind is even yet scarcely capable of responding. For the Byzantines the significance of this tradition became accentuated with generations. We, on the other hand, must discard the very rudiments of our upbringing for its comprehension. As Strzygowski has said, with the seventeenth and eighteenth centuries, " art ceased to touch the life of the people. Even to-day we can hardly know what it can really mean to a man."

If then there be added to this interplay of mystic formalism with living colour, stones, metals, stuffs and mosaic, sufficient in their raw hues and glitter to captivate the heart of a bartering savage; it is not hard to conceive the superlative splendour, speaking not of ſtrained expenditure but effortless reserve, which these materials, ranged in sophiſticated harmony, wrought for Byzantine art. In Conſtantinople, for the firſt and laſt time in hiſtory, an auſtere and intelleƈtual taſte encountered unbridled profusion of wealth, and did not succumb to its temptations. From the flaunting encruſtation of the further Eaſt, Byzantine splendour differs as an ariſtocrat from a parvenu, as an inwardly poised whole from an outwardly intent diversity of body and ornament.

Thus, according to design, magnificence, architectural conception, or technique of craftsmanship, the surviving monuments of Byzantine culture fall into many categories. The pictorial, cradle of European painting, ſtands apart on its own plane of hiſtorical evolution. But the others—and that also, were it but visible through the yellow Turkish wash—are embodied in a single building. This is St Sophia. Though to-day the mosaics, many of them poſt-iconoclaſtic and, therefore, representative of a later period than that firſt-flowering which bore the church, are hid; though ambo and iconostasis are down, carpets skewed Meccawards and Turkish texts aloft; the imagination can reconſtruƈt the old interior, the very pivot of the Byzantine world. St Sophia is the particular visible expression of the firſt coalescence; it exhales the grandeur of Rome, the sanity of Hellas, the myſtery of the Eaſt, and the universality of Chriſtianity. Here, atop the entrant, is no building begun from earth, raised stone by stone upon the plans of an engineer; but a form, a dream abiding, planted entire from heaven. The form, the strength elude. Yet all is clarity, exactitude. The gift of tongues has fallen upon brick and stone. Moslems chant; Christians shuffle boat-footed on the matting. But what the import of obsolete creeds, when here, if ever, Reality is God?

The old church of Constantine was burnt on the 15th of January 532. By February the 23rd, the new was begun. Five years and ten months later, on the day after Christmas, 537, the Emperor Justinian proceeded to its dedication. At a cost computed by a later authority to have been £12,840,000 in bullion, equivalent in present purchasing value to over sixty-four million pounds sterling, the architects Isidore the Milesian and Anthemius of Tralles had erected a church in length and breadth 241 feet by 224, surmounted by a shallow spreading dome 104 feet in diameter and rising, in its eventual form after the earthquake of twenty-one years later, 179 feet from floor to vertex. The whole stood, and stands yet,[1] on a cistern equal, in Byzantine estimation, to the floating of a hundred galleys. " Solomon," apostrophised the Emperor, " I have surpassed thee." With posterity he was not concerned. And what relevant comparison can posterity show? St Peter's, consummate negation of religious inspiration and affirmation of the papal ego,

[1] The building has withstood not only numerous earthquakes, but a city fire in 1755, when the lead from the dome ran molten down the gutters.

breathes empty flesh in every joint of its irremediable classicism. Yet the comparison is relevant after all. It is final. It sums completely the difference between Orthodox and Catholic Europe. The exiſtence of St Sophia is atmospheric; that of St Peter's, over-poweringly, imminently subſtantial. One is a church to God; the other, a salon for his agents. One is consecrated to Reality, the other to illusion. St Sophia, in faſt, is large, and St Peter's is vilely, tragically small.

Six thousand sheep, a thousand each of oxen, pigs and poultry, and half a thousand deer were roaſted at the firſt dedication. The marvel of the Eaſtern lands, enshrining for ever the heart of Greek patriotism, was in being. Let us conceive the interior that caught the allegiance of those early Byzantines, the interior that continues to hold that of their descendants, before it suffered the mutilation of the crusaders and trans-formation to the uses of the Prophet.

The reſtangular doorways, curtained with woven animals, give entrance to a great field of smoky marble, bound in ſtrips of dull carnation green. Surrounding, a syſtem of marble panelling applies to the walls, as we know wood. Sheets of ſtone, cut and cut again so that the veining of each piece may form symmetrical pattern with its neighbour, alternate with bands of other marbles set in delicately notched bevelling. To-day, the miſt of age and seeming disuse films the different colours to a single tone. To Paul the Silentiary, poet of the second dedication, all the glories of nature glimmer about

200

PLATE XI

ST SOPHIA: FACING THE WEST DOOR

him: " Spring green from Caryſtus, and Phrygian polychrome, where flowers of red and silver shine; porphyry powdered with ſtars; crocus glittering like gold; milk poured on a flesh of black; blue corn-flowers growing among drifts of fallen snow ";[1] categorically he enumerates the marble veſture. Supporting the galleries and the walls above them, tiers of pillars, porphyry, verde-antique and every kind of marble, continue the ſtructure of the church. Those beneath, ranged in curves, bear gilded capitals, carved not to deflect the eye, but worked inwardly to carry it up. The curving walls above are similarly wrought in a texture of punctured elaboration, inset with plaques of porphyry. Then gradually, the four triangular pendentives, each bearing the mosaic of a six-winged cherubim, creep out to support the cornice of the dome, whence Christ Pantocrator looks down in majesty to judge the world. Beneath him ſtands the ambo, used for ceremonies such as coronations: a huge jasper pulpit borne by eight pillars and inlaid with ivory and silver. Before and behind, two ſtairways lead to encircling outer walls upon the floor, which support two oemicircles of rose-coloured columns bound in bronze. On these reſt beams, blue and gold, which bear aloft silver crosses in the likeness of the Chi-Rho, and cone-shaped candelabra.

From this boundary, a passage, baniſtered in verde-antique, leads to the iconoſtasis, the great silver screen across the eaſtern apse. Framed at intervals by silver-

[1] Lethaby and Swainson's translation, adapted.

201

sheeted columns bearing pairs of winged angels, broad silver panels exhibit chased circular patterns, monograms of the Apostles and of Justinian and Theodore. Within, a temple of silver gilt, hung with scarlet curtains depicting the same sovereigns prostrate before Christ, and surmounted by a silver tower in the form of an octagonal cone, contains the golden and enamelled altar, "wonder of all nations," which the crusaders will smash and bear away. Around hang the votive crowns of the Emperors, fired with the dull light of cabochon jewels and enamel plaques. And over all, high up on the curving mosaic vault, broods the Mother of God and her Child, blue and white and gold, from a throne of red, and a green footstool.

But it is the light, the formless, unbegotten radiance of no visible source, which brings harmony to these elements—almost, it might be said, transfigures them. In a Gothic cathedral, there are only cavernous shadows and dramatic rays; in a classical, the windows are of blatant, hygienic convenience. But in St Sophia, an exquisite luminous mist seems to envelop the whole church, diffused from innumerable small windows set along the cornice of the dome, and in the walls elsewhere. Shadows are not; only depths. Hence the elusive form, the glory of the building, speaking to all men with the gift of tongues. And at night, in Byzantine days, it is the same. Falling in a gigantic circle from the cornice of the dome, chain upon chain of varying lengths carry stupendous silver discs and

crosses pierced to hold the myriad oil-glasses and their
floating wicks. Sconces in form of bowls and ships[1]
reveal the colours of the marble sheeting. The iconoſtasis flickers athwart the apse. A pendant cross
glows above it. Chriſt in the dome, ruler of the world,
glitters the reflection of invisible lamps atop the cornice.
Outside, alike through winter ſtorms and the velvet
calm of summer nights, the light shines over the sea,
beacon of which every Byzantine sailor carries a spark
in his heart, " beckoning not only the merchantman,
but the way to the living God."

To comprehend the later development of Byzantine
art, the emergence of its pictorial genius and the laſt
efflorescence of Greek painting, it is necessary to take
some ſtock of the diffuse culture which accompanied it,
and without which its peculiar characteriſtics muſt
inevitably have degenerated, as they did elsewhere, into
folk-tainted decoration.

Literacy was no privilege of clerics or the ariſtocracy.
In the themes, popular education was organised under
the auspices of the Metropolitans, as it continued to be
among the Anatolian Greeks until 1923, the prieſtly
or other teachers being paid for their services by the
children's parents. In the capital, schools were officially subsidised; while, for those of noble or, more
accurately speaking, bureaucratic descent, there was a

---

[1] A bronze lamp in the form of a sailing-ship and dating from the
time of Valerius Severus may be seen in the Uffizi at Florence.
Robert de Clary (1204) enumerates 100 discs with 25 lamps each.

bi-sexual seminary within the precincts of the Great Palace itself. A University, founded in the fifth century by Theodosius II, and known as the Octagon, also flourished. Here grammar, rhetoric, dialectic and the classics were studied after the manner of Antiquity. But it stank in the nostrils of the iconoclasts and was closed by the Emperor Leo III the Isaurian, in 727.

Greeks without education are as bees in mid-winter. Moreover, as Rambaud has written, " in the Greek Empire, the humanities seemed indispensable, and at the same time, sufficient, for the formation of civil servants." During more than a century, the study of the humanities was in abeyance. Nor only individuals, but the state services themselves, suffered proportionately. For in Constantinople, as in England to-day, the broadest mental training was considered essential to eventual administrative success. It was to repair the efficiency of the bureaucracy, as previously shown on pp. 127 and 128, to set seal on the iconoclast defeat, and to gratify both his own and the popular craving, that the Cæsar Bardas, brother of the Empress-Regent Theodora, and virtual ruler of the Empire from 856 to 866, refounded the University of Constantinople. Cultured and loose-living, an efficient administrator and dispenser of justice, the typically " Renascence " personality of the Cæsar became the centre of an intellectual clique who impressed their names on history: Photius, afterwards Patriarch of the first schism, and sometimes called the wisest man of the Middle Ages; Constantine, apostle to the Slavs, whose cultural birth through him accomplished was jointly inspired by Photius and the Cæsar; Methodius, parent of the modern Czech; and Leo the Mathematician, Bishop of Salonica, to whose care the new University was entrusted.

First in the revived curriculum came the classics. It is not to be supposed that the part of the Byzantines, *les bibliothécaires du genre humain,* in preserving the writings of Antiquity, was a wholly passive one. More of those fabled books were their possession than are ours. And these lay, not mouldering in cupboards as historians have sedulously preached, but beneath the scrutiny of perpetual copyists, whose volumes were disseminated to student and dilettante alike. It was computed, at one time, that the royal library alone contained 30,000 books. In the higher ranks of society, women were often as well-educated as men.

Simultaneously, the ninth century witnessed an advance in the practical application of science. Greek fire was already discovered. Under the Emperor Theophilus, last of the iconoclasts, Leo of Salonica invented the dial in the Emperor's cabinet, recording the messages of the Asiatic fire-telegraph, and was also responsible for the jewelled birds and golden lions that sang and roared about his throne. Such, in fact, was the fame of Constantinople in this respect, that the Caliph of Bagdad in concluding a treaty with the Greeks, stipulated for the visit of three professors of mathematics to his court; of these Leo was one. At the beginning of the twelfth century, it is recorded that the blinded conspirator, Nicephorus Diogenes, ſtudied geometry by means of figures in solid relief. After the Latin Conqueſt, the mantle of scientific and mathematical learning fell to Trebizond, whither voyaged ſtudents in search of it from every part of the Levant. But the eleventh century was the golden age of Byzantine education. And the width of its ficld may be judged by the subjeɛts of which, at the age of twenty-five, Psellos informs poſterity that he had maſtered the ultimate intricacies: Rhetoric, Philosophy, Music, Law, Geometry, Aſtronomy, Medicine, Magic, and, through Neoplatonism, Platonism.

Music, as a province of the higher culture is seldom mentioned in the Middle Ages. Unfortunately, Byzantine attainment in this sphere is difficult to reconſtruɛt. Music played a large part in military and court ceremonial. Whenever the Emperor moved from the Great Palace, he was accompanied by bands of drums and trumpets; on campaigns, soldiers marched to the sound of flutes; orders were given by the trumpet; and the firſt recorded army bands of Weſtern Europe are said to have been borrowed from the Turks, inheritors of the Byzantine. Mechanical organs gladdened the Empress to her bath; a golden organ filled the throne-room of the birds and lions with myſterious sound at the reception of foreign ambassadors; the faɛtions of the circus had each its silver organ, to be played on a wooded terrace in the palace gardens. The ecclesiaſtical music of the time has survived in numerous manuscripts; but their interpretation is uncertain. The chants appear to have been

akin to Gregorian, of which they were probably the
original inspiration; their rendering by the embassy
of Michael I Rhangabé charmed the Emperor Charlemagne; and they are represented, to some extent, in
the traditional tunes of the modern Greek folk-songs.
Also they formed the basis of Russian church music,
thus lending all Russian tunes and composers their
distinction both from those of Western Europe and
the formless monotony of the lesser Slav peasantries.
To the Chrysanthine system of the modern Greek
Church, they are in no way related; this being a purely
Oriental importation.

In language and literature, the eleventh century
witnessed the further growth of an evolution which
was destined to prove, right down to the present time,
and probably for many years beyond it, the *damnosa
hereditas* of the Greek race. This was the divergence
between the written and the spoken tongue. The
Attic pedantry of schoolmasters lived then as now, and
with disastrous results for the unfortunate language of
which the Attic dialect was formerly a part. To write
even letters in the vernacular was to defy the accepted
canons of taste. And while in the West French,
Spanish and Italian were growing out of Latin, the
youth of Constantinople was still obliged to load its
pen with the jejune purity of classic models. With the
revived study of the humanities, and particularly of Plato,
in the eleventh century, the divergence was rendered
permanent. The language of conversation, unrecog-
nised as a medium of artistic expression, was con-

signed to the limbo of vulgarity. In the phrase of Krumbacher, it was as though the Italian Renascence had subſtituted Ciceronian Latin for the language of Dante. Words evolved, but were never committed to paper. Style became but a heaping of clauses. That, in a thousand years the highly developed Byzantine culture produced no literary work of the leaſt importance, is a convincing teſtimony to the danger of the oft-mourned paſt's survival. Poſterity may be thankful that no such adherence to the models of Praxiteles and Pheidias developed, as it was later to do in Weſtern Europe, a similar ſtrangle-hold on art.

There exiſts, of course, a large bulk of Byzantine literature. Its foremoſt works, the theological, are of too topical an intereſt to attraƈt the attention of subsequent generations. In hiſtory, the Greeks have at all times excelled. Royalty, ecclesiaſtic, bourgeois, each in turn assumed the funƈtion of chronicler. And despite the tedium of form, their outlook is balanced and underſtanding of human charaƈter. The output of poetic hymns, from the eighth century on, was profuse; unfortunately their beauty has not withſtood translation into Ancient and Modern. Apart from such songs as the dirge to the fallen city, quoted on the laſt of these pages, the moſt unique produƈt of mediæval Greek literature is the epic of Digenis Akritas. This poem, dating from the tenth or eleventh centuries, is a romance of the Anatolian border in the days before Manzikert, when the Byzantine dominion stretched almoſt to the Euphrates. There pervades it not only the eternal spark of Greek patriotism, championing the sacred monarchy in Constantinople and its heavenly prototype, but something of the joyous lassitude of Persia, together with the chivalresque caprice of the great captain of the marches. The exploits of the hero, in which history and legend mingle, have penetrated even Russian folklore. Had the Empire endured, and Atticism lapsed, as it must eventually have done, before the need for popular expression, this poem would have occupied, for modern Greeks, the position of the Chanson de Roland or the Canterbury Tales for French or English.

With such measure of culture, save in art, appreciative rather than creative, the Byzantine civilisation reached a climax that lasted from Charlemagne to the crusades. The West lay dark and savage; behind the walls of Constantinople, the classic spirit of humanism waxed and waned, but was never quite extinguished. There alone the amenities of living flourished. Occasionally in architectural form, the Eastern influence went West, as shown at Aix or Périgueux; but more often it was in the products of craftsmanship, in reliquaries of jewellers' and goldsmiths' work, in glass, enamels and fabrics such as were afterwards discovered in Charlemagne's tomb. And it is the splendour, of which these objects were but echoes, which strikes the true note of the age. Something of it remains in the gorgeous colouring of the mosaics of Daphni, accentuated by their intimidating austerity of form. But its outstanding monument is the great church of the monastery of St Luke of Stiris. Here the mosaics, if lacking the conspicuous genius of the former, breathe a cold, vernal brilliance from each shadowed vault above the bevelled panels of dull polychrome marble. In this church alone, situate on a trackless, oleandered spur of Parnassus, is a true interior of the Empire's middle period to be seen. The effect is one, which words, in the absence of analogy, cannot convey.

This splendour, and the material wealth implied, were the sponsors of the Byzantine Renascence, which took place in the eleventh century. To the man in the street, the term " Renascence " conjures various and diverse portents: pagan Italy and Martin Luther; manuscript-mongering scholars and the vanquishing of Gothic; the seed of painting planted out of nothing in Giotto; Columbus in his cockle-shell, Caxton at his press. But in reality the Renascence was a unity of which each force represented by these names was born, and to which each contributed. It was an intellectual impulse, born of reaction against the stale encyclo-pædics of Aristotle and a mysticism no longer synony-mous with, but opposed to, the trend of human progress. The quest of Reality unaided was obsolete; there was need for subsidiary channels. The system of the Ancients, of sensible enquiry into man's proper significance, must be invoked.

Before the West was even thus consciously agrope, in Constantinople, Greeks being Greeks, the logic of humanism, the relating of life's fundamental purpose to the delicious manifestations of the organic world, had never been wholly discredited. And it was thence, from the Byzantines themselves as well as from the ancestral classics in their keeping, that the impulse of the Western Renascence emanated. But the rediscovery of Plato in the East was attended by no such revolution as it afterward produced in the West: the physical odds against which the Empire had now to contend were too great, and the patent abuses of Plato's opponent, the Orthodox Church, too few, to secure his profoundest effect. It was Italy, therefore, that reaped where the Greeks had sown. Save only in painting. In that, the harvest was shared between them.

Although the creative faculties of the Byzantine were mainly guided by the mystic and inspirational, it was, none the less, only its hold on the rational Hellenic perception of sensory values that gave Byzantine culture its uniqueness. Though, from the first, the free exercise of Reason to discover for each individual an interpretation of destiny and duty had been suspect in the eyes of the Church; though the flesh of Hypatia, Neoplatonist of the fifth century, had been scraped from her bones in the streets of Alexandria; though the philosophical schools of Athens had been closed by Justinian in 531, and the University of Constantinople by the iconoclasts two hundred years later; yet always there had existed those who, though not so drastic as the fourth-century Emperor Julian the Apostate in his contempt for the Christian intellect, despite the civil virtues thereby engendered, retained the belief that not only religion, but material phenomena in addition, provided channels of communication with the Affinity of man's perpetual seeking. Of these was the Cæsar Bardas, leader of the anti-Puritan reaction of the ninth century, and precursor, with his learned and influential contemporary, the Patriarch Photius, of a movement which reached its climax at the end of the eleventh. For it was then that the true Byzantine Renascence took place. Psellos, the wisest man of his age and minister of the Empire, advertised Plato.

There now arrives that monstrous, stupid paradox, the rejection of Platonism, fundamentally religious in outlook and classical only in method, by a body of Christian opinion that had long accepted the undiluted materialism of Aristotle. To sum, in a sentence, the difference between the two is a presumption which only the present context can excuse. But holding this in view, it may be said that, in the first place, to Aristotle the conception of an Absolute Reality, external to man, but possessing in him a personal affinity, was unknown; such Reality as he sought was of diverse and impossible elements, such as Justice and Beauty, each possessed of that insulated significance which has proved the greatest curse of the classical incubus. And that, in the second, this limited and scattered Truth was contained for him wholly in objects admitting of sensory perception; his quest, in fact, was a matter of analysis. Plato, on the other hand, discovered God. The "Absolute Reality, external to man, but possessing in him a personal affinity," was the beginning of thought for him; in it "Justice and Beauty" were co-ordinate; the significance of material phenomena was apparent only in terms of it. To Aristotle, material phenomena were as viscera to the analyst; to Plato they were subsidiary to his instinctive location of the element sought. The quest of Reality, a Reality in which the why and wherefore of things had no part, gave him his ideal, and was for him the ideal of man. But the hounds of the pursuit were Reason. And such, for the sake of that very function, was his exaltation of Reason, that the means became confused with the end: Reason became his golden calf, synonymous with God. Hence, while Aristotle, the encyclopædist, chemist delving in the earth for abstractions, was a docile creature in the hands of Christian *doctrinaires*, Plato, glorifying Reason no matter where it led, opened vistas of unlimited heterodoxy. Thus—to trace the sequence of history—the fundamental impulse of the Reformation was the ideal of Plato communicated as an intellectual state. Men must think independently: the quest of Reality is in fact synonymous with logical, independent thought. But Reality is absolute, immutable by speculation. By accepting this doctrine, preserved from idolatry by the latter reservation, the reformed churches regained in some measure the path which the old had lost. But in the Orthodox Church, as distinct from the Roman, whose Absolute, far from being immutable by thought, was the product of an inventive and politically engrossed hierarchy, the path had never been actually out of sight.[1] Had Byzantine civilisation survived, the Platonic element in the future Protestantism might have filtered North-west by means of imperceptible mental contact, in place of violent social upheaval. East and North-west would have been one; and the Roman Church been left to itself, an outcast of the South.

Psellos was the precursor of these incalculable movements. Appointed by the Emperor Constantine IX Monomach (1042-1054) to the chair of a lately founded school of philosophy, he circumvented possible suspicion on the part of the Church by proclaiming Plato a kind of early Father. At first the Œcumenical Patriarch gave the new teaching his blessing. As its fame spread, the whole Levant, like Italy four centuries later, was overcome with excitement; Arabs and Persians hurried to Constantinople. But Psellos, indiscreet with success and incapable of moderation in the cause of his heart, now turned on the Church, accused the Patriarch of practising astrology and magic, and eventually created such disturbance that the Emperor was obliged to close the school. A reaction set in, which resulted, during the last quarter of the eleventh century, in the utterance of official anathemas against the classical philosophers. But the work was done; and the influence of Psellos and his friends remained. The general respect for their learning enabled them to fill

[1] It may be said that while the Orthodox Church alternately blessed and damned the letter of Plato's teaching, the intellectual attitude thereby produced and communicated to the uninitiate, was permitted to flourish.

the chief posts of the administration. And their attempt to weaken the landed magnates of Asia Minor by reduction of the fighting forces, was responsible for the defeat of Manzikert in 1071 and the loss of half the Empire (see pages 96 and 128). Psellos was a complex character, a Hellene and a Byzantine. " I ought," he wrote, " to think only of God; but my nature and my soul's irresistible desire for all knowledge have led me in the direction of science." A tragic apology, semi-grotesque, but at all events consequent. Plato was now read; his works were multiplied, as though with a prophetic view to Italian circulation; and his humanism was reflected in an artistic naturalism which served to enhance rather than obscure the austere ideals of Byzantine representation. Psellos himself wrote letters to officials in Greece, begging them send him statues. He was the first of the pedagogue Philhellenes. Already he pens the familiar phrase: " Must we not love the children for their parents' sake, though, indeed, they reproduce not all their features? " He upbraids the prefect of Athens for finding her provincialism boring. But underneath these admonitions, become odious with time, burns the sacred patriotism, the lamp of the race. " The Byzantine Empire," he writes, " is the Greek Empire."

Thus was inaugurated the last tradition of Byzantine art, which was to survive the Latin Conquest. Prior to that event, however, its implantation in Italy was already accomplished. Its centres in that country were two: the provinces south of Rome, where until the twentieth century Greek was still the language of remote villages, and which were not finally lost to Greek rule till the twelfth century; and Venice, the town which was originally modelled on Constantinople, and which presented, in St Mark's, a continually inspiring, if slightly Italianate, model of Byzantine art. From these sources, gradually diffusing over the whole peninsula a technique become limited and rudimentary from lack of intercourse with Constantinople, Italian painting was born. Vasari, its earliest historian, ascribes its parentage to thirteenth-century Greeks. On the part of such pictures as the Sienese primitives or those ascribed to Cimabue, the direct imitation of the Byzantine icon is not disputed. But in the case of Giotto and his immediate successors, the analogy has not been pursued. Yet it is only necessary to visit the Kahrié mosque in Constantinople, or the churches of Mistra and Mount Athos, to discover unquestionable identity of form, arrangement, and architectural cliché. Henceforth, with the isolation and gradual subsidence of the Empire, Greek and Italian painting went different ways. In Venice alone the legacy remained. There, the colours of the Byzantines, cold blues and vinous reds, survived, though without the principle of their application. And much of Tintoretto, his impressionism and tendency to elongation in the interest of his composition, can only have derived from the impress which the extinct civilisation of Eastern Europe had left upon his home.

Conversely it has been asserted that the Byzantine Renascence of painting owed its origin to contact with Italy. In the sixteenth and seventeenth centuries, when there was no longer a cultural centre in the East, and the Venetians were in Crete, something of the Italian freedom of form was assimilated by Greek artists; though the result, save in the case of isolated icon-painters, seems to have been uniformly unfortunate. But in its initial stages, the advance of naturalism which characterised the last phase of Byzantine art was synonymous with the rediscovery of humanism, which took place in Constantinople some centuries before in Italy. In Constantinople, moreover, the Greeks were deeply attached to the old vehicles of religious expression; naturalism was assimilated to them; it did not displace them as in the West. After the Latin Conquest, Greeks travelled little. And apart from the barrier erected by the mutual hatred of the Orthodox and Catholic Churches, there was little inducement for Italian artists to seek their fortune in the impoverished Empire. Visitors from the West were engaged either in commerce or conquest. Such cultural intercourse as there was flowed from the East, not to it.

The surviving examples of later Byzantine painting have been divided into two categories, the Macedonian and the Cretan schools. The distinction is at first obscure. The mosaics of the Kahrié stand outside both: not only as mosaics, rare in an era of material decline; but in the felicity, almost facility, of their compositions, and the pervading peace and simplicity of their figures. These, almost contemporary, approach very closely the works of Giotto. Next in order of time. as far as dates can be surmised, come the paintings of the Brontocheion and the Peribleptos at Mistra; in these churches the true Byzantine method of coloration by contrast, with which the Cretan school was later to be particularly identified, appears to combine with the quiescent dignity of Macedonian forms. Only in the frescoes of the Pantanassa, painted immediately before the fall of Constantinople in the first half of the fifteenth century, does the Cretan character predominate, in the unique beauty of the colouring. But on Mount Athos, the difference between the two schools is easily perceptible; there, the Macedonian, arriving at the beginning of the fourteenth century, preceded the Cretan by two centuries, employing a separate iconography and a more Westerly technique of colour. Its frescoes exhale an atmosphere of piety and quietude, and a sobriety of light, which, if tending sometimes to weakness, bespeak the dignity of spiritual repose, of unshaken faith in the hidden world amid the mounting catastrophes of this. From these ideals, the Cretan method of expression was far removed. There are strange qualities about this Antarctic of the Greek world. Statesmen of the early twentieth century had cause to recall the seven hundred years of perpetual revolt that comprised the island's latter history. And such, indeed, is the text of its art. A warring of forces, of souls in cataclysm, is born into the conflict of its lines and colours. All that distinguishes Byzantine art from that of the West is riven from its hieratic quiet to form a staccato world of acrid shadow and livid prominence, agog with angry, inner light or swathed in silken tulle of ethereal brilliance. Something possessed these artists, some spirit wrestling with their figures, that we have not. And of their line was born, eighty-eight years after the fall of Constantinople, Domenicos Theotocopoulos. Cretan in birth and personality, he has furnished the epilogue and climax to Byzantine culture.

When, in the last half of the sixteenth century, El Greco came to Italy, the Renascence, that exquisite short song of Gothic spirit in the voice of humanism, had died away. Only the band played on, a ponderous empty symphony in which the heralds of baroque were piping unsubstantial notes. Of its form the Greek borrowed such measure of naturalism as was necessary to conquer naturalism. With this attained, he loosed from its iconographic prison the achievement of a millennium. Settling, at Toledo, amid barren rippling hills like Crete's, and a semi-Oriental culture reminiscent of his own, he gave to the art of his ancestors not a naturalism conventional as their own formality, but freedom, absolute, and vindicated by a consummate ability. Alone he did it, and alone he lived, vouchsafing no explanations, but speaking sometimes, to such as understood his native tongue, of the infallibility of his race. He was the greatest Greek; perhaps, for those who have seen the St Maurice, the greatest artist in all the world. Yet Greeks to-day, puffed of their earthy speculators, scarcely know him. Meanwhile European art pursued another road; and when he died, only his colour remained for Velasquez to dilute. A dubious posterity has thought to discern an astigmatism in his eye. Let it grieve, also, for that same astigmatism, which, for thirty generations, afflicted the artists of Byzantium: the astigmatism of fixation on Reality. Are not we, too, after four centuries, again infected?

CHAPTER X

THE JOYOUS LIFE

THE structure of the Empire, its commerce and wealth; its religious idea; its learning and creative artistry: the stable, the transcendental, and the cultural elements; prefaced by a suggestion of history; into these has the anatomy of Byzantine civilisation resolved. But like a house, civilisation is more than its structural components, than bricks and plan and paint; it is a unity, an atmospheric environment, implied not in the category of its blessings, but in their common reaction; to be judged by the tenor of Monday rather than Saturday. The outline is limned, even the shape ; there remains to impress the reader with the very colour of Byzantine life. Those, who seek, may find it still, lurking in the coves of the Ægean, softening the brown castellated ranges of Anatolia; wrapped in the treeless decay of Venice; glancing about the flowered monasteries of Athos; glowing, as through a smoked glass, over all Constantinople. And whence its light? The light is in the air; and the air holds the print of lesser things, of common round and average character, of the immediate concerns of individuals. The evidence is scattered; materials await the researches of a profounder scholarship than this. But irrelevant as the following details seem, to some extent they fill the void.

221

The names take life and the bodies move. Without them, the mediæval Greeks muſt ſtand divorced in myſtery for ever, insoluble as the Chinese. Whereas it is of their wedding with the paſt and future of Eaſtern Europe that this book purports to tell.

Of royalty, nobility and bourgeois, isolated pictures emerge.

The hub of the world was Conſtantinople. Within it was another hub, an immense walled precinct on the point of land at the foot of the Bosporus between the Golden Horn and the Marmora, and ſtretching in terraced decline from the plateau of the Hippodrome and St Sophia to the three waters. Here, overlooking the sea to the Asiatic mountains, dwelt the Greek Emperors. Here, set among groves of trees and planted gardens, a vaſt concourse of buildings, churches, ſtables, banqueting-halls, fountains, accouchement-chambers, schools and barracks, enshrined that un-ending ritual, the life of "the Autocrat of the Romans faithful in Chriſt." Of that ceaseless liturgy, from birth in the porphyry pavilion at the water's edge; of the landmarks, coronations, marriages and triumphs; of the everyday procedure corresponding with the religious calendar, the processions, services and inveſti-tures; of the banquets, feſtivities, and races in the Hippodrome; to the laſt ceremony of interment at the church of the Holy Apoſtles, record survives.[1] But

---

[1] In the *De Ceremoniis* of the Emperor Constantine VII Porphyro-genitus.

occasional scenes stand out, to speak not of ostentation, frivolity and immobility, but a profound and subtle beauty. The being of Byzantine royalty was set in as lovely a frame as man and nature could devise. Political theorists, blind to the temperaments of peoples and the sanctification of the state in symbols, may cavil. But whatever the faults which posterity discerns in the Byzantine sovereignty, the lethargy commonly associated with excessive formality is not one of them.

The hall of great banquets was the Triclinos of the Nineteen Settees. And it was here that took place the Christmas dinner in the reign of the Emperor Constantine VII Porphyrogenitus, of which the ambassador Liutprand, afterwards Bishop of Cremona, has left an account. The Emperor, if the ordinary custom was observed, was surrounded, in imitation of his heavenly prototype, by twelve chosen companions ; while the rest of the company, to the number of 216, was disposed in parties of twelve at the remaining eighteen tables. The plate was of gold; and the weight of the three gold vases of dessert necessitated their arrival on three scarlet-upholstered chariots, whence they were hoisted to table by ropes descending from a ceiling of golden foliage, and wound on to a revolving machine. The ambassador, though disconcerted, as the modern visitor to Greece, at the oil cooking and resinous wine of the people, bears testimony to the excellence of occasional dishes. The meal was followed by a display of acrobatics, in which two boys ascended a pole twenty-four feet high,

balanced on a man's head. A second banqueting hall
was the Chryso-Triclinos, a domed octagon supported
on eight arches leading to eight apses. The walls were
covered with a mosaic of flowers, framed in a tracery
of carved ciphers bound in silver. The doors were of
silver; the feet of the guests trod on a crush of roses,
rosemary and myrtle; the plate was of gold, the tables
of gold and silver; and both were enamelled and
jewelled.

Later than these was the Magnavra, situate on a
terrace of tall trees by the sea, and containing the famous
throne-room of the iconoclast Emperor Theophilus,
decreed for the reception of foreign ambassadors. At
the end of a long hall, hung with silver chandeliers and
echoing with the music of a golden organ, sat the
Emperor at the head of six steps, guarded by golden
lions and griffins, and shaded by trees of gilded bronze,
in whose branches glittered jewelled and enamelled
birds. As the ambassadors approached, the lions
moved towards him; their mouths roared; their tails
twanged the ground; while, above, the birds gave forth
the twitters of their kind. As the eyes of the visitor
were bent in prostration, Emperor and throne were
wafted bodily into the ceiling; to descend, ere the
stranger's head was raised, with the former newly
arrayed in the hieratic vestments of his office. These
bewildering devices, to the weight of 200 pounds of
gold, in value £43,000, were melted down by Theophilus' extravagant son, Michael III, and afterwards
minted into a special coinage by his successor Basil I.

But a curious light is thrown on the movements of dispersed Byzantine treasure in the narrative of Clavijo's embassy to Samarcand in 1404-6. On the occasion of a visit to Tamerlane's chief wife, Clavijo remarked a pair of doors "covered with plates of silver gilt, ornamented with patterns in blue enamel. . . . All this was so finely wrought that evidently never in Tartary nor, indeed, in our Western land of Spain, could it have been come to. In the one door was figured the image of St Peter, while in the other was St Paul. . . ." These, reported by the Tartars to have been found among the treasure of the defeated Turkish Sultan Bajazet at Brussa, were plainly Byzantine. But more astonishing still in this capital of central Asia, there appeared, within the tent, " a golden tree that simulated an oak, and its trunk was thick as might be a man's leg. . . . This tree reached to the height of a man, and below it was made as though its roots grew from a great dish that lay there. The fruit of this tree consisted of vast numbers of balas rubies, emeralds, turquoises, sapphires and common rubies with many great round pearls of wonderful orient and beauty . . . while numerous little birds, made of gold enamel in many colours were to be seen perching on the branches." [1]

---

[1] A similar tree to that of Theophilus graced the court of the Abbassid Caliphs in the tenth century. Its branches numbered eighteen, and it was attended by phalanxes of mounted knights draped in silken uniforms and also moveable. On the subject of any mechanism, Clavijo (see bibliography) is silent. But this, after five or six hundred years, was probably in need of repair.

It was in the Emperor's cabinet in the Magnavra, adjoining the throne-room of the birds and lions, that the messages of the Asiatic fire-telegraph were recorded. To the unsleeping sentries on the Pharos, the island lighthouse at the entrance of the Bosporus, the signals were transmitted from the Eastern coast of the Marmora, having come hill-top to hill-top from the interior. And their import, by the invention of Leo of Salonica, was determined by the hour marked on a clock in the Emperor's cabinet, constructed to keep exact time with a fellow on the Cilician frontier. Each hour, it was arranged, should represent a different message. Hence perhaps arose the Western legend that Virgil, in the rôle of necromancer with which the Dark Ages invested him, had fashioned for Augustus a set of twelve images called " Salvatio Romæ." Each of these, representing an imperial province, bore a bell in its hand. When that province was in revolt, the bell struck. Here, possibly, in the guise of a traveller's tale turned history, is a clue to the nature of Leo's " dial."

In the latter part of the ninth century arose the new palace of the Emperor Basil I the Macedonian, surpassing in splendour all that had ever been seen. The chief hall took the form of a basilica supported on eight columns of verde-antique alternating with another eight of red onyx decorated with reliefs of vines and animals. The Emperor's bedroom adjacent was wholly covered with mosaic: on the ceiling, starred with gold, a cross of brilliant green dominated the room; on the walls, above a floral wainscotting, the imperial family were ranged on a background of gold; on the floor from a medallion of a peacock, there radiated four diagonal strips of green marble to four smaller medallions containing eagles. There was also a summer-bedroom, having one side open to the garden and the others adorned with mosaic hunting scenes. Byzantine art was continuing the secular tradition inaugurated by the iconoclast magnificence of the Emperor Theophilus.

Thus, like the Greek Augusti themselves, the reader may wander for ever between the walls of marble and gold, crushing the scent of flowers and herbs, opening the doors of silver and ivory, brushing the scarlet curtains woven with animals, dazzled with the traditional palace-vista of gold and silver chandeliers. Through the churches of the Palace precinct: the Oratory of the Saviour, with its floor one sheet of silver inlaid with niello and its walls of silver gilt set with pearls and cabochons; the New Church of Basil I, with its six bronze domes glowing in the sun; and the Church of our Lady of Pharos, pendant with doves of white gold studded with emeralds, and carrying cruciform sprigs of pearls in their beaks; past the innumerable fountains: the " Mystic Phiale " of the Sigma, its golden pineapple spouting wine into a silver-bound basin full of almonds and pistachios, where the Emperor enthroned received the delegates of the circus factions and reviewed the horses before the races, as kings shake hands with Cup-tie finalists in modern England; the similar pineapples on long shafts in the courtyard of the New Church, one of red porphyry surrounded by dragons, the other of iridescent marble in the company of rams, goats and cocks in expectorant bronze. Among the schools, cadet-corps, and sentries in gilded armour and red aigrettes. Along the polo-ground. And down at last to the artificial port of the Boucoleon, with the royal yachts and barges lying at anchor. Here the days of the monarchy's affluence were passed. Here the delegates of Christ planned and prayed and loved. Here evolved that ritual of courts and royal divinity, which governed Europe till the twentieth century; and which even our sons will scarcely understand.

The place of women in the social structure of the Byzantines was of an independence which a world of competitive modernity may flatter itself on having lately reintroduced. And this is particularly apparent in the lives of the Greek Empresses. Once chosen, the affianced of the Emperor was crowned, not after, but before, her marriage: the sacred essence of her royalty emanated from God and not her husband. Henceforth a separate household was at her command; her fortune was subject to none but her own control; and she was empowered to summon the great ministers of state to conference, and to confer her own insignias on whom she pleased. Following her marriage, the populace hailed her as " the Augusta chosen of God "; and from now on, her every action was attended by a ritualistic publicity which can only be compared to that perfected by Louis XIV at Versailles. She was followed by the whole court to the bridal bed; the consummation

228

of her marriage was celebrated by a banquet; and on
the day following, court and city formed a double line
to see her to her bath, whither she was borne to the
music of organs. Grand dignitaries, servants bearing
scents and bath-robes, and three ladies-in-waiting
carrying red enamel apples encruſted with pearls,
brought up the rear. A similar pomp assiſted the
arrival of imperial heirs in the porphyry chamber by
the sea conſtructed for their purple-bearing.

Of the Byzantine ariſtocracy and its division into
bureaucrats and territorial magnates, something has
been said. But titles were not hereditary; so that, in
faᴄt, it was only the latter who developed the hereditary
pride of a separate class. Name was the true criterion
of birth. And such a superscription as Ἀνδρόνικος ἐν
χῷ τῷ Θῷ πιστὸς βασιλεὺς καὶ αὐτοκράτωρ Ῥωμαίων Δύκας
Ἄγγελος Κομνηνὸς ὁ Παλαιολόγος καὶ νέος Κωνσταντίνος[1]
illuſtrates the importance which even the Emperors
might attach to their connecᴛion with the moſt
prominent families of the Empire. The significance
of the connecᴛion, often commemorated by the
retention of the maternal name, was with power, not
pedigree. For caſte nobility there was no feeling.
Until 1922, many of the famous Byzantine names
were ſtill to be found among the Greeks of Anatolia,
often in diſtricts of which they were once the glory.

In the provinces, by the eighth century, a feudal
syſtem had arisen which tended, as later happened in

[1] Millet, *Inscriptions chrétiennes de l'Athos*, No. 359.

the West, to absorb the land of the smaller proprietors. While the Isaurian and Macedonian dynasties reigned, legislation was enforced to prevent this; the Emperor Basil II Bulgaroctonos even undertook personal tours to relieve the magnates who disturbed his peace of their possessions. But with regional recruiting converted, for fear of rebellion on the part of local leaders, into monetary payment, the smaller owners fell still further into the hands of the greater, owing to the financial assistance which, in bad years, only the latter could afford them for their share of the scutage. Thus the process continued; what the nobles lost in levies, they gained in land; till the Frankish crusaders could remark the resemblance between the conditions of Byzantine land tenure and their own. Finally, after the extinction of the Macedonian dynasty in 1057, the throne itself became the property of the landed aristocracy.

The potential wealth of Anatolia, should that region ever again see peace and be inhabited by a settled and industrious people, may be judged by the fortunes of the Smyrna merchants before the Great War, which were derived almost entirely from an unsystematic peasant agriculture covering a mere fraction of the available land. In Byzantine days, the stock of a smaller proprietor consisted of 600 oxen, 100 plough teams, 800 horses out to grass, 80 saddle horses and mules, and 12,000 sheep. In the middle of the estate stood the manor-house, dispensing universal hospitality, and having wooden furniture inlaid with metal and ivory. The country palaces of the great contained many courtyards; their rooms glittered with mosaic or were hung with tapeſtries; they had baths, pools and walled gardens, such as attach to the Moorish caſtles of Spain. But from the eleventh century on, this prosperity was gradually deſtroyed by the Eaſtern invasions. The coming of the Seljuk Turks is a landmark in the economic hiſtory of the world; by their agency one of the richeſt territories known to man was transformed, for all praćtical purposes of European well-being, into a desert. A certain revival in agriculture was effećted by the Nicæan Emperor, John III Vatatzes, after the fourth crusade. By his own example he sought to induce the ariſtocracy to live on their eſtates as praćtical farmers. He improved the breed of cattle and horses; grew food for the court and charities of his temporary capital; and from the sale of his private eggs derived sufficient profit to buy his wife a tiara of pearls.

The classic tale of Byzantine feudalism is the epic of Digenis Akritas, one of the great hiſtorical romances of the Middle Ages. The ſtory, a mixture of legend and truth, is set among the dark, sweeping ranges and bird-haunted marshlands of Cappadocia, a frontier of fortified passes at the desert's edge, where there is no cognisance of the opposing Eaſt and Weſt. Here, like the Weſtern Palatines, the great vassals raided and fought, unthinking of monarch and miniſters in the capital. " Akritas " means a Warden of the Marches; and " Digenis," twin-blooded; for while the hero's

mother had been a Dukaina of the famous family of
Dukas, his father was a Moslem prince from Edessa, or
as some think, one of the Puritan sect of the Paulicians.
For love of his wife, he was converted to Orthodoxy;
and their son, child of Eurasia, grew into the perfect
type of Byzantine chivalry: soldier, hunter, lover; and,
over all, the patriot-knight—φιλόπατρις—of Christendom, defender of the Empire and proud servant of its
rulers.

In appearance this youth was fair; his hair was
blond and curly; his eyebrows contrastingly black;
his complexion ruddy; and his chest broad and white
as crystal. He was clothed in a red tunic, embroidered
with pearls and fastened with gold buttons. Round his
neck hung a collar of amber and pearls. His boots were
embroidered with gold, his spurs inset with stones.
Holding a green Arab lance written over with golden
characters, he sat a white horse, bridled in enamelled
gold, upon a saddle-cloth of green and rose. The mane
of the horse was powdered with turquoises and golden
bells.[1]

Such a figure was it that fired the leisure of Byzantine humdrum. And the life was in accordance.

---

[1] A very accurate portrait of a young Porphyrogenitus of about
the same period is preserved on an ivory casket now in Troyes Cathedral
and is reproduced in Hayford Pierce and Royall Tyler's *Byzantine Art*
(London, 1926). The rider has the seat of an English cavalry officer ;
the bridle is without a bit. On the other panels are hunting scenes :
a boar attacked by hounds wearing heavy collars ; and a lion, with
two arrows protruding from its neck, springing upon the rider, who
defends himself with a short sword.

Famed in childhood for his slaying of wild beasts, Digenis Akritas, after enrolling in a brigand band, abducted a Dukaina cousin from her father's palace. (There is the stamp of truth in this cousinship; the family was too distinguished for the incident to be apocryphal). Refusing a dowry, he retired alone with her into the desert to hunt monsters; and the fame of his prowess provoked a visit from the Emperor himself, Romanus I Lecapenus. Next, he conducted a love affair with a Saracen princess, left shiftless by a Greek, whom she had released from prison. But conscience-stricken at the remembrance of his marriage vows, he restored her to him; to little purpose; for he immediately fell victim to the seductions of an Amazon queen, whom, like Siegfried, he had conquered in battle. Eventually, in a garden of flowers, trees and singing birds by the banks of the Euphrates, he built a palace. In the centre, scene of splendid feasting, stood a great hall in the form of a cross, decorated with mosaic figures of the romance-pantheon of Christian Hellenism, of Samson and Achilles, David and Alexander, Ulysses and Joshua.

These were but wild oats. Ultimately he became a famous general; won battles for the Empire; received presents from the soldier Emperor, Nicephorus II Phocas. But his delight was always in solitude, wandering by the flowing river with only his beloved. Then, at the age of thirty-three, he died. Within a century Manzikert was lost, the themes of the East fell to the Turks and beyond the frontier was barbarism. The palaces were overwhelmed; the romantic, chivalresque life hardened and disappeared. What monuments of it may survive, archæology has yet to discover.[1] But Turks till recently have been known, who assume the designation " Roumbeyoglu," implying descent from a " prince of Romania "; and who claim, not that their ancestor was governor of a European province in the early Ottoman Empire, but that he was a Byzantine noble, who turned Moslem with the advancing tide, and who occupied precisely that same castle which remains in his family to-day.

Aristocracy, as a class, derives its prestige from the country. The Byzantine bureaucracy was essentially town-bred, for the most part Constantinopolitan, and was recruited, since there was no caste-line, from the bourgeoisie and lesser nobility alike, they themselves being entirely intermarried. Hence arose that cultured liberalism which is only the product of large towns, but which, being product of Constantinople, was inevitably linked with religion. And there survive, to illustrate its germination in the family circle, two character sketches of mothers left by distinguished sons. In each case the mother appears as the preponderant factor in the solution of the problems that beset the family. For it was not the Empress alone who enjoyed

---

[1] The one exception, though Syrian, is the eighth-century palace of Kusejr 'Amra, adorned with frescoes of the Byzantine Emperor Chosroës King of Persia, Roderic King of the Spanish Visigoths, and Negus of Abyssinia. See bibliography, A. Musil.

an independence which the women of such countries as Spain may still envy. Under the Greek Empire, the property of a wife was in no way confused with that of her husband. She was legally admissible to the status of guardianship. And the conditions of divorce, though subject to occasional alteration, always remained substantially the same for both sexes.

The first of these Byzantine women whom parentage has brought fame, was the pious Theoctista, Constantinopolitan of the late eighth century, and mother of Theodore of Studium. A rigid, unswerving application to the work of salvation, both for herself and those around her, was the dominant interest of her life. She abstained from the ostentatious toilets of her station; not a feast-day passed, but that some outcast sat at her table. And on these occasions, her servants, who habitually fed on bread, bacon and wine, were given fish, fresh meat, chickens, and better wine. At other times she would beat them; then, overcome by remorse, fall on her knees before them. Her nights were spent in acquisition of knowledge which she might impart to her children. Conjugal intimacy she discouraged, so as better to prepare for the eternal parting of death. Finally, she persuaded herself, her husband, her three brothers-in-law, and her children, to give themselves absolutely to God. A few friends were invited to a farewell party; the house was sold for the poor; the servants were dismissed; and the whole family retired to their country estate in Bithynia, where they lived on a wooded, well-watered plateau overlooking the sea.

Upon their denouncing as sinful the second marriage
of the Emperor Constantine VI—though his bride was
actually a relative of Theoctista's—they were forcibly
dispersed; but were later reinstated by the iconodule
Empress Irene.

The picture has a dour, repelling stamp. The
temperament of Theoctista lacked the typically Byzantine mystic element which alone can render religious
fanaticism either palatable or intelligible to those who
do not possess it. And it was the age of the iconoclasts.
All the latent bitterness of piety was uppermost.

About two and a half centuries later, at the beginning
of the eleventh century, lived Theodota, mother of
Psellos the Hellenist. From his account of her emerges
a character sympathetic as Theoctista's was not. Her
outlook was serene and mystic; charity was instinct in
her, rather than consciously derived from the letter of
Christian commandment; moreover, she was type of
an eternal verity, the mother anxious for her children's
worldly advance. Possessing little education herself,
beyond the ability to read and embroider, it was through
her machinations and endeavours, fortified by dreams
and messages from the Above, and nights spent weeping
before the Virgin's icon in St Sophia, that Psellos
obtained the intellectual training which was to leave
his name as the originator of the European Renascence. She was happy in marriage; her husband was
endowed with good looks, clear eyes and a patrician
ancestry, and was without affectation. Like Theoctista,
she received the poor at her table, served them herself

and washed their feet. She had one daughter. This girl, casting about for a neighbour to love as herself, lighted on a prostitute who lived near by. In answer to the latter's query: if she gave up her trade, how should she live? Psellos' sister took her into her house and shared with her all she possessed. She taught her to blush; to forsake jewellery and coloured shoes. But despite these renunciations, there came a lapse, and to her reformer's horror and indignation, the reclaimed girl was brought to bed of a child. Psellos, meanwhile, had left the capital in pursuit of new learning. His sister died soon after. And he describes how he returned, without having heard the news, to encounter the funeral by chance. Theodota was overwhelmed, and, despite the entreaties of her husband, decided to take the veil. So fixed was her whole being upon contact with the other world, that she neglected the barest necessities of this. After her novitiate, she gradually sank. And ultimately followed her daughter to eternity, regretted by the whole populace of the city.

The story of the prostitute indicates the whole tenor of Byzantine society. That society was one in which practice of the true Christian ideal was possible; not of a tithe to the poor or the turning of the other cheek; but of the sympathy for others, of the understanding into fellow-beings born of the Greek instinct to scatter the pretensions of one man above another. The nauseating moral hypocrisy which distinguishes a woman who gives her body for pleasure from one who does so for bread did not govern Constantinople.

While the prostitute had a soul, she remained within the pale of human fellowship; the world did not avert its cognisance of her. And this raises the whole much discussed question of Byzantine character and morals. It may be that the rigid standard of purity enforced both by law and public opinion under the iconoclasts was exceptional; that in another age Constantine VI's divorce would not have forfeited him his throne. But there can be no doubt that behind the rebukes administered to profligate Emperors by subsequent Patriarchs, the real force lay in popular disapproval. The question is not one of comparison with the contemporary West, with the harems of Frankish kings or the state-run brothels of London; but of judgment by modern standards. The Byzantines could be cruel and unscruplous; but scarcely more so than Irish cattle-maimers or those who burn negroes alive in the southern United States. If the worst aspects of their character were sometimes intensified, it must be remembered that during the eleven hundred years of its existence, the Eastern Empire was scarcely ever free from the danger of invasions which, should they have succeeded, must have destroyed it utterly; that over long periods the capital itself was beset by terrific forces; that its first capture was the outcome of Western devilment such as had no parallel in the whole of Greek history; and that during its last two and a half centuries, throughout the lives of eight generations from father to son, the Greek Empire was fighting not for its boundaries, but for the being of its civilisation against

238

the threat of barbarism. For eight generations, from the cradle up, every Greek child knew that the extinction of all that made life liveable, of freedom, faith, art and learning, was drawing nearer. "'Aνάγκη ἦν— it had to be." But he learnt also to combat it by every means that ingenuity could devise. And if, in this necessity and under this unceasing strain of nerves from birth to death, his principles were not those of an Anglo-Saxon gentleman, who shall blame him? As for his morals, it is hard to think that they could have been worse than those of our whitest men. For he had a Christian ideal; and we are only snobs.

As the days move along, in palace, town and country, sped by the amenities that only civilisation can offer, their survey is incomplete without thought as to the actual appearance of these people. The hero Digenis Akritas was fair, with skin of snow; it was these attributes, in a world of dark people, that added to his romance. For miniatures and frescoes depict the Byzantine Emperors as swarthy men, adorned, after youth, with tapering beards and long black hair. Some exhale the effrontery of the camp, some the mysticism of ascetics; others, in their whiteness, a venerable sanctity. Of the great Emperor, Basil II Bulgaroctonos, there survives a warrior portrait, showing legs planted apart, beneath a kilt, in tall pearl-embroidered boots; a corselet, sword and javelin; together with a squat, square diadem, having pendent strings of jewels at either side. But for the most part, the Emperors and

239

Empresses stand, crowned and rigid, beneath straight metal-woven robes reaching to the floor. " The imperial diadem, or tiara," wrote Anna Comnena, " was like a semi-spherical close-fitting cap, and profusely adorned with pearls and jewels, some inserted and some pendent; on either side at the temples two lappets of pearls and jewels hung down on the cheeks. This diadem is the essentially distinctive feature of the imperial dress. But the coronets of the Sebastocrators and Cæsars are but sparingly decorated with pearls and jewels, and have no globe." Over all the Byzantine portraits that survive, there fleets a strange unlikeness to familiar human form, dissimilarity which is the result of more than mere formalisation, such as that to which the kings of the mediæval West were also subject. The Byzantines, educated in the hollowness of naturalism, saw their fellows not in the classical light, as versions of the ideal body, but as harbourers of a divinity ever straining loose from the restrictions of flesh and blood. Can it be that by the same assimilative psychological process which moulds the body to the shape of fashion, the Byzantine frame assumed an elongated non-earthly appearance? The monks of Byzantine monasteries to-day preserve the same tradition.

One of the first impressions recorded by Benjamin of Tudela, was that, by the standards of the West, all the inhabitants of Constantinople were arrayed as princes. Nowhere in the world, save perhaps in China, has the magnificence of clothes surpassed that which prevailed in Constantinople before the thirteenth century. Of the robes embroidered and woven with metal thread, and the patterned silks valued beyond price, sometimes even signed and dated; of the scarlet of the Emperor and the lilac of his brothers and the Patriarch; of the blue of the other princes; each assumed by the Emperor as fancy or ritual prescribed; of the woven insignias of rank and office: the sovereign eagles and crosses; the roses of the patriciate; the ivy-leaves of magistrates; of the embroidery with jewels, which caused the Emperor Isaac Angelus to be described as " decked like a shrine," and in which the Latin Emperor Baldwin sought to validate his claim to the East Roman throne; ivories, enamels and miniatures convey but a faint version of the gorgeous reality. Each pattern was a symbol, corresponding to the epaulette or chevron of to-day. And the problem of their meaning raises also that of Byzantine heraldry of the symbols of the state itself. The *labarum* of Constantine, the Chi Rho surmounting portraits of the reigning sovereigns, continued to lead the Byzantine armies through their most glorious campaigns. And the eagle inherited from Rome descended not only to the last Christian Emperors of Constantinople and Trebizond, but, as a mark of his temporal power, to the Œcumenical Patriarch, by whom it was not relinquished until 1923. Under the Palæologi, however, though the Emperor Andronicus II of that family appears to have adopted as his badge the " lion rampant, crowned and holding an upright sword," till recently to be seen on a wall of the harbour of Koum Kapoussi,

241

the device of the throne was the cross and four B's reproduced on the title page of this book, of which the legend is supposedly:

ΒΑСΙΛΕΥϹ ΒΑСΙΛΕΩΝ ΒΑСΙΛΕΥΩΝ ΒΑСΙΛΕΥΟΥϹΙ.

Examples of this may be seen in the woodcut borrowed from the Nuremberg Chronicle opposite page 78; on the imperial galley in Filarete's bas reliefs to the doors of St Peter's, where it is accompanied by other armorials; on an inverted shield in the courtyard of the church of the Panaghia of Souda in Constantinople; and as a pennant on a piece of pottery unearthed by the expedition of the British Academy in 1927. And it is presumed to have been in imitation of this, that the Serbs and Montenegrins adopted their cross and four C's to stand for: *Samo Sloga Srbina Spasova.* Pero Tafur asserts that the royal arms before the fall of Constantinople to the crusaders were " checky," since he himself, being descended from a Greek royal prince who had taken refuge in Toledo, still bore them; and that these could " still be seen on the towers and buildings of the city, and when people put up their own buildings they still place the old arms upon them." To his enquiries on the subject, the Emperor John VIII replied that the sovereign (Michael Palaeologus) who had delivered Constantinople from the Latins " could never be prevailed upon to relinquish the arms which he formerly bore, which were and are two links joined; but that the matter was still being debated between himself and the people." Can " two links joined " signify a Byzantine B?

With Western chivalry came new fashions, causing the Nicæan Emperor John III Vatatzes to express his disapproval of Latin garments on patriotic grounds. But even in poverty, Byzantine dress retained its distinctive splendour to the end, arousing the admiration of the Parisians upon the visit of the Emperor Manuel II Palæologus, and rendering the Palæologus hat, with its high ribbed crown and peaks before and behind, an artistic convention throughout Europe for the depiction of unfamiliar potentates. A curious mystery surrounded the last Emperors of the East in the eyes of the awakening West. The sovereignty of Trebizond became a cliché among dramatists to denote dominion over the other ends of the earth. And a detail of its owners' dress has also descended, to invest them with a reality which their contemporaries almost denied. Clavijo, sailing the Black Sea on his way to Samarcand, describes the Emperor and his son as wearing " hats of a very high shape, which had cordings of gold running up the sides with a great plume on the top made of crane feathers; further these hats were trimmed with marten fur." But the climax of astonishment was reached on the occasion of the Council of Florence, when, for two years, the north of Italy was traversed by the retinues of Eastern Christendom. Of the impressions of contemporary artists, the most famous is that of Benozzo Gozzoli in the Riccardi Palace at Florence. But this was not painted till

twenty years later, and the headdress of the Emperor
John VIII bears no likeness to anything that was ever
seen in Constantinople. It is in the frescoes of Piero
della Francesca at Arezzo, and on the bronze doors
of St Peter's at Rome by Filarete, that the astounding
costumes of the later Byzantine court are truly represented, in works almost contemporary with their
advent. At Arezzo, the army of Heraclius, fighting
to regain the Cross from Ctesiphon, is clothed in the
uniforms of eight centuries later, which are strangely
reminiscent of those which the Turks eventually
adopted from the Greeks and which are now preserved
in St Irene at Constantinople. On the doors of St
Peter's a series of scenes depicts sucessively, the
departure of the Emperor John VIII Palæologus from
Constantinople in a galley armed with many rowers
and flying the imperial eagle; his reception by the
Pope, before whom he kneels, while an attendant
carries the familiar hat; a sitting of the actual Council,
where he is absorbed in thought; and his departure
and re-embarcation for the East again. During these
proceedings, Pisanello, it is thought, must have achieved
actual communication with the Emperor. A more
convincing proof of this than the medal reproduced
opposite page 184, is a drawing by that artist in the
Louvre, which depicts with an exquisite suggestion of
modelling, the same man in the same hat as shown on
the medal. Posterity could have desired no more
vivid memorial to the type of Byzantine aristocracy.
Beneath the long, delicately built nose, appear the full

PLATE XII

THE LATER BYZANTINE COURT

The Emperor John VIII Palaeologus departs from Florence and embarks for Constantinople; by Filarete, from life

lips of an ancient Greek statue, yet expressing, in place of the implied vacuity, great sensitiveness combined with an almost mystical impassivity. It is a type that strikes the extreme of contrast with the facial coarseness of the contemporary Italian nobility who were Pisanello's chief patrons.

In the case of women, the arts of the Byzantine toilet were not far removed from those of the twentieth century. The Empress Theodora, whose past is still the subject of eternal witticism, slept late and bathed for her complexion's sake. While the blonde Empress Zoë, who could attract a third husband to share her throne at the age of sixty-two, discarded the imperial robes for lighter draperies and passed innumerable hours in a bedroom fitted like a laboratory with cosmetics and scents. Such practices were viewed in the West with horror. The Byzantine ritual which Theophano, daughter of the Emperor Nicephorus II Phocas and wife of Otto II, introduced into the Holy Roman court, alienated both Germans and Romans from her son, Otto III. And Venice, mirror, if any, of Byzantine custom, was scandalised by the diabolical innovations of the Greek Dogaressa Selvo. She wore gloves. She ate meat, carved by eunuchs, with a golden fork. Her complexion was artificial; her body wasted with perfumes and toilet waters. At length, as a just retribution, she died abandoned by all.

The traveller Bertrandon de la Broquière, courtier of the Burgundian Duke Philip the Good, has left a portrait of the last of the Greek Empresses to reign in

Constantinople, Maria Comnena, sister of the Emperor
Alexius IV of Trebizond and wife of the Emperor
John VIII Palæologus. He had seen her during a
service in St Sophia; and determining to repeat the
experience, waited all day without food or drink for
her reappearance. A fine hack, richly saddled, was led
to a bench, whence the Empress mounted behind the
screen of an outstretched cloak, and seated herself
astride. Attending her were a body of eunuchs, a few
elderly courtiers, and two ladies-in-waiting, likewise
riding. She wore a long cloak, and a pointed Greek
hat, presumably of the familiar Palæologus type, down
the peak of which were fastened three golden plumes.
Her face was painted, " of which she had no need, for
she was young and fair." From her ears hung gold
clasps, large and flat, set with jewels.

The life of individuals was both reflected in, and
the reflection of, the capital in which they moved, or to
which, as citizens of the Empire, they looked. By
position the most delectable of cities; planted with
trees and gardens; Constantinople, in the days of her
prosperity, when the population ranged from 700,000
to 1,000,000 as it does now, was at pains to deserve
the title of " queen of cities," which her inhabitants
habitually bestowed on her. Unlike anywhere else in
the world, an organised hospitality was accorded to
visitors: free access was allowed to foreign ships on
principles which formed the basis of the now universal
navigation laws; in Justinian's time, enormous hostel-

ries were built for the shelter of travellers to the
capital engaged in commerce or litigation; definite
colonies of foreign traders were accorded capitula-
tion status; and it may be mentioned in passing
that the mosque which the Latin soldiers so in-
dignantly burnt, had been built at state expense for
the benefit of Mohammedan residents. Throughout the
Middle Ages, Constantinople was almost the only town
in Europe that was lit at night. A regular system of
sanitation augmented the extraordinary natural healthi-
ness of the place. And to preserve the purity of the air,
rules concerning the height and proximity of buildings
were enforced under the iconoclasts, with a strictness
which extended even to the Emperor's brother-in-law.

The outstanding triumph, however, of Byzantine
municipal organisation, was the abundance of its water-
supply. Water was brought to Constantinople by
aqueducts and stored in immense underground reser-
voirs situated mainly in the centre of the city round
about or actually beneath, St Sophia. Fifty-eight of
them are still known to exist, of which only four or five
are at present accessible; and even those have never
been archæologically explored. That which Philoxenus built for the Emperor Constantine the Great, is
supported on 224 columns, each twin-jointed and
fifty-four feet in height. The present Yeri-Batan Serai,
begun for Constantine and finished under Justinian,
has an area of nearly one and a half acres. While
those under St Sophia, constructed, after the unwanted
columns of old Byzantium had all been exhausted in

the building of the others, on square pillars of brick, were reported by Dr Covel towards the end of the seventeenth century, to contain water to the depth of seventeen feet, leaving six and a half feet to spare between the roof and the surface. Similar arrangements for storing water are found as far as the East Roman boundaries stretched, and may still be seen, though on a smaller scale, in such fortified towns as Mistra and Monemvasia. In the case of the former, which is planned in terraces, almost every house rests on a vaulted cistern.

The Turkish bath is in reality a direct offspring of the Roman through the Byzantine; and regular bathing, considered in the West, until fifty years ago, effeminate and ridiculous, was recognised in Constantinople as one of the essentials of comfortable living. Within a hundred years of the city's foundation, eight public and 153 private baths had been installed. In the original treaty with the early Russian traders, it was stipulated that they should have free baths while in residence. And there is still extant the charter signed by the Empress Irene Dukaina to found the convent of Our Lady of Mercy, in which it was laid down that each inmate should take one bath a month, and more if the doctor should so order. In the Emperor John II Comnenus' hospital of the Pantocrator, every patient was to have a bath twice a week and at Easter be given an extra allowance to buy soap. And Robert de Clary speaks of the "*paieles d'argent que les dames de le chite portoient as bains.*" Similar provision was made for the army. The baggage of the Emperor in the field contained a kind of leather suit for vapour baths. And an Arab chronicler of the ninth century records that at the warm springs of Dorylaion in Asia Minor, the authorities had constructed indoor baths for the simultaneous laving of 7000 men.

The pivot of popular recreation in Constantinople was the Hippodrome. Sharing the central tableland of the city with St Sophia, and topping the declivity of the Great Palace, it completed the triple symbolism of Emperor, Patriarch and People at the core of the Empire. Here was celebrated every manner of public function, from the triumph of a victorious general to the torture and execution of a criminal. Here mobs gathered; revolts were hatched and loosed. Here all the passion of popular leisure was focused on the chariot-races and public games. For us to-day, witness of the round world girdled in the white rails of race-courses, and such words as " Derby " and " football " proclaiming the first stage of Esperanto, it is not hard to visualise the frenzy that possessed the Byzantine crowd as it swayed in its seats with the teams. The town was divided into two factions, of which member-ship was of three classes: those who paid annual sub-scription to the actual club; the drivers and racing personnel; and the unregistered masses. Each faction had its president, treasury, stables, stud-farm, chariots and attendant army of employees and mummers. And representatives of each occupied a definite place in court ritual.

249

The performances were occasions of tense enthusiasm; every chance was studied, every point of driver and team. The day was opened with the arrival of the Emperor, to the music of organs and the hymn-singing of choirs. Betting began in the imperial box. For the ordinary spectator it was perhaps sufficient thrill to belong to one faction and to watch, on the opposite seats, those of the other with whom, at the close of the programme, he would be engaged in perhaps a literal battle to the death. As Rambaud says, there was little reason to regret the savage shows of Antiquity, which Christianity had abolished. ". . . What gladiatorial combat in the very heyday of Rome could have equalled that magnificent sedition of Justinian's reign, when 40,000 bodies strewed the tiers and the arena of the circus?" This was the Nika, when half the city was burnt as well. Such a crisis, it is true, has not been engendered in an Anglo-Saxon stadium. But in a time of civil discontent, what more probable than that the long-heralded revolution shall march on monarchy and constitution from between the goal-posts of a football field?

With course of time, the scenes of violence lessened. But devotion to the horse as an instrument of sport continued to infect all classes. The aristocracy borrowed from Persia a form of polo, which they played within the precincts of the palace on a ground known as the Tzycanistirion. In the ninth and tenth centuries, the cult of the stable reached its apogee. The Emperor Michael III the Drunkard, took the reins in the

PLATE XIII

BYZANTINE HUMOUR

The Patriarch Theophylact, summoned, in a previous miniature, from celebrating the divine mysteries, is received by the proud mother.

Hippodrome himself; and on one occasion, to the
scandal of sober people, refused to interrupt a race to
receive news of a defeat on the Euphrates. His
successor and murderer, Basil I the Macedonian,
hailed from his ſtable, and owed his firſt chance in life
to his skill as a horse-breaker. He met his death on
horseback from the attack of a hunted ſtag. The
classic figure of equinity for all time was the Patriarch
Theophylaƈt, who, in place of the humble ass, maintained a stable of 2000 horses, fed on fruit, washed in
wine and perfumed. The younger son of the Emperor
Romanus I Lecapenus, he became head of the Church
at the age of sixteen, and remained in that position for
twenty-three years: the neareſt approach to a Borgia
that Orthodoxy ever achieved. Under his ghoſtly
sovereignty, the anti-Puritan reaƈtion of the tenth
century reached its zenith; he introduced symbolic
dances into the services of St Sophia, so that, according
to the censorious Liutprand, they came to resemble an
operatic speƈtacle; and the ſtory is recorded of how
the Patriarch, informed at the altar of the accouchement
of a favourite mare, hurried to her side and was yet
able to return to the church in time to take part in the
final procession. He, too, loved hunting. But his
joyous career was cut short by an unmanageable horse
againſt a wall in 956. The Hippodrome remained in
full use until the fourth crusade. In 1111 Sigismund,
King of Norway, witnessed the games, which were
accompanied by fireworks, organ-playing and flying
men. Fifty years later, Benjamin of Tudela saw a

display of juggling and wild animals. After the first incursions of the crusaders, jousting and tournaments were introduced. And according to Clavijo, the place was by no means derelict at the beginning of the fifteenth century. The Sultans themselves used it for occasions of public ceremony: there exist in the library of the Serai miniatures of the Turkish court assembled in proximity to the three-headed serpent of Delphi. Ultimately, such portions of it as were still standing were employed in the construction of the gigantic Sultan Ahmet mosque in 1610, where the original pillars of the sphendone, that appear in all the sixteenth century maps and drawings, may still be seen in the courtyard.

In a society such as the Byzantine, much thought was taken for the sick and destitute. The foundation of hospices and shelters by the pious rich was as common as of institutions wholly religious. By such means also the Emperors might win, not only eternal life, but the more immediately important affection of the people in addition. And no comparison reveals the West of Europe, right up to the nineteenth century, in so unprogressive a light, as that of its charitable organisations with those of the Greek East [1] before the Turkish Conquest.

The whole conception of charity unsupported by the state was a Christian one. After the Edict of Milan, the original clandestine hospital of the early faith spread

[1] Their tenor and methods, though but indirectly connected with charity, survive on Mount Athos.

PLATE XIV

THE HIPPODROME ABOUT 1450

rapidly over the Levant. The greatest of them, and prototype of many to come, was founded at Cæsarea in 372 by Bishop Basil, and was as big as a town. There was a resident staff of doctors and priests; orphans were trained and apprenticed; and even lepers were admitted. Another form of public benefit undertaken by private individuals was the institution of rest-houses for travellers, where they might be ensured food and warmth. In Constantinople, works for the unfortunate could depend for support on the generosity both of the state and of individuals. This reached its height in the twelfth century under the Comneni.

The Emperor Alexius I, second of that family to occupy the throne, built a hospital on the Golden Horn dedicated to St Paul, which is described by his daughter Anna, as a vast medley of institutions containing every kind of inmate, orphans, blind, and wounded in war, to the number of several thousand. This example was followed by his son, John II, whose monastic hospital of the Pantocrator was as complex an organisation as the advance of science could demand. The smallest regulations for its management were laid down. Separate wards, each furnished with two lavatories, were set apart for the different sexes and diseases, the latter dictating the nature of the heating, which was lit every evening. Lady doctors attended the female wards. And special inspectors of the food, which was mainly vegetarian, went the rounds every morning to receive the complaints of the patients. To each bed were attached floor-mat, pillow, mattress, and quilt, the latter being doubled in winter; also a comb and a *vase de nuit;* while for the preservation of general cleanliness, brooms and sawdust were prescribed. Arrangements for washing were elaborate. Each patient had the use of sponge, basin and slop-pail; and in each ward was a copper basin at which the doctor might cleanse his hands before proceeding to the next. For the bi-weekly baths with their paschal soap (see page 248), two each of face-towels, hand-towels and bath-towels were provided. Attached to the hospital were dispensary, kitchens, bakery and wash-house. A special herbalist was installed, together with a professor of medicine for the instruction of new doctors. There was also a machine for the cleaning and sharpening of surgical instruments.

Certain additional details of administration emerge from the rules of the hospital adjoining the convent of the Redemption of the World, founded by the Sebastocrator Isaac, a younger son of the Emperor Alexius I Comnenus. Each pillow was stuffed with wool; and each patient had his own plate, porringer and cup. No bed was allowed to lie empty. Funerals were decently conducted. There were baths outside for all, which on Wednesdays and Fridays were reserved for women. These proved of much benefit to the neighbouring residents; though in their case an entrance fee was charged.

As the thirteenth century opened on Constantinople, the political barometer, if temporarily depressed, gave no more alarming hint of impending cyclone than had often been seen before. Though the Angeli Emperors held power which it passed their wit to use; though trade was slipping to the Italians and the revenue proportionately diminishing; though crusaders were established in the ancient territories of the Empire, and the poise of Europe was deranged by the mutual detestation of Latin and Greek; nevertheless, for Greek men and women, the halcyon life continued, guarding still unsevered the traditions of classical humanism and the Oriental quest of God. Gold might be less; but the endowment of the city with public works, churches and treasures, had reached the zenith of magnificence. Born to splendour, environed in beauty, the inhabitants pursued their lives, confident in state and God. Upon this society, upon the cumulative security of 874 years, there fell, in the April of 1204, destruction. The army of the fourth crusade, diverted from its proper objective by the cupidity of the Venetians, assaulted Constantinople and took her. The unthinkable had happened. And the Byzantine state, already in decline, was precipitated into chaos. When its equilibrium was recovered, the ballast of political stability was lost.

Much has been written of the fourth crusade. And even those authors whose understanding of the Byzantines is least, and contempt for them consequently greatest, have found small means of extenuating the conduct of the Franks. Robert de Clary, their own chronicler, cannot but regard the later disasters as just retribution for the " bad faith they had used towards the poor people of the East, and the horrible crimes they had committed in the city after they had taken her." The first negotiations, the sack of Zara, and the disregard of the papal interdict; the arrival at Constantinople, the incendiarism which gutted half the city, and the final capture; the barbarisms of the sack: the destitution of noble and wealthy Greeks fleeing over the countryside, accompanied by the Patriarch "without scrip or staff"; the rape of women, of matrons, virgins, nuns, whom even the Saracens were wont to spare; the organised plunder, of which the French share, smaller than that of the Venetians, amounted, according to Gibbon, to "seven times the annual revenue of the kingdom of England"; the calculated sacrilege: the loading of church plate on mules brought to the very altars; the violation of the imperial tombs; the caparisoning of horses in sacred vestments; the enthronement of a prostitute in the patriarchal chair of St Sophia; from first to last the transactions were such as to leave the Byzantines incredulous at the wickedness of them, and inexorable in their unforgiveness; and to reveal to a judicial posterity, how frail the hold of Christianity on the grim mediæval populations of the West. Plunder and women, in the fever of assault, we could all enjoy. In a freebooting age, which of us, had the richest city in the world suddenly appeared as though by magic on the horizon, might not have been tempted to the attack? But the long-engineered plot, the constructed immorality of rulers assembled in a cause from the sacredness of

which they had not the intellectual attainment to absolve
themselves; the bestial sacrilege of the rank and file;
and the systematic pillage, often for its objects' very
holiness, conducted not in the heat of battle, but when
order had been restored; these place the fourth crusade
alone in the annals of historical crime. Writes Nicetas:
" They have spared neither living nor dead; they have
insulted God; they have outraged his servants; they
have exhausted every variety of sin." The repetition
of 1453 refuses parallel altogether. And for the Turk,
an alien religion and the Mongol tradition plead com-
prehensible excuses.

While soldiers were apportioning the piled loot of
gold, warehoused in three churches, others were casting
the most renowned statues of the Ancient World into
portable specie. Few tears have flowed for the icons
and enamels, the jewelled gold and silver of thirty
generations of craftsmen, of which a tittle still adorns
the treasury of St Mark's in Venice. But all the world
has lamented the Helen of Lysippus and the Hercules
whose thumb was big as a man's waist; the wolf of
Romulus and Remus; the sphinxes, crocodile, and
elephant with trunk that moved, from Egypt; the
group of Paris and Venus; the Juno of Samos, whose
head taxed the strength of four horses to draw it to
the pot; the gigantic Scylla, with her thighs vomiting
" the monsters that threw themselves on Ulysses' boat
to make meal of his unfortunate companions "; the
eagle of Apollonius, through whose outstretched feathers
the sun told the hour on a dial; and even the Byzantine

Anemodulion, the brass obelisk adorned with pastoral reliefs and bearing a weathercock in the form of a silver woman.

But even more than precious metals, it was the relics of the holy that attracted the crusaders' cupidity. By the gift of one of these to his church at home in the West might each individual expiate the breaking of his solemn oath not to bear arms against fellow-Christians. For the possession of a sainted bone brought church or monastery, not only sanctity, but prosperity as well. Pilgrims would flock to the fame of it, donations swell, and a fee could be charged for the privilege of its worship. Constantinople, considered impregnable in a world of growing insecurity, had become a repository of relics for the whole Levant. A special legislation, whence arose the Western law of sacrilege, was devoted to their care. But the savage commercialism which, spurred the Latins to their acquisition so far surpassed the much ridiculed devotion of the Greeks as to provoke comment even from a Latin chronicler.

The largest single share of these talismans was apportioned to Venice. But the whole of Europe was scattered with them, and the preponderance of towns revised with their advent. The Cross was rationed by the Latin bishops; the blood and tears which it had occasioned suffered wide distribution. Amalfi received the body of St Andrew; Cluny, Halberstadt, and Amiens, the heads of St Clement, St James the brother of Christ, and St John the Baptist respectively. Soissons secured those of St Stephen and St Thaddeus,

together with the Virgin's girdle, the robe worn by
Jesus at the Last Supper, and the finger which St
Thomas intruded into his wound. Single thorns of
his crown, already recognised as a coveted factor in
Byzantine diplomacy, were now so widely diffused
that their enumeration and subsequent vicissitudes
have occupied a book. Meanwhile, Latin priests,
fired by the exports of the crusaders to their native
countries, were hurrying out to join the search. The
supply of relics only failed to meet the demand, when
the traffic was prohibited by order of the Lateran
Council of 1215. Enough, however, remained of the
Crown of Thorns for it to be sent in pawn to Venice
during the reign of the Latin Emperor Baldwin II.
Thence it was rescued by St Louis of France in 1239,
who not only redeemed its pledge, but paid Baldwin, at
that time in Paris, a sum equivalent to £20,000 for its
possession. For five centuries it remained in the Sainte
Chapelle; but was eventually removed to St Denys,
where it met the Revolution. Even this upheaval
sufficed only to break it in three. The pieces were
ultimately discovered in an empty box in the Cabinet
de Médailles, and are now in Notre Dame.

During the fifty-seven years' existence of the Latin
Empire, the queen of cities was as dead. Two generations of Greeks saw their capital sinking deeper, instead
of recovering from, the poverty and squalor which the
conquest had inaugurated. Of the life which the
Franks introduced in the provinces, glimpses abound
in the incongruously familiar fortresses which crown

the hills of Greece and the Asia Minor littoral. But the Greeks refused to assimilate them; the lords and ladies of the Levant, and their children and grand-children after them, remained always foreigners, holding the tradition of an alien chivalry among the eternal ranges overlooking the sapphire sea. The romance of two Europes, of failing East, and West still unformed, surrounds them. They soften to the new land, to the colour of the country and the joy of Greek life. Simultaneously they form a school of knighthood, so that hundreds flock to climb the cobbled streets of Mistra in the train of a Villehardouin. As good French was spoken at the court of the Dukes of Athens as in Paris. To Pope Honorius III, Greece was " the new France." Yet who, in the light of history, were these Frankish nobles? They took no root; they brought no peace; they built no bulwark against the advancing East. At a time when Europe was beginning most to rely upon it, they had undone the political structure of the Byzantines for ever. They rendered possible, two centuries later and for four centuries to come, the extinction of a complementary civilisation to that of Western Europe, of the influence towards perennial happiness of the Greek lands. In compensation they bequeathed posterity nothing. Let posterity judge them.

Meanwhile at Nicæa, within her red walls, the threads of the old days were gathered to a smaller capital. In place of the Bosporus was a lake, where fish were caught and holidays observed in the shade of rustling trees. Emperors of royal connection, competent as their predecessors had been puny, conducted the administration and the wars of reclamation. And as the Latin State, born in decline, sank below the horizon, proportionately the Star of Nicæa rose. An ally was found in the West in the person of Frederick II of Hohenstaufen. This German Emperor, precursor of the Western Renascence, had aroused the violent hostility of the Roman Church by the enlightened culture of his court in southern Italy. Like the Greeks, he drew upon himself the envy and hatred which crude mediævalism, in the name of religion, ever displayed at the prospect of a superior civilisation. Nowhere could more sympathetic enmity towards the Papacy be found than in Nicæa. Negotiations were set on foot, conducted in Greek by Frederick himself. In 1244, his daughter, Constance, was married at Brussa to the Emperor John III Vatatzes. Though, in the end, it was one of her ladies-in-waiting that so captured the latter's fancy that she was allowed to disport herself in scarlet buskins, the German Empress attained such influence that, on his accession, Michael VIII Palæ-ologus wished to divorce his wife and make her his consort. Then, in 1261, Constantinople was retaken. And the Empress Anna, as she was known, finding no place in the new court, forsook the Greek lands, to die, after many wanderings, in 1313 at Valencia in Spain, where her epitaph may still be read : " *Aqui Yaçe D^a Costāça Augusta Emperatriz de Grecia.*"

The vitality of Hellenism had triumphed. And for

all but two centuries longer the Byzantine mode resumed dominion on the Golden Horn. But with a
difference. Though the machinery of the state was
mended, the former security was gone; with the
encroachments of Turks on the East, Slavs on the
West and Italian traders at the centre, each day added
colour to the threat of extinction. Conditions in the
capital were changed. The population that had fled
never came back. Such as remained grew less. The
monastic absorption continued undiminished. And by
the beginning of the fifteenth century, as large an area
within the walls was occupied by fields and orchards as
by houses. The churches were refurnished; the re-
parations of St Sophia undertaken on a large scale.[1]
But dilapidation prevailed and, with time, increased.
The Great Palace, though still used after the re-entry,
was gradually forsaken for that of Blachern, situate on
the walls at the back of the city, where King Amaury
I of Jerusalem and his suite had marvelled at the baths
and stoves and other luxuries in 1171. The old enter-
tainments were discontinued. For the reception of
foreign princesses, laments a contemporary, " when
there is no money, it is impossible to celebrate the
fêtes or give the banquets which etiquette prescribes."
At court, many of the jewels are glass, much of the
gold, silver gilt; till even they are gone. Peasant

[1] Pero Tafur (see bibliography) says: " Inside, the circuit is for
the most part badly kept, but the church itself is in such fine state
that it seems to-day to have only just been finished." This was
in 1438.

262

rebellions against the land-owners disrupt the remaining provinces. The Byzantines are living the epilogue of the Empire in a stricter fashion, consciously, on a note of sadness. Hellenic patriotism reverts to old forms. The Emperor, hitherto Autocrat of the Romans— Αὐτοκράτωρ τῶν ῾Ρωμαίων, becomes King of the Greeks —Βασιλεὺς τῶν ῾Ελλήνων. The names of classic heroes make more frequent appearance. With the exception of a long civil war, resulting from the loss of power on the part of the central authority, the capital shows little sign of the generally accepted demoralisation. According to Sir Edwin Pears, " neither in la Bro-quière's account nor in that of any contemporary . . . is there anything to show that the diminished population was other than an industrious and sober people."

Impelled by the Empire's desperate helplessness, there set sail, at the opening of the fifteenth century, an embassy which took the last representatives of East European civilisation to see the emerging nationalities of West. The West knew nothing of what lay dying in the East; the Easterners could scarcely guess that the West already bore the seed of world-dominion. But for us, who observe the moment inserted between the previous and the subsequent, there is something elegiac in this final contact.

Throughout the fourteenth century attempts had been made to obtain help from the West against the advancing Turk. In 1396, these had culminated in the crusade of Sigismund King of Hungary and the

Comte de Nevers, which was annihilated at the battle of Nicopolis. Three years later, the Marshal Jean de Boucicault had arrived in Constantinople with reinforcements. And he was about to return during a lull in the hostilities, when the Emperor Manuel II Palæologus, attended by a numerous suite, decided to accompany him, in order to seek in person the assistance from outside which alone could save the Empire.

Scholar, philosopher, letter-writer, and soldier, the Emperor Manuel, adorned with a long and pointed white beard, presented a fine example of a Byzantine. Leaving wife and children at Mistra in the care of his brother, the Despot Theodore, he landed in Italy, whence, after a series of receptions which bear witness to the prestige which the Eastern Emperor still enjoyed, he arrived at the outskirts of Paris. Escorted from the bridge of Charenton by 2000 mounted citizens, he was met in state by King Charles VI and the whole nobility; he was presented with a white horse; and at the age of fifty-two, attired in a long robe of white silk, woven, it may be imagined, with the same golden pattern depicted by Benozzo Gozzoli on the dress of his successor, he vaulted into the saddle without the aid of stirrups. His stay in the French capital was diverted by such incidents as the wedding of the Comte de Clermont and the astonishment caused by the celebration of the Orthodox service. In a letter to a friend, he describes the difficulties of linguistic communication and the beauty of the Flemish tapestries with which his room was hung. After a few months he crossed the channel, in its proverbial state of disturbance, to England, where he was received by Henry IV with the utmost magnificence at Blackheath.[1] The two sovereigns spent Christmas together in the royal palace of Eltham. And Manuel, in a letter, describes the island as " a country which one might call another world." After a month he returned to Paris, where he remained more than a year, until the arrival of the news of the Turkish Sultan Bajazet's defeat by Tamerlane. At that he set out posthaste for Constantinople, fortified by 200 men and the promise of a pension from the King of France.

The impressions of the Emperor and his suite were later recorded by the historian Chalcocondylas, whose notices of the nations among whom they moved seem curiously modern in their application. The Germans, he says, are the most numerous of peoples, patient and brave, whose strength, if united, would be irresistible. Their industry excels in the mechanical arts. The French he describes as ancient and opulent, esteeming themselves the first of Western nations. But this foolish arrogance has lately been humbled by the English. Britain may be considered as one or three islands. In populousness, power and luxury, London stands pre-eminent over all the cities of the West. The long bow and the fixity of land tenure also attract his notice. But, he adds, with no conceivable partiality to belie the truth of his countrymen's experiences, " the most singular circumstance of their manners is their disregard of conjugal honour and female chastity. In

[1] See Thomas Walsingham's *Historia Brevis*.

their mutual visits, as the firſt aċt of hospitality, the gueſt is welcomed in the embraces of their wives and daughters; among friends they are lent and borrowed without shame; nor are the islanders offended at this ſtrange commerce and its inevitable consequences." " Informed," continues Gibbon, " as we are of the cuſtoms of old England and the virtue of our mothers, we may smile at the credulity or resent the injuſtice of the Greek . . . but his credulity and injuſtice may teach us an important lesson: to diſtruſt the accounts of foreign and remote nations and to suspend our belief of every tale that deviates from the laws of nature and the charaċter of man." Thus the pseudo-hiſtorian pens, in measured category, as downright a condemnation of his own work as can ever be devised. And the Greek, as though under premonition of the future defamation of his people and the nationality of its foremoſt detraċtor, unconsciously takes his revenge.

CHAPTER XI

FROM the inauguration of Conſtantinople as the capital
of the Chriſtian world till her fall to the Sultan of the
Ottoman Turks eleven centuries, twenty-three years
and eighteen days later, the Byzantine Empire was un-
ceasingly at odds with nomadic peoples impelled Weſt
by convulsions in their Eaſtern rear. In the beginning,
while the Helleniſtic Eaſt held its own, the Weſt of
Europe was overwhelmed. But the mental charaɗer-
iſtics of its conquerors were of an indefiniteness which
permitted their Europeanisation. Slowly they settled
down to assimilate the remnant of Roman civilisation
and to evolve that of the present world. Meanwhile,
within two centuries of their advent, the more immediate Eaſt was launching into a new ſtride. The
Eaſt—denoting, in common parlance, a temperament
and intelleɗ alien to our own—had already won a
spiritual battle with Chriſtianity over classicism. It
was now to engage on physical ground. From 634 to
1453, Conſtantinople remained successively the barrier,
the ſalient and the isolated outpoſt of the European
front. By the time the laſt Greek arms were fallen, the
laſt manuscript sold, Europe was saved. But by what
small margin, only those who saw the Turks before
Vienna in 1683 could realise.

Mohammed was born at Mecca in Arabia in 570 A.D. The Arabs of the time were without political or spiritual organisation. Christian, Judaic and Zoroastrian converts were to be found among them; but the majority lacked any form of religious expression, either in ritual or speculation. Mohammed, a mystic, subject to seizures and spasmodic asceticism, recognised one God in all religions, and grafted to his teaching such of their principles as filtered over the desert to his unlettered ear. Immorality and idolatry were condemned; forgiveness of injuries preached; and a theory of resurrection, divided between a mediæval Hell and a heaven of complacent women, formulated. Disliked by the Meccans, the Prophet, at the age of fifty-two, took refuge with a neighbouring community of Judaised Arabs at Medina, of whom he assumed political leadership. From their influence arose the mosaic spirit of exact observance, and the identification of civil with religious life, which were destined to pervade Islam. In 625 began a war with Mecca. But in Medina, at last, was the germ of an organisation. Its strength grew. By 629, the Prophet could boast as large an army as 3000 men, which came into first contact with the Byzantine troops of Syria in the north-west. In 630, he captured Mecca. Two years later he died.

The Arabs were now aware of a political focus, whose emergence coincided with their country's economic decline and their own consequent impulse towards expansion. The original impetus of Islam was religious only in so far as its political machinery bore a religious complexion. Byzantine rule in Palestine and Syria was detested for its weight of taxation and religious persecution. The Moslems offered freedom from both. The Arab tribes on the northern border, deprived by Heraclius, owing to the financial burden of the Persian war, of their annual subsidies for good behaviour, enlisted themselves in the new community; and in unison the Arabs marched north, defeated the imperial troops, and, aided by the welcome of the native populations, became masters of Damascus, Baalbek, Emessa, Aleppo, Antioch, and ultimately of the Hellenised stronghold of Jerusalem. Ten years later Ctesiphon was taken and Persia lay at their feet. Only the Caucasus brought them to a standstill. Simultaneously they spread south. Forcing the Greeks to evacuate Alexandria, they seized Cyprus and built a navy, defeated the Emperor Constans II on the sea, and besieged Constantinople every year from 673 to 678. The attacks culminated in that supreme effort by land and sea of 717, which was repulsed by the Emperor Leo III the Isaurian. For the time, Islam had found its limit.

Though troubled by civil war, the Moslem Empire now began to achieve definite political form. The Caliphate, descended office of the Prophet as secular and religious chief, became hereditary. And a system of taxation was applied to Moslem and Christian alike. Expansion continued along the coast of North Africa, which ended in the occupation of most of Spain and that immortal skirmish with Charles Martel in 732, known as the battle of Tours. It was more than a century later that the Saracens gained their footing in Sicily and south Italy, whence they were ultimately ousted by the Macedonian Emperors of Conflantinople and the Normans.

Change meanwhile had arisen at the centre. In 750, the Persian Abbasids, champions of a purer and wholly theocratic Islam, wrefted the Caliphate from its Umayyad holders and moved the capital of an Empire which now extended from the Indus to the Atlantic, from Damascus to Bagdad. The next eighty-three years were an era of far-famed prosperity. The Persian conception of absolute sovereignty reacted on the Caliphate as it had formerly on the Roman Empire. And it was now that the splendours of the Eaft, emanating in a stream of cultural and commercial intercourse from the Bagdad of Harun al Raschid, left their deepeft imprint on Conflantinople. But all was not peace. And the tide was not turned in favour of the Greeks until the campaigns of the Emperor Nicephorus II Phocas at the end of the tenth century. Even then, a new force was ftill to come out of the Eaft.

Islam seemed on the point of disintegration. Its Caliphs had became pawns in the play of Persian Emirs; it was rent by heresy; everywhere, independent ftates were growing. But in the third decade of the eleventh century, ravaging Armenia and Georgia with such ferocity that the kings of those countries were obliged for safety's sake to submit to Byzantine vassalage, came a new race of terrifying firft impression. "They worship the wind

and live in the wilderness. . . . They have no noses.
And in lieu thereof they have two small holes, through
which they breathe." Set a Jew[1] to describe a Mongol.
For these were the Seljuk Turks from beyond the
Oxus, who in 1055 delivered the Caliph at Bagdad
from his puppetship and made him proclaim their
leader Sultan. Sixteen years later they inflicted on the
Byzantines the disastrous defeat of Manzikert, and
overran Asia Minor to the very shores of the Marmora,
leaving desolation in their wake and a scattered population of permanent settlers. But their first great
Empire, in which the ferrymen of the Oxus were paid in
" drafts on Antioch," lasted scarcely a hundred years.
By the middle of the twelfth century, the western
themes were reconquered by the Comneni Emperors,
and the Turks themselves had split into innumerable
dynastically ruled communities, who looked to Bagdad
as their theoretical centre, the home of science, art and
literature. Even this slight equilibrium was shattered.
In 1258, the Mongol Hulagu, bred in the tradition of
Jenghis Khan, whose armies are believed to have caused
the death of eighteen millions of people in China alone,
overthrew Bagdad, murdering the Caliph and 800,000
inhabitants. The pivot of the Moslem world shifted
to Cairo. Here the Caliphate survived till 1517, when
it was transferred from the Abbasids to the dynasty of
Othman reigning in Constantinople.

This first Mongol terror, though it submerged
Russia and penetrated even Hungary and Poland, was

[1] Benjamin of Tudela.

271

ephemeral as that of Tamerlane. Two years after the capture of Bagdad, the hitherto invincible hordes were defeated in open battle by the Mameluke Sultan of Egypt. Their history henceforth lies in the north of the Eurasian continent. In the Levant, for the fourteenth and fifteenth centuries, the balance between East and West hung as before: between Greek and Turk. It was the advent of the Turk that had saved the immediate East not only from Byzantine encroachment, but from that of the Frankish crusaders in addition. But the Franks had stabbed their fellow-Europeans in the back. And had the Mongol advance reached Nicæa, the rallying-point of the Greeks, while the Latins were in occupation of Constantinople, the East must have conquered then and there. As it happened, the Mongol incursion so weakened the divided Moslem Sultanates as to avert the decision of the struggle for two centuries more.

When, in addition to this eternal pressure from the East, it be recalled that the Slav peoples of Russia and the Balkans to the north-west constituted a menace scarcely less persistent, it is not surprising to discover that, in the perpetually defensive Byzantine state, war was regarded not as the fortuitous means of advancing the personal prestige of princes and feudatories, but as a conscious art, regulated by text-books and calculated to achieve communal security rather than individual glory. Certainly the spirit of chivalresque adventure was not always absent; such it was that fired the exploits

272

of the border wardens and the dashing campaigns of the Emperors Romanus IV Diogenes and Manuel I Comnenus. But back of the iconoclasts, of the great generals of the Macedonian era, of the indefeatable Nicæans and of the last of the Palæologi, was the modern concept of the use of the state machine for state purposes. The workings of that primary factor in Byzantine stability, the imperial defence, deserve some analysis.

Until the reign of Justinian, the army was organised on the familiar Roman model; though after the defeat of the Emperor Valens at Adrianople with the loss of 40,000 men, the supremacy of cavalry, which was to remain unchallenged till the invention of gunpowder, was recognised by the incorporation of the mounted archers of Asia Minor in the imperial forces. But at the end of the sixth century came a change. The Byzantine entity was crystallising, its frontiers becoming consolidated. The mercenaries were discarded. Henceforth the armies of the Empire were recruited from within its confines. They fought not for gain, but for Christ, Emperor, and civilisation. For five centuries, until Manzikert, they remained to all intents and purposes invincible. And although, after the ravaging of the Asiatic themes, the hire of foreign troops was again necessary, the principles of the system endured to the end.

The numbers of the standing army, from its re-organisation at the beginning of the eighth century till the invasion of the Seljuk Turks at the end of the eleventh, varied from 120,000 to 150,000. Of these,

24,000 were permanently stationed in the capital and
70,000 in Asia. These figures may be compared with
those of Britain in 1914, when the strength of the
regular army was 162,251, and of the British troops in
India, 77,500. Foreign expeditionary forces numbered
from 5000 to 20,000. As with ourselves, in the heyday of the Empire military service was voluntary. To
the Greek, civilised individualist, universal conscription was detestable. In this lay the crux of the whole
problem. Byzantine history might be written in terms
of the struggle between its avoidance and necessity.

At no time, however, was the burden of defence
wholly centralised. The troops of the different themes,
varying in number from 8000 to 12,000 infantry and
4000 to 6000 cavalry with the size of each, were
charged upon their respective inhabitants. They were
divided into brigades, regiments, companies and
platoons, commanded by officers corresponding to
those of a modern European army. Proficiency with
bow and javelin was encouraged in all ranks of society.
And there existed some sort of organisation corresponding to a provincial militia. But as a general rule
the obligation to bear arms was commuted by pay-
ments in kind and money on a scale that may be judged
by the record of the Peloponnese in 935. That district,
in addition to the £4280 in bullion mentioned on page
141, contributed in lieu of individual service, a thousand horses saddled and bridled, of which, apart from
private persons, the Archbishops of Corinth and Patras
gave four apiece, the other bishops two, and the monas-

teries two or one according to their means. The monetary tax, for the poor, was reduced by half.

The army was recruited mainly from the small yeoman farmers, whose absorption by the larger proprietors was forbidden under the iconoclast and Macedonian Emperors by special legislation. Superficially, its outstanding feature was the fact of its being uniformed, in accordance with the Roman system, which was not reintroduced into Western Europe till the sixteenth century. The armour of a trooper consisted of a mail-shirt stretching to the thighs, steel shoes and gauntlets, and a steel cap supporting a tuft which matched, in the colour of the regiment, a pennant and a linen surcoat. Each was armed with bow and quiver, axe, broadsword and dagger. Such as could were recommended to bring servants and camp-followers with them, to relieve them of chores and ensure the smartness of their turn-out. Importance was attached to morale. "If," says a military treatise of the tenth century, "they are to sally forth, joyous of soul, brave and content of heart, to risk their lives for our holy Emperors and the whole community of Christendom," soldiers must be accorded special privileges above the ordinary citizen, and immunity from taxation. In later years the encroachments of the aristocracy were resisted by the grant of land tenures for life to distinguished soldiers. These, as in the West, frequently became hereditary.

A large tactical literature existed for the regulation of the army's movements. Its aim was defence; its basic principle, to save men and money by the cunning employ of ambushes and night attacks, and the knowledge of different enemies' peculiar weaknesses. It was a maxim, for example, that the Frankish knight was invincible when mounted, but helpless on the ground, owing to the weight of his armour; aim, therefore, should be directed against his horse. Similarly, Orientals, being susceptible to the cold, should be attacked in bad weather. The Franks complained of the Greeks' duplicity. Yet in the military handbooks of the latter, the violation of treaties, the rape of female prisoners and the slaughter of non-combatants was forbidden; and to these rules the Byzantine armies, with few exceptions, adhered. Those of the Franks did not.

The frontiers of the Empire were guarded by a series of forts, which were strung by Justinian " from Tunis to the Euphrates, and Armenia to the Danube." These, in case of attack, were connected, through concentration camps, with the headquarters of the theme and ultimately the capital, by a regular system of communication, of which the fire-telegraph was an example. The auxiliary forces of the army in the field were organised with an elaboration unknown till comparatively modern times. The mounted members of the ambulance corps could earn a fixed reward for each seriously wounded man brought off the scene of battle to the military doctors at the base. The commissariat marched with the infantry, bringing biscuit, cooking-pots, spades and pickaxes in carts. Camps were always pitched behind trenches, the carts being disposed so as to form a kind of "laager" in the middle. There was also a special section of engineers. "For the passage of broad rivers, where a Western army would have been forced to march until a ford was reached, the Byzantines constructed sectional boats, of which the numbered parts could be borne on the backs of transport animals, and then put rapidly together and caulked when the stream was reached." [1]

This efficiency reached its climax on occasions when the Emperor himself took the field. His dining-tent and his sleeping-tent, two of each, to precede him on alternate days, and furnished like the palace to which he was accustomed; his stoves, water-heaters, chandeliers and candles; his medicines, massage-unguents, perfumes and sweet-burning pastilles; his table linen, uniforms, underwear, arms and insignia; his silver clock and writing parchment; his chapel and icons; his travelling library on war, weather, portents and religion; his oils, wines, vegetables, cheese, salt, fish, and caviare, with their animate complement of sheep, cows, goats, geese and chickens, assisted from the rivers by a band of skilled fishermen; all the necessities of imperial travel, down to the very water beakers for the chickens when on horseback, are enumerated in the *De Ceremoniis* of Constantine VII Porphyrogenitus. For the transport of the whole, 685 horses and mules were requisitioned, partly from the imperial farms, partly from the clergy, the monasteries and the functionaries

---

[1] Baynes, *Byzantine Empire*, page 142.

of the court. An extraordinary care was lavished on these favoured beasts, who could only enter the imperial service between the ages of five and seven. Each one, branded with the royal mark, was caparisoned in scarlet and furnished with a separate groom, who must produce a marked check to procure its evening ration. Medicines of wines and vinegar, resin for saddle sores, feeding-bags, buckets and shovels, were among the regulation equipment. And a special inspector was appointed to see that each was properly rugged at night and was not overloaded in the morning. Animals too old or ill for further service were put out to grass in the royal paddocks till their death, " according to very ancient usage."

It is not to be thought that these imperial peregrinations were conducted with those galaxies of mistresses and unblushing preference of diversion to business, which characterised the campaigns of Louis XIV. Once in enemy country, the routine changed; the officials of the palace gave the custody of the Emperor's person into the hands of picked guards; and the greater part of the baggage was discarded. Nothing can better illustrate the astonishing mobility of the Byzantine forces and the efficacy of their care of animals, than the famous march of the Emperor Basil II Bulgaroctonos from Bulgaria to Aleppo in the midwinter of 994-995. With 40,000 men, of whom 17,000 were actually with him on arrival, he traversed the diagonal length of Asia Minor in a fortnight. The whole force was mounted on mules picked for their swiftness, each man having a second beast in reserve.

The prowess of Byzantine arms was not confined to the land. And the initial barrier with which they confronted Islam after the beginning of the eighth century was largely a naval one. In this sphere, the evidence of contemporary and subsequent chroniclers shows that the recent invention of " Greek fire " had revolutionised warfare scarcely less than did gunpowder 700 years later. This weapon, whose secret even the Church conspired to defend by the formulation of anathemas against its potential betrayer, consisted of an inflammable liquid projected through a series of directable tubes, and lit either by the agency of some slowly burning substance at their mouth, or by direct contact with the air. In the fleet which the Emperor Nicephorus II Phocas led against the Saracen pirates of Crete in 960, 2000 battle-ships were armed fore and aft with these siphons, as the tubes were called, protruding from the mouths of metal beasts. In vain might the enemy ships erect screens of metal and keep their decks piled with sand in readiness to quench the flames. Not less devastating than the actual damage, was the moral effect, to which Mussulman and Latin alike have testified. The reputation of Greek fire was prodigious; it was said to burn in the water and to consume whole battallons of men; the Russian besiegers of Constantinople in 941 jumped into the sea to sink in full armour rather than face it; by its agency were counteracted the mines of Bohemond of Antioch at the siege of Durazzo in the reign of Alexius I Comnenus; on occasions its employment was accompanied by detonations; and the fumes could be such that day became night. Another method was to launch it upon the enemy decks, or the defenders of a beleaguered town, in huge metal cauldrons, which exploded, as they travelled, into clouds of liquid flame. It was also used, on a smaller scale, in "hand-siphons" and glass or metal grenades.[1]

The ultimate decline of Byzantine defence was due to no marked decadence in the national character, but to the loss of both the military and maritime themes of Asia Minor, whence the personnel of the army and navy had been mainly recruited. Mercenaries and hired ships reappeared. And as the resources of the treasury dwindled throughout the fourteenth and fifteenth centuries so as to preclude the invocation even of these, the alternative conscription produced an inevitable lack of discipline. None the less, the nucleus of the army, shrunk to piteous dimensions, remained to fight to extinction within the walls of Constantinople. There we may smile to the last upon Gibbon's grotesque dictum, that "the vices of the Byzantine armies were inherent, their victories accidental." And thither the scene shifts.

---

[1] An Arab MSS. in the Bibliothèque Nationale shows a battleship armed with pots of Greek fire. And a book in the Bibliothèque d'Arsenal, written for King Louis XI, contains an illustration of a siege of Constantinople, in which one of the defenders is holding a funnel-mouthed pipe about five feet long, whence flames are protruding.

During the early stages of a struggle in which 1453 was one climax and 1922 another, religious fanaticism, on the Asiatic side at least, was unknown. After the eleventh century, when the Seljuk settlements in Asia Minor were an accomplished fact despite their temporary reincorporation in the Greek Empire by the Comneni Emperors, friendly intercourse with Mohammedan neighbours became a voluntary principle of Byzantine policy. The Greek populace even attempted to defend the mosque of the Saracen merchants in Constantinople from the ferocious bigotry of the Latin knights. Furthermore, the dominance of Islam in western Asia was yet by no means wholly assured. The Tartars, who were at the root of all the Westward migrations, had no religion; but Jenghis Khan was married to a practising Christian; and many were the tales of Prester John, the great Christian ruler of the Mongolian plateaux, whose legend, though never historically identified, illustrates the scope and influence of Nestorian Christianity. Even among the original Turkish invaders, the channel of faith was still in balance between the Son of God and his Prophet. A few years after the recapture of Constantinople by the Greeks, a neighbouring Sultan, in response to a popular outcry against the Patriarch for having permitted Holy Communion to his children, and to himself the use of a Christian bath, officially offered to eat the flesh of the pig in order to demonstrate his non-adherence to Islam. The religious *élan* of Mohammedanism developed only after the political decline of the Christian state with which it was primarily in conflict. Uncommercial; agricultural only from hand-to-mouth necessity; instinct with no desire for settled institutions or the acquisition of property; heedlessly destructive, yet fundamentally hospitable and honest; the Turkomans who first came knocking on the diminishing boundaries of the Empire, differed in no essentials from the dying race we see to-day, laced bodily and mentally into the frock-coat and bowler hat of the inevitable West. Only intermediately were they missionaries. And with this vocation they were not imbued till the accession of the Sultan Murad I in 1359.

Among the chieftains who took part with Jenghis Khan and his successors in the Mongol incursions to the West, were some who made their permanent home with the colonies of Seljuk Turks already in existence. Of these was Ertogrul, father of Othman, who succeeded him in 1277, and from whom sprung the Ottoman dynasty and the Ottoman Empire, the longest-lived Mohammedan power that the world has known. The reason for its endurance is plain. The Ottoman Empire was the Byzantine Empire, identical in geography; but with this difference: that with the expansion of the Byzantine marched civilisation, and with the expansion of the Ottoman, its negation; that with the diminution of the Byzantine, civilisation disappeared, and with the diminution of the Ottoman, another, its affinity, advances. The living heart of the Byzantine state was the city of Constantine; and from this source also circulated the cohesive strength of the

Ottoman. Without Constantinople, the vast dominions
of Murad II and Bajazet were fluid and ephemeral as
the Tartar lordships. With her, with the ineffaceable
tradition of Roman stability conferred, the hapless
organism assumed the dignity of Empire. Supported
by a bureaucratic and military organisation directly
borrowed from the Greeks, with whom the Turks had
been in immediate contact for two centuries before the
fall of the capital; with the élite of its army recruited
from the sons of Christians; with its rulers bred and
suckled by their daughters; the Ottoman Empire
stood. But from 1453 on, the Turk, nomad and
countryman, lover of horses and gardens, was fettered
to a town. The revealed precepts of his religion, its
boundless arrogance and condonation of wholesale
sexual licence, to the detriment of male character
and the extinction of female; these, titillated by
the most delectable environment that earth could
furnish, called to the surface that latent inertia which
a life of mobility had formerly counteracted, and which
should henceforth prevent him, for all his political
effect, from contributing one grain to the general convenience of mankind. Like a new tree in a forest,
which shades and stifles all the others with the quick-
ness of its growth, then decays itself from the richness
of the soil, he was made and unmade by Constantinople.
But the world still waits his 1453.

With the advent of Othman, the surviving outposts
of Greek life on the Asia Minor littoral began to dis-
appear. Migration from the central East was increasing.

283

Forcing himself as suzerain upon the scattered Turkish principalities already existing, Othman assumed the title of Sultan. His advance westwards was contested; but in every engagement the Byzantines, who had vainly looked forward to a new era of prosperity following the regaining of their capital, were helplessly outnumbered. In 1306, at the invitation of the Catalan mercenaries who had turned against the Emperor Andronicus II Palæologus and were ravaging Thrace and Greece proper, the subjects of Othman made their first crossing into Europe. Two years later they captured Ephesus, behind Smyrna, whose ruins still bear the impress of arrogant municipality beneath the brambles and bulrushes that obscure them. In 1326, Brussa suffered the same fate, while the young Emperor Andronicus III Palæologus was away in the north Balkan fighting the Tartars. A year later, Othman died. And there at Brussa, on a spur of Bithynian Olympûs overlooking the rich plains of figs and mulberries to the sea, he and many of his line after him lie buried. He was succeeded by his son Orchan.

In the same year, after a heroic defence, Nicæa, city of the creed and former Greek capital, fell also. Yet still there was no persecution of the Christians. Their religion was respected. Taxation for them was less under Turkish than Byzantine rule. A regiment of them fought for the Sultan. And Orchan himself espoused the daughter of the Emperor John VI Cantacuzene, who was allowed the free exercise of her religion. But the pressure from behind was not relaxed, and still the Turks continued to advance. With the capture of Nicomedia and Angora, land-communication between the capital and the further East was severed. At Orchan's death in 1359, the Turkish rule over Asia Minor was complete. Further, the Ottoman Turks were definitely a nation.

A crucial point in their development had now arrived. The successor of Orchan was his son Murad. And it was he who first imbued his people with that fanatic detestation of Christians, which was to render odious the future centuries of Turkish rule in Europe, to contrast them horribly with the enlightened Moslem civilisation that once prevailed in Spain, to vitiate the character of his nation in the process, and to incise with sharp hatred the hitherto romantic border between East and West. The taxation of Christians under Ottoman rule, as opposed to Moslems, was increased; and the corps of Janizaries instituted by the forcible recruitment in early childhood of one in every five Christian male children. The footing of the Turks in Europe was once and for all established, Adrianople and Sofia were captured, Macedonia, Epirus, Thessaly and parts even of the Peloponnese reduced, and the parodies of Empire set up by the Serbs and Bulgars destroyed. The Greeks themselves were weakened by a long civil war, whose disunited factions in face of increasing odds from outside illustrate the breakdown of the central authority since the Latin Conquest, and recall the conditions of the War of Independence four and a half centuries later. The Emperor John V Palæologus, rendered helpless by his son's insubordination, was obliged to proclaim himself the Sultan's vassal. And a final coalition of Serbs, Hungarians, Wallachs, Dalmatians, and Albanians, was utterly routed at the first battle of Kossovo-Pol in 1389. But, in the very moment of victory, Murad was assassinated by a Serb.

Seven years later, Bajazet, Murad's son, met the only real crusade that the West ever undertook to stem the Turks, at Nicopolis on the Danube. The Christian army, of 52,000 men, led by King Sigismund of Hungary, and recruited from every state in Europe in response to papal proclamation, was almost entirely annihilated. Budapest was threatened; and Bajazet expressed the hope that his horses should feed from the altar of St Peter's. Yet still the Greeks, despite the inherent vices of their armies, held out, when all the might of the West was failing. They were assisted by the fleet of the Admiral Jean de Boucicault, despatched by the Venetians and Genoese to aid their merchant communities in Galata across the Golden Horn.

The fall of Constantinople seemed imminent. And in 1399, the Emperor Manuel II Palæologus left for the West on a last errand, as he thought, to fetch help. The progress of his embassy has been described (pages 263 to 266). But in 1402 came a respite. Tamerlane's Tartars attacked the Turkish rear; Bajazet was utterly defeated at Angora; and his empire was thrown into temporary confusion. Order, however, was gradually restored by his son, Mohammed I. This Sultan seems to have felt an almost superstitious respect for the unflinching resistance of the isolated city. A close friendship developed between him and the Emperor Manuel; visits were exchanged; and the latter was left guardian of his younger sons. The eldest, Murad II, was willing, on his accession, to continue these amicable relations. But the Byzantines, in opposition to Manuel's advice, refused. Was it that, with the true resilience of Greeks, they felt a return of strength? Or that, lightheaded with the strain of their position, they wished to force an issue? War followed, and a siege, from which the Greeks emerged victorious. In 1425, Manuel, a great Emperor in adversity, died.

The reign of John VIII, his successor, and last Emperor but one, was devoted wholly to obtaining help from the West by the unification of the Orthodox and Latin Churches. A glimpse of him appears out hunting, just prior to his departure for Florence, when he and the Empress and Pero Tafur with them on horseback " killed many hares and partridges and francolins and pheasants, which are very plentiful here." During his absence, the Turks were so far apprehensive of the outcome of the negotiations, (see p. 185), that they refrained from attacking Constantinople. In 1430, they had captured Salonica; and the monastic republic of Mount Athos, to preserve its independence as the ultimate fortress of a vanishing civilisation, had voluntarily admitted their suzerainty. But in 1442 and 1443, the armies of Murad II were defeated by an alliance of Serbs, Hungarians and Poles. A ten years' truce was proclaimed, which was immediately broken by the

Christians at the instigation of the Roman Church, in
the person of the Cardinal-Legate Julian. At Varna
and the second battle of Kossovo-Pol, all the advantage
gained was lost. And the Emperor John died of the
news. A delegation was despatched to Mistra, where
his brother, the Despot Constantine Dragases, was
holding the Peloponnese. There, in the Metropolitan
Church of St Demetrius, overlooking the Eurotas valley
and the site of ancient Sparta, the last successor of
Constantine the Great received his coronation. In 1448
he reached the capital. And in 1451 Sultan Murad II,
to whose strict observance of treaties even the Greek
historians pay tribute, was succeeded by his son,
Mohammed II at the age of twenty-one.

The fifteenth century had passed its middle year,
Donatello was an old man, Caxton middle-aged,
Columbus and Botticelli were boys. Thirty years more
and the earth should bear the small feet of Erasmus,
Michelangelo and Martin Luther. Joan of Arc was
dead, and the Middle Ages with her. Should their
complement in the East survive? Should those attenu-
ated, steeple-hatted Byzantines, born half spirits,
traitors of the classic speech, enter the new heaven of
reason, representation and revival? In truth the Turks
were but the instrument of righteous evolution. Constantinople, Paris of the East, was become old-fashioned.

Yet still the walls, fourteen miles in circumference,
were standing as they had stood a thousand years,
lapped for ten miles by the three seas, and overland,

THE SULTAN MOHAMMED II
by Gentile Bellini, from life, November 25th, 1480

across the four-mile base of the triangle, rising and
falling with hill and valley in a triple line: the hinder
40 feet in height, 14 feet thick, and swelling into towers
60 feet high at intervals of 60 yards; the next, separated
by a terrace 20 yards across, 25 feet high, with towers
at similar intervals; and then, after another similar
terrace, the moat, 20 yards broad, that once had been
filled with water regulated by sluices. Still they ſtood,
and ſtill to-day they ſtand, exhibiting the breaches of
the laſt siege, with Mohammed's ſtone cannon balls
interrupting the careful lettuce-planting of peasants in
the disused moat. 24,000 troops was the number
calculated necessary to man the fourteen miles in case
of attack. In 1453, it was computed, by requeſt of the
Emperor, that the Greek combatants within the city
did not exceed 5000. And the total of the defenders,
including the Italians, was at no time more than 8000.
Without, lay encamped an army of 150,000 men,
supported by 50,000 camp-followers—almoſt the entire
able-bodied male population of the Turkish nation. In
the Bosporus and the Marmora, rode a fleet of between
three and five hundred, as opposed to " nine galleys
and thirty other ships," ſtationed to defend the chain[1]
which barred the entrance to the Golden Horn. Yet
on the eve of the final assault, despite these over-
wænning advantageo, despite the faƈt that his army was
in the prime of its early ellicacy, Muhammed was on tho
brink of retreat, and was only dissuaded from that
course by the report that his soldiers were one and all

[1] Still preserved in St Irene.

in favour of attack. The fighting quality of the laſt Byzantines asks no further teſtimony.

In time and the course of things, the city muſt have capitulated. But the explanation of the immediate disaſter of 1453 lies in two faƈtors: Mohammed's artillery; and the diminution of the Greek population.

The fall of Conſtantinople, as became the doyen of Chriſtian mediæval civilisation, was the firſt event of cardinal hiſtorical importance to be wrought by the primary weapon of modern warfare, gunpowder. Cannon, it is true, had been used in European battles since Crécy; but rather in the manner of an Eaſtern potentate's elephants, to alarm by unfamiliarity, than for the worth of their damage. The young Sultan now determined to put this worth to the teſt. Upon the arrival in his camp of Urban the Hungarian, who had left Conſtantinople discontented with the terms offered by the impecunious Byzantine Emperor, preparations were set on foot for the conſtruƈtion of such an engine of bombardment as the world had never seen. Inner and outer mould were beaten of the finest clay. And there was caſt in bronze a cannon 26 feet long, 9 feet in circumference, and 4 feet in total diameter, which was capable of launching a stone ball 88 inches round and weighing 1200 pounds. Drawn by 60 oxen, supported by 200 men, and preceded by a band of 200 road-menders, its transport from Adrianople to its emplacement in the Lycus valley, before the walls of Conſtantinople, occupied two months. Accompanying it were some 200 smaller guns ranged in batteries of ten or twenty, among which the two chief seem to have been scarcely inferior to that described above. Juﬅ as the walls of the Greek capital were without equal, so were the inﬅruments of Mohammed's attack on them. Bravely the defenders sought to lessen the impaﬅ of projeﬅiles, which no masonry could withﬅand, by means of skins, earth, and sacks of wool. The whole population of the city was called to repair the breaches with temporary barricades, which the exiguous force within was ﬅill further ﬅrained to man. Taking in consideration the narrow margin of Turkish success, as revealed by the Sultan's final doubts, it can he said that, but for the artillery, the siege of 1453 muﬅ have failed.

A more fundamental weakness of the Greek cause, and one that muﬅ ultimately have proved fatal to it was the decline of population. By the fifteenth century, more than half the area enclosed by the walls of Conﬅantinople was bare of houses. And contemporary travellers bear witness to the utter desolation, accentuated by vaﬅ ruins, which had overtaken the Balkan peninsula and Asia Minor. Yet Greek hiﬅorians record no such wholesale massacres on the part of the Turks as attended the campaigns of the Mongols. The only explanation, though a hypothetical one, for this complete and sudden devaﬅation, is to be found in the plague.

It is only lately that the Engliﬄ chroniclers of the Black Death have been proved correﬅ, by the examination of manorial rolls and parish records, in their much ridiculed assertions that half the population of England was carried off in the years 1348 and 1349. On this occasion alone, Oxford lost two-thirds of her inhabitants. In the Levant, from 1347, when the pestilence made its first appearance in the Greek capital, till 1431, the date of its last, there were nine outbreaks. Apart from a volume of contemporary evidence concerning the disastrous nature of these visitations, Muratori, the Italian scholar (1672-1750), computed that, all told, Constantinople lost eight-ninths of her population. His authority for this statement is unknown. But in reconciling Villehardouin's assertions, that in 1204 the city contained ten times as many people as there were in Paris—in other words, considerably over a million— and that, in the third of the fires which devastated the city after the Franks' arrival, more houses alone were burnt than there were in the three greatest cities in France; in reconciling these with the statements of Critobulus and Leonard, Archbishop of Mytilene, that the Greek captives after the fall in 1453 numbered less than 60,000 men, women and children, Muratori's figure is undeniably corroborated. For slaves were included in the Turkish soldiers' legitimate booty, and the 60,000 must be taken as a more or less accurate total of the able-bodied persons remaining in the city. The Latin Conquest and subsequent depression of trade must be reckoned with as factors in the process of depopulation. But even so, it can, and in fact, must be supposed that the plague, falling nine times on a crowded town considerably nearer the seat of the disease than England, was the chief agent. If its effect, despite their nomadic outdoor life, was the same on the Turks, their ranks would inevitably have been filled by pressure from the East.

Thus, when, within a year of his accession, the Greeks learnt from Mohammed's building of the fort of Rumeli Hissar on the European shore of the Bosporus, that they were destined to a siege distinct in the calculating patience of its mover from the many which had preceded it, the position was as follows:— A population of not more than 80,000 souls, of whom not 6000 were competent to fight, together with a fleet of forty sail, were called upon to repair and defend fourteen miles of walls against a fleet of 400 and an army of 150,000; to fight side by side with 2000 Italians, whom they detested more than the Turks; to witness the gradual disappearance of their soldiers, the consumption of their food, and the desiccation of their fortifications at a pace which they could not retard; and, in the event of inability, despite these odds, to hold the city, to contemplate the total extinction of Greek nationality and civilisation, of which they alone remained trustees. Yet that siege lasted fifty-three days, more than seven weeks. And at the last, not only did the Sultan's courage, but even the assault itself, waver in the balance.

The tale of that April and May has summoned the attention of many writers; to the least understanding of them, it has communicated an emotion which the heroism and suffering of individuals have never kindled. The gauds of drama, dear to the historian, shine with an inner light. The struggle of a handful of people in an isolated town; the suppression of a nationality; the elegy of a paralysed empire; such accidents are found in many chronicles. Here, with conscious delibera- tion, was conducted the funeral office of a millennium, of thirty generations of men bent in one co-ordinate endeavour to harmonise the material ideals of civilisa- tion with the search for Reality. . . . We may watch, as the Greeks watched from their vantage-points within the city, the course of an obsequy, than which no race, institution or faith ever achieved more fitting:—the coming of the Turkish army on the 5th of April, and the pitching of the Sultan's red and gold pavilion; the entrainment of the cannon and the beginning of the bombardment; the safe harbouring of three Genoese ships bringing reinforcements, which had fought their way into the Golden Horn through the whole Turkish fleet, with the Sultan cursing aloud from a horse knee- deep in the sea and the beleaguered citizens straining every prayer and hope on the walls above; the trans- portation of sixty-seven Turkish ships, sails unfurled, bands playing and oarsmen rowing, down a wooden tramway over the hill behind Galata into the Golden Horn; the failure of the Greek attempt to destroy them with fireships, and consequent necessity of extending still further the thin line of the defence; the growing assaults on the land walls; the frustration of Turkish mines by the German John Grant; the calling of monks, old men, women and children to pile every available substance into the breaches; the non-arrival of ex- pected help from the West; the chivalrous return of the ships sent out to seek it; and at laſt the supreme preparations. On May the 26th, the whole length of the Turkish camp below the walls was illuminated. There were feaſting and singing; and for two days more, faſting and preparation for death, broken only by the herald's proclaiming the three days' plunder that muſt ensue if the city falls. Meanwhile, Mohammed in his tent debates whether to raise the siege.

Within the city, while the adolescent Sultan, sensualiſt, ſtudent of Ariſtotle, and ruler of men, takes his final decisions, it is realised that the day so long and miraculously averted is approaching; and another sovereign, Conſtantine XI Dragases Palæologus, laſt of the eighty-eight Chriſtian Emperors who have ruled the Greek empire of the Eaſt, walks the ſtage as a charaĉter ſteadfaſt and unaffeĉted, but coloured with a fatality born of greater events than lie in man's control. It is he who has persuaded, by personal requeſt, the Italian soldiers to join in the defence of the city. And his rôle has been one of mediator between the Greeks and those Latins who now make tardy reparation for the fourth crusade. Repeatedly, during the siege, he has been urged to leave the city by every shade of opinion, to rally aid from the Albanians and the Weſt. The Italian commander has placed ships at his disposal. But his answer has been: " What would the world say of me? Ask me to remain with you. I am ready to die with you." And invoking the example of the Good Shepherd, he ſtays.

Monday, the 28th of May, dawns, and the city

wakes conscious of crisis. All day long the bells of the churches clang in dolorous and irregular cadence, calling to the ramparts; soldiers tramp to and from their posts; the rest of the world is building up the breaches. Without the walls is silence. As the afternoon arrives, a huge procession forms, the epitome of all those innumerable processions of triumph and despair that have trod the hallowed streets. Orthodox, Uniate and Catholic, till this moment rending one another for the misfortune visited upon the community by an improperly supplicated God, now unite in the chant of Kyrie eleison, Lord, have mercy; the relics and icons are brought out; and with the invocation of celestial aid, hope revives. " Thus," says the Archbishop Leonard, " comforted regarding the issue of the day of battle, we awaited it with good courage."

At the finish of the procession, the Emperor addresses[1] the assembled officials, nobles and generals, Greek and Latin together. He speaks, as men have often spoken, of the duty to die, for Christ, for Greece, and for those most beloved. He speaks of their city, " the pride and joy of every Greek and of all who live in the Eastern lands, the queen of cities, the city which in happier times has conquered nearly all the countries under the sun, and which the enemy now covets as his chief prize." He speaks of their ancestors, the Greeks and Romans, " whom we honour, as posterity, if we conduct ourselves aright, must honour us." He speaks

---

[1] The two accounts of this address, written independently by men who heard it, agree.

of their faith: "The Turks have their artillery, their cavalry, their hordes of soldiers. We have our God and Saviour." Himself, he will die for and with his people. Finally, he addresses separately the Venetians and Genoese.

Then the Emperor, the court, the generals, and the populace, enter St Sophia.

Look while you may. The great church, forsaken in bitterness since the union of the Churches was there celebrated on December the 12th last, is open. Once more, and only once more, the marbled walls, the mosaic vaults, the ambo and iconostasis, the hangings, the plate, the lamps and the vestments, assist the familiar ritual. Patriarch and Cardinal, with a crowd of ecclesiastics representing both the Orthodox and Catholic Churches; Emperor and nobles, remnant of the once gorgeous and brave Greek aristocracy; priests and soldiers intermingling; and the crowd of citizens, Constantinopolitans, Venetians, Genoese; all are here together. For the last time the Byzantines assemble. They receive the divine mysteries. Emperor and Patriarch bid public farewell: the temporal state doomed to extinction and the Church that must live. Then all go to their posts. And stationing themselves between the first and second walls, lock the doors behind them, so that retreat is impossible.

Constantine, accompanied by his friend Phrantzes, at whose marriage he had in past years stood best man, rides the length of the city to his palace of Blachern up on the walls to the north-west, where they begin descent to the Golden Horn. In the manner of kings, he asks pardon of his dependants. " Had a man been made of wood or stone," wrote Phrantzes later, " he must have wept." The night is dark and clouded. A noise sounds from the Turkish camp; enormous drops of rain herald a storm; then both subside. After midnight the Emperor rides the rounds. Everything is in order. From a tower he discerns the sound of muffled preparations. At length he and Phrantzes separate.

The assault begins before the dawn, between one and two in the morning. As the dull light filters in the sky, a vast din shakes the earth: the yells of the attackers to the accompaniment of cymbals and flutes; the metallic ring of weapons, the boom of cannon, the tremor of resounding shot; and over all, the church bells, faster now, calling and calling to the walls. The end comes with the mortal wounding of Justiniani, the Genoese commander, who is carried on board ship to die at Chios. A local panic ensues, and the Turks effect an entry. The cry goes up that they are in. The Emperor, accompanied by Theophilus Palæologus, Don Francisco of Toledo, and John of Dalmatia, gallops to stem the inrush; but seeing it hopeless, dismounts, throws off the imperial insignia, and plunges into the combatants, leaving as his last recorded words," The city is taken, and I am still alive." The body is later identified by scarlet boots embroidered with the Roman eagles.

Thus Constantinople falls. The sack, as promised, continues three days. The plunder of the churches is divided; the libraries are trampled or sold. A few of

PLATE XVI

THE SULTAN MOHAMMED II
by Costanzo, from life, 1481

the Greeks escape by sea; the rest, stripped even of
their clothes, are roped together like cattle, the property of the soldiers, to be auctioned in the provinces.
Mohammed enters in triumph, and with his own sword
strikes the fool who would injure St Sophia. A number
of illustrious prisoners are executed. While those of
either sex, whose beauty warrants it, are placed in the
Sultan's harems. Silence overspreads the town, a great
emptiness, only to be repaired by forcible repopulation.
But the setting of empire remains. St Sophia, unchanged even in name, shelters new worshippers. The
walls of Theodosius enclose them. Still, on those walls,
the invocation may be read: "CHRIST O GOD GUARD
THY CITY FROM TROUBLE AND WAR. CONQUER THE
WRATH OF THE ENEMY." But now at last the heavens
are deaf. The age of Reason is at hand.

The latter Byzantines were no race of heroes, as we
understand heroes. Have they so appeared, it is owing
to the seeming superfluity of recapitulating those un-
ending foibles of which historians have already been
lavish in their revelation. Under the strain of the last
years, the faults of the unchanging Greek had pushed
to the surface. Greedy of money, mentally exercised
over the very chaff of theology, seeking compensation
for misfortune in overweening conceit, these men were
scarcely average. Even in their appearance there was
something unearthly: the Florentines, at the Council of
1438, regarded with astonishment their demeanour of
pedantic vanity, their long beards and painted eye-

brows, their flowing mantles and outlandish hats. Yet their art was fresh; their religion held no germ of that sinister bigotry which should characterise the Puritan and Counter Reformations, simultaneous reactions against a paganism engendered in Italy by writings of which they, the Byzantines, had always been possessors; and they had courage. They fought, fought to the last, when, had they acceded to Mohammed's demands, life and property might have been theirs.

In two spheres, however, the conquest was not yet complete. In the Peloponnese, the Despots Thomas and Demetrius Palæologus, brothers of the Emperor Constantine, still retained their independence. The growth of Hellenic sentiment at the beginning of the fifteenth century had made possible, with the exception of a few fortresses, the reclamation of the whole centre of the peninsula from the engrafted feudalism of the Latin invaders. And the organisation of the country had been the object of personal supervision from the Emperor Manuel II. But prosperity was slow in reappearing; and the prevalent misery and confusion bear witness to the impotence of the last period of Byzantine administration. In the writings of Gemistos Plethon, the foremost Platonist of his day and occupant of a judgeship at Mistra, strange socialist remedies are proposed for the amelioration of social evils, the oppressive taxes, debasement of coinage, and maladministration of justice. Mohammed, busy with the affairs of his new capital, was prepared, in return for the payment of a tribute and the recognition of his sovereignty, to confirm the *status quo*, provided that peace was forthcoming as a result. Unfortunately, it was not. In each valley, on each range, the land of eternal feud gave evidence of a new quarrel. The brothers made war on one another; their subjects revolted against them. In 1460, after the despatch of several subsidiary expeditions, Mohammed marched south in person, received the submission of Mistra, and reduced the country to some state of order. We may imagine, some thirty miles north of the Gulf of Corinth, the Turkish soldiers in the small town of Calavryta. There, 361 years later, the banner of a small monastery was hoisted by an Archbishop to proclaim the Greek War of Independence.

Meanwhile, at Trebizond, on the south coast of the Black Sea, a last offshoot of the vanished monarchy was represented by the Grand Comnenus, King and Emperor of all the East, whose eagles were now the rallying-point of Greek disaffection. The nineteen Emperors and three Empresses of the dynasty founded after the fourth crusade by Alexius Comnenus, grandson of that Andronicus whom the Constantinople mob tore asunder in the Hippodrome in 1185, had reigned two centuries and a half. The extent of their dominion, which had reached even Georgia and the Crimea, was ordinarily some 7000 square miles contained in a narrow strip along the shore. And their capital, since the destruction of Bagdad by Hulagu, had been famed for its mart of wares from the further East. Venetians and Genoese, as at Constantinople, had their outposts there;

301

and many travellers have left passing impressions of the place. An English embassy of 1293 wore its shoes to ruin on the cobbled streets. Another Englishman, in the time of Richard II, describes the royal palace: its marble audience chamber in the form of a pyramid; its frescoed banqueting hall; and its library of scientific and historical works. To the city's continued prosperity in the fifteenth century, the writings of Bessarion, the Trapezuntine Cardinal, are witness.

In 1456, the Emperor John VI had recognised the overlordship of the Sultan in Constantinople. The stock of which he came was famed for its good looks; the admiration of a Frenchman for one of its princesses has already been noticed (page 246); and the Emperor himself was known on this account as Kalo-Joannes. The beauty of his daughter, the Despoina Catherine, was celebrated from Italy to Persia; and when Usan Hassan, chief of the neighbouring Turkomans of the White Horde, sent offering "not only his army, but his treasure and his own person," in case of a struggle with Mohammed, she was despatched to become his wife. Their grandson was the Shah Ismail, creator and first ruler of a united Persia. Meanwhile Kalo-Joannes had died, and his small son's throne been usurped by his brother David. The alliance with Hassan was continued; and aid was sought from Venice, Genoa and the Vatican. At length, in 1461, Mohammed lost patience with these intrigues and himself marched on the city, which incontinently surrendered, while Hassan remained discreetly in the interior. A third of the population was sent to repeople Conſtantinople; a third sold into slavery; and the reſt suffered to remain. The Emperor David, his wife and their seven sons were exiled to Adrianople, where, two years later, all save the Empress were ſtrangled. The Despoina Catherine, ruling magnificently in Asia Minor, did not cease, as long as she lived, to incite her husband to avenge her family.

All veſtiges of Greek independence had disappeared. Byzantine civilisation was extinct; and, other than that of El Greco, its future influence, outside the ſterile confines of the Ottoman Empire, was deſtined to be little. Yet, with the fall of Conſtantinople, two countries, were most immediately affected. These were Italy and Russia.

The ancient theory that, with the entry of the Turks into Conſtantinople, a multitude of scholars debouched by an opposite gate to flood Europe with their manuscripts and cause the Renascence, is no more. The germs of that movement had already appeared among the Albigenses and the Hussites, and at the south Italian court of the Hohenſtaufens. But these early symptoms had been eradicated by the Papacy. And nothing illuſtrates more clearly the difference between Eaſt and Weſt Europe, than the attitude of their respective Churches towards the writings of Antiquity. By the Orthodox, despite spasmodic opposition to Plato, they were treasured for the moſt part as a genuine source of spiritual inspiration; by the Catholic, knowledge of them was held to discount all hope of salvation. In the latter sphere, the standpoint of the fanatic of Cordova, who cried: " Let the foaming and bespittled grammarians belch, while we remain evangelical servants of Christ," was general; Faust, it will be remembered, sold his soul to the devil for the learning of the ancients; and if all Europe had gone the way of the Italians, who in the first ecstasies of humanistic individualism, reverted not only to paganism, but to a level of political and sexual immorality that defies belief, the standpoint of the fanatic might have been justified. As Symonds says, " The tendencies of the Renascence were worldly; its ideal left no room for a pure and ardent intuition into spiritual truth." The Italians rediscovered the language, collected the manuscripts. But when, with Reuchlin and Erasmus, the new-found critical spirit advanced north of the Alps, it passed from the control of dilettanti into the hands of men whose search for that truth nothing could divert. The result was the Reformation.

In the agency of this upheaval, which was to bury the Middle Ages, to recover in one glorious burst the freedom of man's mind, and to settle into a degraded sediment of classical imitation, the part of the Byzantines was no small one. With their language, something also of the spirit of their society was communicated to the Italians. National consciousness, in which that people now excels, was dissolved in the " cosmopolitan ideal of the human family, one in culture." Distinctions of birth gave place to those of talent, so that cities and princes contended for the bodies of scholars, living or dead. All the world was united in a frenzied search for loſt authors, of which the discovery " was regarded almoſt as the conqueſt of a kingdom." Italian officials in the Levant reaped fortunes by the sale of manuscripts.

The craze began with Petrarch, who died nearly eighty years before the fall of Conſtantinople, and whose intuition was the firſt to prediſt that the immediate future of humanity lay with the knowledge of Greek. This, by his advice, Boccacio acquired. Meanwhile, Byzantine importunity for Italian aid was increasing. In 1389, Manuel Chrysoloras, friend and correspondent of the Emperor Manuel II Palæologus, disembarked at Venice on his way to Rome; and in 1396, he was induced to accept a Greek chair at the University of Florence. A passion filled people: professions and property were forsaken for the satisfaſtion of mental cravings by possession of a language which alone could interpret the dreams that were in every one's head. The Council of Florence added to the ſtimulus. Gemiſtos Plethon, the Platoniſt, who had ſtudied philosophy not only at Conſtantinople, but at the Moslem schools at Brussa and Adrianople, was among the Greek delegates. He it was, spiritual descendant of Psellos, who revived Plato's vision of God to attack the ecclesiaſtically manipulated materialism of Ariſtotle. And to him was aſtually due the revival of Platonic ſtudies in the Weſt. In 1450, he died at Miſtra. And five years later, juſt before the

305

reduction of that stronghold by the Turks, the bones of one so great were exhumed by Sigismondo Pandolfo Malatesta, and reinterred at Rimini.

A long list of names reveals the Byzantine tutors of the Renascence: John Argyropoulos; George of Trebizond; John Lascaris, who took service with France, became ambassador for Louis XII, and collected Francis I's library at Fontainebleau; Filelfo, husband of a Byzantine, who assures us that the noble matrons of Constantinople spoke the purest Attic; and, in Rome, Bessarion, the outstanding Greek of the period, who had attended the Council of Florence as Archbishop of Nicæa, and was created Cardinal by Pope Eugenius IV. His palace in Rome, after the fall of the Greek capital, became the centre of all fresh agitations for a crusade. And here assembled many of the unfortunate refugees, among them the historian, Phrantzes.

Of the two Palæologus Despots, Demetrius and Thomas,[1] the former was granted a substantial pension by the Sultan, and ended his days as a monk at Adrianople; while his daughter, Helen, entered the harem of

[1] A monument in Llandulph church, near Plymouth, displays the following inscription : " Here lyeth the body of Theodoro Paleologus of Pesaro in Italye descended from ye Imperyall lyne of ye last Christian Emperors of Greece being the sonne of Camilio ye sone of Prosper the sonne of Theodoro the sonne of John ye sonne of Thomas second brother to Constantine Paleologus the 8th of that name and last of ye lyne yt raygned in Constantinople until subdewed by the Turke—who married with Mary ye daughter of William Balls of Hadlye in Souffolke gent & had issue 5 children Theodoro John Ferdinando Maria & Dorothy & depted this life at Clyfton ye 21st of January 1636."

the Sultan. The latter, with his wife and children, had escaped to Italy. As a passport to hospitality, he brought with him the head of St Andrew from Patras. A great reception was accorded this relic by the Romans, which, though spoilt by the rain on the first day, resulted, on the second, in a march of two miles on foot for Pope Pius II, and the burning of 30,000 candles. Thanks to the influence of Bessarion, the Despot received an allowance of 500 *écus d'or* a month, which was continued, after his death in 1495, to his children. Bessarion supervised their education, the regulation of their household, doctors, chaplains and tutors, and the maintenance of their servants and horses. His efforts were to little purpose. Andrew, of whom a portrait by Pinturicchio survives in the Vatican, side by side with the mounted figure of Prince Djem, a refugee son of Mohammed II, who had arrived at the Borgia court in 1488 and set a fashion for Turkish fancy dress, espoused a prostitute and died childless in 1502, bequeathing his imperial claims to Ferdinand and Isabella of Spain. His younger brother Manuel returned to Constantinople, where, thanks to the generosity of Mohammed, he was able to maintain "a decent harem." There remained, however, a sister, named Zoë, renowned throughout Europe for her wit. In 1467, Ivan III of Muscovy sent requesting her hand. And the face of the Russian monarchy was changed.

Of the influence of mediæval Greek civilisation on the Balkans, it is sufficient to say that it was only by the imitation of Byzantine institutions, the assumption of Byzantine titles and the borrowing of Byzantine culture, that the conscious nationalities of Bulgars, Serbs and Rumanians, were evolved and were able to withstand the extinction threatened by Turkish enslavement. In Russia, however, the Greek foundations were deeper; the existing political structure more peculiar; and the complexion of the resulting edifice so wholly removed from any sphere of comparison, that even now its effects on the history of the world are incalculable.

In the ninth century, the missionaries, Constantine and Methodius, by the invention of the Slav alphabet, had reinforced in perpetuity the cultural barrier between East and West Europe. This work was still further assisted by the Orthodox Church in permitting celebration of the liturgy in the vernacular to the successively Christianised Slav races. The particular conversion of Russia was the work of Olga, daughter-in-law of Rurik, the founder of the Russian state, and of her grandson Vladimir. Olga, who visited Constantinople in order to " learn about God," was baptized with the Emperor Constantine VII Porphyrogenitus as her godfather. Vladimir, Prince of Kiev, brought aid to the Byzantine monarchy during the minority of the Emperor Basil II Bulgaroctonos against the rebellion of Bardas Phocas; and was rewarded, despite his 300 concubines, with the hand of Basil's sister. At Cherson, whither he came to meet her, he was baptized on the spot occupied by the allied trenches before Sebastopol in the Crimean War; and thenceforth, from 988 onwards, Christianity became the state religion. Relations with Constantinople were continued; marriages between the two royal families were frequent; and it was not until the fifteenth century that Greek bishops ceased to preside over the Russian dioceses. Only in 1587, was the shifting of political gravity thought to justify the creation of the Patriarchate of Moscow, which was extinguished in 1723 by Peter the Great, and only reconstituted by the Provisional Government in 1917.

The political unit of early Russia was the city state. Kiev and Novgorod, the main centres, were diminutive Constantinoples; their buildings were designed after Greek models and were often decorated by Greek artists; their law, the Pravda, was simply a Slav edition of the digests of the Isaurian and Macedonian Emperors; and their whole existence was dependent on the maintenance of trade with the markets of the Greek capital. For the strength of their rule over the countryside was economic, instead of based, as in the West, on a feudal land-tenure. But, with the Tartar invasions of the thirteenth century, the growing civilisation fostered in the cities, was driven into the interior to develop of itself; and the economic basis of the Russian state, divorced from commerce, became agricultural. During this period, it was only the Byzantine cultural foundation that saved the Russian identity from total immersion by the Oriental migrations.

At length, by the end of the fifteenth century, the princes of Muscovy were loosening their dependence of the Golden Horde. And in the person of Zoë Palæologina, henceforth known as Sophia, there came to them a princess in whom all the character, ability, and pride derived from centuries of worshipped royalty, had accumulated. Was not she, whose father and brothers suffered themselves to remain pensioners of a Pope detested in Russia more even than in Greece, the inheritor of the Roman Empire? Her signature, embroidered by her own hands on a sheet in 1498, may still be read, with the appellation " Tzarevna Tzaregerodskaia—Princess of Constantinople " attached. The end of that imperial line was yet to come, in the house of Ipatiev at Ekaterinbourg. Disliking the familiarity of the Boyars, she introduced the ceremonial of her ancestry, the coronation and reception rites; the bureaucracy, the titles, and the custom of employing and ennobling foreigners, followed. In 1480, the rule of the Tartars was finally discarded. The Kremlin, in imitation of the Great Palace of Constantinople, was built at Moscow. And the Prince assumed the double-headed eagle and the title of Samoderzetz, Autocrat, borne for 1100 years by the successors of Constantine the Great. All connections with the former Greek capital were revived, all channels of descent. And when, in the middle of the sixteenth century, Ivan the Terrible finally adopted the ancient style of the Emperors of the East, he had his pretention ratified by the Œcumenical Patriarch of Conſtantinople and hierarchy in full council. Thus was the Prince of Rus, who was formerly honoured with the title of " Table-dresser to the Emperor," advanced. Well might the monk of Pskov write that henceforth Moscow was the third and final Rome. The Russian claim to the Byzantine inheritance, which the Europe of the nineteenth century was conſtrained to dispute, boaſted ancient pedigree.

Yet the true heirs of Conſtantinople owed their claim not to the journeys of scholarship and the inflation of barbarous kings. They remained, in the Levant, among the people who created Byzantine civilisation and its capital. To the underſtanding of the Greek entity, this analysis of the Byzantine civilisation has been attempted; and to that end, the hiſtory of its inheritors deserves to be continued. Already, lament for the past was echoing, handed by mouth from father to son, in the counting-houses of foreign merchants, on the beaches of forgotten islands, amid the craggy faſtnesses of honourable brigands:—

" The Lord has signified, the heaven and earth have signified,
And Saint Sophia, that has four hundred sounding-gongs and sixty
And two loud bells with each its priest and every priest his deacon,
The mighty church has signified, to interrupt the service
When sounds the Song of Cherubims, that Christ the King retire.
A dove is come from out the midſt of heaven, bidding muffle
The Song of Cherubims and lower down the holy objects.
' Ye priests bear them away with ye, and candles be ye dimmed,
Since God decrees dominion of the Turk upon the city.
Despatch ye only message to the West, that ships come hither,

311

A trio, one to bear away the cross, the next the gospel,
And last, the finest of the three, to take our holy altar
Before the dogs can steal it from us and pollute it for us.'
And troubled was the Lady Virgin ; weeping were the icons.
' Now Lady Virgin, hold thy peace, and icons weep no longer.
Again, with journeying of years, again shall they be yours.' "

NOTES ON THE ILLUSTRATIONS

PLATE I

COMMERCE IN THE GOLDEN HORN, frontispiece,

Extract from a panorama in the British Museum, about seven feet long and eighteen inches broad, by Gerard Hofsted van Essen, printed in sections, 1713. This is perhaps the best view of Constantinople that exists, since photographs convey no impression of the place, and all earlier panoramas of Stambul from the heights of Galata are entirely inaccurate, being based on that of Dilich (see note on plate III). The present extract shows St Sophia and St Irene, and part of the sea-walls now demolished. The aspect of the shipping could have changed little since Byzantine days.

PLATE II

THE CITY OF CONSTANTINE, to face p. 70,

An aerial photograph, provided by the Central Aerophoto Company. The site of the Hippodrome is indicated by the line of municipal bedding that runs above the Sultan Ahmet mosque. Careful scrutiny will distinguish the obelisk of Thothmes III at the southern end, and next it the hole containing the Delphic serpent. The obelisk restored by Constantine VII Porphyrogenitus is hidden by a minaret. The Kaiser's fountain, vulgar and pretentious as its donor, interrupts the northern flower-bed. The long street running to the top of the picture was the main thoroughfare of the Byzantine city, and may be identified in plate XIV. The column of Constantine stands on the north side of it, half way up.

PLATE III

A WOODCUT OF CONSTANTINOPLE and THE LAND WALLS TO-DAY, to face p. 78,

The former reproduced from Hartmann Schedel's *Weltchronik*, Nuremberg, 1493, the latter from E. Diez: *Alt-Konstantinopel*, Munich, 1920.

313

NOTES ON THE ILLUSTRATIONS

The woodcut, despite its gothicised version of St Sophia, illustrates the following points :—

The complete circuit of the walls with their double towers,
The Palæologus shields with the four B's,
The imperial eagles over the gateways,
The palace of Blachern up on the land walls, where they start descent to the Golden Horn,
The dehabitation of the city after the Latin conquest,
Three windmills,
The equestrian statue of Justinian,
And the chain guarding the entrance to the Golden Horn.

Whatever the accuracy of the picture, it is interesting to note that these features existed in the imaginations of Western contemporaries.

Numerous topographical panoramas of Constantinople, taken soon before or after the Turkish capture, survive, and their merits are summarised in E. Oberhummer : *Konstantinopel unter Suleiman dem Grossen aufgenommen im Jahre* 1559 *durch Melchior Lorichs aus Flensburg*, Munich, 1902. The earliest is that of Buondelmonti, dating from about 1420, of which various versions exist. This shows the chief columns and monuments, but has no artistic value. A century later, Vavassore, a Venetian, executed another, of which innumerable copies spread over Europe. Then follow the views of Lorichs, to which Oberhummer appends an interesting Turkish map of about the same date. The earliest of the long panoramas from Galata is that reproduced in W. Dilich : *Eigendtliche Kurtze Beschreibung und Abris, der weitberühmten Keyserlichen Stadt Constantinopel*, Cassel, 1606. This likewise spread and was elaborated ; but despite the fact that Dilich visited the city, it is largely imaginary. Of a similar type, but accurate, and a work of art, is that of Gerard Hofsted van Essen (see note on plate I). A series of frescoes dating from 1536 in a church at Moldovita in Rumania, represent the Turkish siege, and illustrate :—

The cannon of both sides
The procession of icons
The rain of blood.

314

NOTES ON THE ILLUSTRATIONS

PLATE IV

ROMANUS II AND HIS FIRST WIFE EUDOXIA, to face p. 114,

Reproduced, by courtesy of Messrs Ernest Leroux and Professor J. Ebersolt, from the latter's *Les Arts somptuaires de Byzance*, Paris, 1923.

This ivory, now in the Cabinet de Médailles, illustrates the difference between formalisation and mere formula, and the absurdity of the contention that the Byzantines " could not draw." The feet of the Christ anticipate those of Signorelli. Greek typographers, instead of poring over Periclean inscriptions, might study with advantage the elegance of the Byzantine lettering.

The sovereigns depicted have been generally assumed to be Romanus IV Diogenes, captured at Manzikert, and his wife, Eudoxia Makrembolitissa. For their proper identification, see Royall Tyler and Hayford Peirce : *Byzantine Art*, London, 1926, p. 39. Romanus II was the adored son for whom the Emperor Constantine VII Porphyrogenitus wrote his *De Ceremoniis*, and whom he celebrates as the glory of the world on the obelisk still standing in the Hippodrome. His first wife was Eudoxia, illegitimate daughter of Hugo King of Italy ; his second, Theophano, who poisoned him, after a reign of four years, in exchange for Nicephorus II Phocas. He excelled in physical beauty, and his days were divided between the tennis-court and the hunting of boars. He was the father of Basil II Bulgaroctonos and of Anna, who married Vladimir, *fornicator immensus*, Grand Duke of Russia. Her granddaughter became the wife of Henry I of France. Thus, as Gibbon observes, the blood of the Macedonian dynasty of Constantinople still flows in the veins of the Bourbons.

PLATE V

THEODORE METOCHITES, GRAND LOGOTHETE, to face p. 123,

Reproduced, by courtesy of Messrs Ernest Leroux and Professor J. Ebersolt, from the latter's *Les Arts somptuaires de Byzance*, Paris, 1923.

This figure is taken from the mosaics of the Kahrié and represents their donor offering his church to Christ enthroned. The inscription reads : " The founder, logothete of the central treasury, Theodore Metochites." His headdress is white with pink bands, his inner tunic of gold, and his mantle of green woven with red ivy-leaves. These

315

mosaics, completed before 1321, occupied some twenty years in execution, and were part of the general movement to restore the glories of Constantinople after the expulsion of the Latins. They excited the admiration of contemporaries, and their founder himself has left a poem on them.

Theodore Metochites has descended as one of the most vivid figures of the later Byzantine age. Born at Nicæa, he studied philosophy and literature with a view to a career, and first made his mark as an orator. He was known as the handsome Metochites, and combined elegance of figure and repartee with a capacity for hard work, which he brought to the study of Plato, science and astronomy, the composition of poetic and historical works, and the conduct of the state; so that contemporaries marvelled at the application of this intellectual to his duties at the palace. Like Psellos he was a Hellenist, and he wished to reform the language after the ancient model. As a true Byzantine, he condemned both aristocratic and democratic government, and supported the ideal of a monarchy constitutionalised by a bureaucracy trained in the humanities. Among his poems is a lament on the unhappy condition of the Empire and the beloved provinces of Asia.

As he rose by stages to the chief offices of the state, his riches increased proportionately and his daughter married a nephew of the Emperor. But like Clarendon's, his good fortune was too great. In the civil war between Andronicus II and Andronicus III, he championed the former; the troops of the latter entered the city; his palace was pillaged and he himself exiled. He returned only to take the vows of the monastery that he had so generously endowed in the days of his prosperity, and to die on March 13, 1332. " Weep, choir of Muses," wrote his friend, Nicephorus Gregoras, " This man is dead, and with him, all wisdom."

Plate VI

APOCAUCOS, HIGH ADMIRAL, to face p. 122,

Reproduced, by courtesy of Messrs Ernest Leroux and Professor J. Ebersolt, from the latter's *Les Arts somptuaires de Byzance*, Paris 1923.

This miniature is contained in a manuscript of the works of Hippocrates executed for Apocaucos and now in the Bibliothèque Nationale. The legend above the sitter's head reads : " Grand Duke Apocaucos." This title denoted the office of High Admiral, and since, to English ears, it implies a heredity which it did not possess, the latter is thought to be the better translation.

Notes on the Illustrations

Apocaucos was the chief supporter of the Empress-Regent Anna of Savoy during the minority of John V Palæologus, and the opponent of Cantacuzene, who afterwards became Emperor as John VI. As prefect of the capital he exercised a virtual dictatorship, till murdered by his own prisoners, among he had ventured unarmed, in 1345. He enjoyed a reputation for learning.

PLATE VII

CONSTANTINOPLE, THE GOLDEN HORN, AND GALATA, to face p. 132,

Reproduced from J. G. Grelot: *Relation nouvelle d'un voyage de Constantinople*, Paris, 1680.

PLATE VIII

CHRIST, RULER OF THE WORLD, to face p. 172,

Reproduced, by courtesy of the Oxford University Press and Mr O. M. Dalton, from the latter's *East Christian Art*, Oxford, 1925. The photograph was taken by the late Mr S. H. Barnsley, and the original negative is in the possession of Mr R. W. S. Weir.

This eleventh century mosaic of Christ Pantocrator, placed in a rainbow circle about fifteen feet in diameter, occupies the central dome of the church of Daphni near Athens, and is the most absolutely spectacular example of Byzantine representational art extant. Even to-day, in a ruined church, with the motor ticking outside, it terrifies. The effect of its majesty, during an Orthodox service, upon those who lived in ultimate expectation of the actuality, can scarcely be imagined.

PLATE IX

THE EMPEROR JOHN VIII PALÆOLOGUS, to face p. 184,

Reproduced from a medal by Pisanello in the British Museum.

The legend reads: " John King and Emperor of the Romans the Palæologus." The reverse shows the Emperor on horseback and bears a double legend in Latin and Greek: " Work of Pisano Artist."

Doubts have been cast on the authenticity of this medal in A. Calabi and B. Cornaggia : *Pisanello*, Milan, 1928. The authors have reproduced the drawing of the Emperor by the same artist, referred to on page 244, and have contrasted its delicacy with the hardness of the medal. But such a contrast is only the natural outcome of a drastic translation of medium ; and the greater authority of Mr G. F. Hill, of the British Museum, may be invoked in the medal's favour. Another version, in which the famous hat is furnished with the spiked crown so essential to the artists of the period in their depiction of the kings of the East, is preserved in Paris and Naples, and in all probability is no more than a later pastiche. The bust in the Museo di Propaganda at Rome may be considered a nineteenth century forgery.

PLATE X

ST SOPHIA WITH TURKISH MINARETS, to face p. 190,

Reproduced from J. G. Grelot : *Relation nouvelle d'un voyage de Constantinople*, Paris, 1680.

PLATE XI

ST SOPHIA : FACING THE WEST DOOR, to face p. 200,

Reproduced from C. Fossati : *Aya Sofia Constantinople*, London, 1852.

Photographs of the interior of St Sophia give an impression of indescribable architectural confusion, punctured by staring loopholes of sunlight. Fossati's coloured plates manage to convey something of the exquisite radiance that pervades the building, and something of its architectural harmonies. The marble panelling is visible, and the mode of artificial lighting, though the lamp-holders are modern, is essentially the same as in Byzantine days. Fossati was an Italian architect called in by the Sultan Abdul Medjid to restore the church after an earthquake. Previous to his additions, such as the ornate balustrading of the galleries and the stencilled designs on the vaulting and dome, the interior was plainer. During the repairs, the mosaics were disclosed, and Victorianised copies of them may be seen in W. Salzenberg : *Altchristliche Baudenkmale von Konstantinopel*, Berlin, 1854. Posterity may at least be grateful to Fossati for his attempt to preserve their general colouring in his over-wash.

NOTES ON THE ILLUSTRATIONS

PLATE XII

THE LATER BYZANTINE COURT, to face p. 244,

From a bas-relief on the doors of St Peter's, Rome, by Filarete,
Reproduced from M. Lazzaroni and A. Muñoz: *Filarete, scultore e architetto del secolo XV*, Rome, 1908.

The series of reliefs on these doors relating to the Emperor John VIII Palæologus are described on page 244. Not less remarkable are two others depicting the arrival and reception of the Abyssinian abbot. Filarete was in Florence in 1439 and began work on the doors of St Peter's almost immediately afterwards. The Bakst-like costumes of the court, and of the officials illustrated on plates V and VI, are corroborated by the frescoes of Piero della Francesca at Arezzo, where the soldiers of Heraclius, uniformed like Russian Boyars, have astonished observers ignorant of the fact that both the court of the Tzars and the Florentine artist drew their fashions from Constantinople.

PLATE XIII

BYZANTINE HUMOUR: THE PATRIARCH THEO-PHYLACT, to face p. 250,

From a manuscript of Skilitzes' history, variously attributed to the twelfth and fourteenth centuries, in the National Library at Madrid,
Reproduced, by courtesy of Messrs Benn, Professor G. Millet, and Mr R. Tyler, from *Byzantine Art* (Kai Khosru Monographs' series), by the latter and H. Pierce, London, 1926.

PLATE XIV

THE HIPPODROME ABOUT MCDL, to face p. 252,

Reproduced from O. Panvinio: *De Ludis Circensibus*, Venice, 1600.

This engraving is stated by the author, in 1580, to show the remains of the Constantinople Hippodrome at the time of the Turkish conquest. Presumably redrawn from an older sketch, the central monuments, in which Panvinio was most interested, have been revised to suit the taste of the age, one of the obelisks removed from its base, and the Delphic serpent between them transformed into a column with a Corinthian capital. The mound at the northern end probably denotes the remains of the *spina*. The vaults of the sphendone, at the other, still exist; the pillars above them were used in the construction of

319

the Sultan Ahmet mosque in 1610. For comparison with the aerial photograph, facing p. 70, see note on plate II. Pieter Koeck van Aalst, a Dutch artist, has left a series of woodcuts dating from the year 1553, which give a more intimate view of the ruins and monuments, slightly improved in accordance with the classical canon.

PLATE XV

SULTAN MOHAMMED II, to face p. 288,

Reproduced from a picture in the National Gallery by Gentile Bellini, who visited Constantinople at the Sultan's invitation. Excessive cleaning has removed most of the detail.

PLATE XVI

SULTAN MOHAMMED II, to face p. 298,

Reproduced from the medal by Costanzo of Ferrara in the British Museum.

Costanzo also visited Constantinople. The legend reads : " Equestrian portrait of Mohameth, Emperor of Asia and Greece, in the field. Work of Constantius." The obverse, showing the Sultan's head, gives the date 1481.

THE MAPS have been copied from the Spruner-Menke *Hand-Atlas für die Geschichte des Mittelalters und der neueren Zeit*, Gotha, 1880, with the exception of that of the themes on page 125, which is borrowed from G. Schlumberger : *Un Empereur byzantin au 10ᵉ siècle : Nicephore Phocas*, Paris, 1890.

BIBLIOGRAPHY

The following list of authorities, for matters subsequent to the foundation of Constantinople in 330 A.D., is intended to assist those who interest themselves in Byzantine civilisation for the sake of its relation to the general evolution of Europe. Students of isolated periods and compartments will find it far from complete, and should refer to the bibliographies of the Cambridge Mediæval History, 1927, volumes I and IV, and of Mr Norman Baynes' Byzantine Empire, London, 1925. The former gives complete tables of original sources. Here only about half a dozen are included on account of their vividness of description and comparative ease of access. The books and pamphlets mentioned are to be found, almost without exception, in either the British Museum, the library of the Victoria and Albert Museum, the London Library, or the Korais Library at King's College in the Strand.

CHAPTER IV: THE WORK OF CONSTANTINE.

BATIFFOL, P., *La paix constantinienne*, Paris, 1914.

BRÉHIER, L., and BATIFFOL, P., *Les survivances du culte impérial romain*, Paris, 1920.

Cambridge Mediæval History, Vol. I, chs. I, IV and V.

FIRTH, J. B., *Constantine the Great*, New York, 1905.

MAURICE, J., *Numismatique constantinienne*, Introduction, Paris, 1911.

STEIN, E., *Geschichte des Spätrömischen Reiches, I. Vom Römischen zum Byzantinischen Staate*, Vienna, 1928.

CHAPTER IV: TOPOGRAPHY AND MONUMENTS OF CONSTANTINOPLE (for St Sophia see ch. IX).

CASSON, S., *Preliminary report upon the excavations carried out in the Hippodrome of Constantinople in 1927: the Excavations*, Oxford, 1928.

321

Bibliography

CURTIS, C. G., *Broken Bits of Byzantium*, 2 parts, with interesting lithographs of objects now disappeared, particularly a series of bas-reliefs depicting the races in the Hippodrome, by Mrs M. A. Walker, Constantinople, (?) 1887.

—— *Constantinople according to the Greek Anthology*, mainly architectural inscriptions illustrating the Byzantines' enjoyment of their surroundings, Constantinople, 1878.

EBERSOLT, J., *Constantinople byzantine et les voyageurs du Levant*, Paris, 1918.

—— *Le Grand Palais de Constantinople et le Livre des Cérémonies*, Paris, 1910.

—— *Rapport sur un mission archéologique à Constantinople*, Paris, 1921.

GROSVENOR, E. A., *Constantinople*, London, 1895.

LABARTE, J., *Le palais impérial de Constantinople*, Paris, 1861.

MORDTMANN, A. D., *Esquisse topographique de Constantinople*, Lille, 1892.

THIERS, A., and EBERSOLT, J., *Les églises de Constantinople*, Paris, 1913.

VAN MILLINGEN, A., *Byzantine churches in Constantinople*, London, 1912.

—— *Byzantine Constantinople*, London, 1899.

CHAPTER V : GENERAL HISTORY.

BAYNES, N. H., *The Byzantine Empire*, a brilliant sketch containing a great deal of information, London, 1925.

BURY, J. B., *History of the Eastern Roman Empire* (395-565), London, 1889.

—— *History of the Later Roman Empire* (802-867), London, 1912.

Cambridge Mediæval History, Vol. I, all but chs. VII, IX-XI, XIII-XV.

Cambridge Mediæval History, Vol. IV.

CHALANDON, F., *Essai sur le regne d'Alexis I Comnène*, Paris, 1900.

—— *Jean II Comnène et Manuel I Comnène*, Paris, 1912.

DIEHL, C., *Byzance*, Paris, 1919.

—— *Etudes byzantines*, Paris, 1905.

—— *Histoire de l'Empire byzantin*, Paris, 1919, English translation by G. B. Ives, Princeton, 1925.

—— *Justinien et la civilisation byzantine au 6ᵉ siècle*, Paris, 1901.

FINLAY, G., *History of Greece*, edited by H. F. Tozer, Oxford, 1877.

BIBLIOGRAPHY

FULLER, G. T., *Andronicus or the Unfortunate Politician*, perhaps the earliest English Byzantine study, London, 1646.

GFRÖRER, A. F., *Byzantinische Geschichten*, Graz, 1874.

GIBBON, E., *The History of the Decline and Fall of the Roman Empire*, edited by J. B. Bury, London, 1896.

HERTZBERG, F., *Geschichte der Byzantiner und des Osmanischen Reichs*, Berlin, 1883.

HOLMES, G. W., *The age of Justinian and Theodora*, London, 1905.

OMAN, C. W. C., *The Byzantine Empire*, London, 1897.

PAPARREGOPOULOS, K., Ἱστορία τοῦ Ἑλληνικοῦ Ἔθνους, edited by P. Karolides, Athens, 1903.

RAMBAUD, A., *Etudes sur l'histoire byzantine*, Paris, 1912.

—— *L'Empire grec du 10ᵉ siècle : Constantin Porphyrogénète*, Paris, 1870.

SCHLUMBERGER, G., *L'épopée byzantine à la fin du 10ᵉ siècle :*—

I. *Jean Tzimiscès, Basile II* (969-986).

II. *Basile II* (989-1025).

III. *Les Porphyrogénètes, Zoé et Théodora* (1025-1057), Paris, 1896-1905.

VOGT, A., *Basile Ier, Empereur de Byzance*, Paris, 1908.

CHAPTER VI : CONSTITUTION AND ADMINISTRATION.

ANDRÉADÈS, A., *La vénalité des charges est-elle d'origine byzantine ?* Nouvelle Revue Historique du Droit, Paris, 1921.

—— *Le recrutement des fonctionnaires et les universités dans l'Empire byzantin*, Extrait des Mélanges de Droit Romain, Paris, 1926.

BRÉHIER, L., and BATIFFOL, P., *Les survivances du culte impérial romain*, Paris, 1920.

BURY, J. B., *History of the Eastern Roman Empire* (395-565), London, 1889.

—— *History of the Later Roman Empire* (802-867), London, 1912.

—— *The Constitution of the Later Roman Empire*, Cambridge, 1910.

—— *The Imperial Administrative System in the Ninth Century*, London, 1911.

BUSSELL, F. W., *The Roman Empire : Essays on the Constitutional History* (A.D. 81-1081), London, 1910.

BIBLIOGRAPHY

DIEHL, C., *Etudes sur l'administration byzantine dans l'Exarchat de Ravenne*, Paris, 1888.

RAMBAUD, A., *L'empire grec du 10ᵉ siècle : Constantin Porphyrogénète*, Paris, 1870.

VON LINGENTHAL, K. E. Z., *Geschichte des griechisch-römischen Rechts*, Berlin, 1892.

WALTON, F. P., *Historical Introduction to the Roman Law*, Edinburgh, 1920.

CHAPTER VII : COMMERCE AND WEALTH.

ANDRÉADÈS, A., *De la monnaie et de la puissance d'achat des métaux précieux dans l'Empire byzantin*, Liège, 1924.

—— *Le montant du budget dans l'Empire byzantin*, Paris, 1922.

—— *Les finances byzantines*, Paris, 1911.

COSMAS INDICOPLEUSTES, *Topographia Christiana*, English translation by J. W. McCrindle, London, 1897.

DIEHL, C., *Venise*, Paris, 1918.

HEYD, W., *Histoire du commerce du Levant au moyen âge*, Leipzig, 1885.

HODGSON, F. C., *The Early History of Venice*, London, 1901.

—— *Venice in the Thirteenth and Fourteenth Centuries*, London, 1910.

KLUCHEVSKY, V. O., *A History of Russia*, Vol. I, chs. V and VI, London, 1911.

CHAPTER VIII : ORTHODOX CHURCH GENERAL HISTORY.

Those wishing to study this subject and its particular aspects are warned against the numerous works of English Roman and Anglo-Catholics. Under cover of spurious erudition and pretended impartiality, they exhibit a feminine spite, which makes the reader realise, after perhaps hours of attention, that he has been wasting his time.

ADENEY, W. F., *The Greek and Eastern Churches*, Edinburgh, 1908.

BRÉHIER, L., *Cambridge Mediæval History*, Vol. IV, chs. IX and XIX.

—— *L'église at l'Orient au moyen âge*, Paris, 1907.

DIEHL, C., *Cambridge Mediæval History*, Vol. IV, ch. I.

DORNER, J. A., *History of Development of the Doctrine of the Person of Christ*, English translation by W. E. Alexander and D. W. Simon, Edinburgh, 1894-8.

BIBLIOGRAPHY

HARNACK, A., *A History of Dogma*, English translation by N. Buchanan, E. B. Speirs and J. Millar, London, 1894-8.

HEILER, F., *The Spirit of Worship*, English translation by W. Montgomery, an excellent and wholly impartial comparison of the different ideals of the Christian Churches, London, 1926.

LUCHAIRE, A., *Innocent III et la question de l'Orient*, Paris, 1907.

NEALE, J. M., *A History of the Holy Eastern Church*, London, 1850.

OECONOMOS, L., *La vie religieuse dans l'Empire byzantin au temps des Comnènes et des Anges*, Paris, 1918.

PARGOIRE, R. P. J., *L'église byzantine* (527-845), Paris, 1905.

STANLEY, A. P., *The Eastern Church*, London, 1869.

TOZER, H. F., *The Church and the Eastern Empire*, London, 1897

WIGRAM, W. A., *History of the Assyrian Church*, London, 1910

—— *The Separation of the Monophysites*, London, 1923.

CHAPTER VIII: ICONOCLASM.

ARNOLD, T. W., *Painting in Islam*, ch. I, analysing the anti-representational impulse of Mohammedanism, Oxford, 1928.

BRÉHIER, L., *La querelle des images*, Paris, 1904.

GFRÖRER, A., *Der Bildersturm*, Vol. II of *Byzantinische Geschichten*, Graz, 1874.

SCHWARZLOSE, K., *Der Bilderstreit*, Gotha, 1890.

TOUGARD, A., *La persecution iconoclaste d'après la correspondence de saint Théodore Studite*, Revue des Questions Historiques, Paris, July, 1891.

CHAPTER VIII: MONASTICISM.

BUTLER, E. C., *Cambridge Mediæval History*, ch. XVIII.

BYRON, R., *The Station : Athos, Treasures and Men*, London, 1928.

GARDNER, A., *Theodore of Studium*, London, 1905.

HANNAY, J. O., *The Spirit and Origin of Christian Monasticism*, London, 1903.

LAKE, K., *Early Days of Monasticism on Mount Athos*, Oxford, 1909.

MARIN, L., *Les moines de Constantinople*, Paris, 1897.

BIBLIOGRAPHY

MEYER, P., *Die Haupturkunden für die Geschichte des Athosklöster*, Leipzig, 1864.

CHAPTER IX: GENERAL CULTURE.

ANDRÉADÈS, A., *Le recrutement des fonctionnaires et les universités dans l'Empire byzantin*, Extrait des Mélanges de Droit Romain, Paris, 1926.

KRUMBACHER, K., *Greek Literature : Byzantine*, in the current Encyclopædia Britannica.

—— *Geschichte der Byzantinischen Litteratur*, Munich, 1897.

RAMBAUD, A., *Michel Psellos, philosophe et homme d'état*, Revue Historique, Paris, 1877.

SYMONDS, J. A., *Renaissance in Italy*, Vols. I and II, London, 1898.

ZERVOS, C., *Michel Psellos*, Paris, 1920.

CHAPTER IX: ART AND ARCHITECTURE.

See also Chapter IV : Topography and Monuments of Constantinople.

ANTONIADES, E. M., Ἔκφρασις τῆς ἁγίας Σοφίας, Paris, 1917.

BEYLIÉ, L. M. E. DE, *L'habitation byzantine*, Paris, 1902.

BREASTED, J. H., *Oriental Forerunners of Byzantine Painting*, Chicago, 1924.

BRÉHIER, L., *L'art chrétien : son developpement iconographique*, 2nd edition, Paris, 1928.

CADAFALCH, J. P. Y, FALGUERA, A. DE, and CASALS, J. G. Y, *L'arquitectura Romànica a Catalunya*, Barcelona, 1909.

DALTON, O. M., *Byzantine Art and Archæology*, Oxford, 1911.

—— *East Christian Art*, Oxford, 1925.

DIEHL, C., *Manuel d'art byzantin*, 2nd edition, Paris, 1925-6.

DIEHL, C., and others, *Les monuments chrétiens de Salonique*, Paris, 1918.

EBERSOLT, J., *La miniature byzantine*, Paris, 1926.

—— *Sainte Sophie de Constantinople : étude topographique d'après les Cérémonies*, Paris, 1910.

JACKSON, T. G., *Byzantine and Romanesque Architecture*, Cambridge, 1913.

BIBLIOGRAPHY

LETHABY, W. R., and SWAINSON, R., *The Church of Sancta Sophia*, London, 1894.

MILLET, G., *L'école grecque dans l'architecture byzantine*, Paris, 1916.

MILLET, G., *Le monastère de Daphni*, Paris, 1916.

—— *Monuments byzantins de Mistra: matériaux pour l'étude de l'architecture et de la peinture en Grèce aux 14 et 15ᵉ siècles*, Paris, 1910.

PIERCE, H., and TYLER, R., *Byzantine Art*, London, 1926.

SCHULTZ, R. W., and BARNSLEY, S. H., *The Monastery of St Luke of Stiris, in Phocis*, London, 1901.

STRZYGOWSKI, J., *Origin of Christian Church Art*, English translation by O. M. Dalton and H. J. Braunholtz, Oxford, 1923.

CHAPTER X: SOCIAL LIFE.

BEYLIÉ, L. M. E. DE, *L'habitation byzantine*, Paris, 1902.

BURY, J. B., *The Nika Riot*, Journal of Hellenic Studies, London, 1897.

CHALANDON, F., *Essai sur la regne d'Alexis I Comnène*, Paris, 1900.

—— *Jean II et Manuel I Comnène*, Paris, 1912.

CHAPMAN, C., *Michel Paléologue, restaurateur de L'Empire byzantin*, Paris, 1926.

CLAVIJO, *Embassy to Tamerlane* (1403-6), English translation by G. le Strange, Broadway Travellers' Series, London, 1928.

COMNENA, PRINCESS ANNA, *The Alexiad*, English translation by E. A. S. Dawes, London, 1928.

DE LA BROQUIÈRE, B., *Voyage d'Outremer*, Paris, 1892.

DE MÉLY, F., *La Sainte Couronne d'Epines à Notre Dame de Paris*, Paris, 1927.

DIEHL, C., *Choses et gens de Byzance*, Paris, 1926.

—— *Figures byzantines*, 2 series, Paris, 1906 and 1913.

—— *Justinien et la civilisation byzantine au 6ᵉ siècle*, Paris, 1901.

EBERSOLT, J., *Le Grand Palais de Constantinople et le Livre des Cérémonies*, Paris, 1910.

—— *Les arts somptuaires de Byzance*, Paris, 1923.

—— *Sanctuaires de Byzance*, Paris, 1921.

FORCHEIMER, P., and STRZYGOWSKI, J., *Die Byzantinischen Wasserbehälter von Konstantinopel*, Vienna, 1893.

BIBLIOGRAPHY

HOLMES, G. W., *The Age of Justinian and Theodora*, London, 1905.

JEANSELME, E., and OECONOMOS, L., *Les œuvres d'assistance et les hôpitaux byzantins au siècle des Comnènes*, Anvers, 1921.

LIUTPRAND, Bishop of Cremona, *Histoire de l'Empire d'occident*, containing extremely amusing accounts of his two visits to Constantinople in the tenth century, French translation by L. Cousin, Paris, 1684.

RAMBAUD, A., *Etudes sur l'histoire byzantine*, Paris, 1912.

—— *L'Empire grec au 10ᵉ siècle : Constantin Porphyrogénète*, Paris, 1870.

RIANT, P., *Des dépouilles religieuses enlevées à Constantinople au XIIIᵉ siècle par les Latins*, Paris, 1875.

—— *Exuviae Sacrae Constantinopolitanae*, Geneva, 1877-8.

SCHLUMBERGER, G., *L'épopée byzantine à la fin du 10ᵉ siècle* :—

    I. *Jean Tzimiscès, Basile II* (969-986).

    II. *Basile II* (989-1025).

    III. *Les Porphyrogénètes, Zoé et Théodora* (1025-1057), Paris, 1896-1905.

—— *Un Empereur de Byzance à Paris et Londres*, Paris, 1916.

TAFUR, P., *Travels and Adventures* (1435-1439), English translation by M. Letts, Broadway Travellers' Series, London, 1926.

TOY, S., *The Aqueducts of Constantinople*, Journal of the Royal Institute of British Architects, London, Nov., 1928.

VOGT, A., *Basile Ier, Empereur de Byzance, et la civilisation byzantine à la fin du IXᵉ siècle*, Paris, 1908.

CHAPTER X: THE LATIN SETTLERS AND INVADERS.

An enormous literature exists and is fully set out in the bibliography of the Cambridge Mediæval History, Vol. IV. For the Venetians, see Chapter VII : Commerce and Wealth.

BRÉHIER, L., *L'église et l'Orient au moyen âge : les Croisades*, Paris, 1907.

BUCHON, J. A., *Collection des chroniques nationales françaises*, Paris, 1826.

—— *Recherches historiques sur la Principauté française de Morée*, Paris, 1843.

BIBLIOGRAPHY

DU CANGE, C. DU FRESNE, *Histoire de L'Empire de Constantinople sous les empereurs françois*, 1657, edited by J. A. Buchon, Paris, 1826.

HOPF, C., *Chroniques gréco-romanes*, containing Robert de Clary's account of the fourth crusade and description of Constantinople, and others, Berlin, 1873.

LUCHAIRE, A., *Innocent III et la question de l'Orient*, Paris, 1907.

MILLER, W., *Cambridge Mediæval History*, Vol. IV, ch. XV.

—— *Essays on the Latin Orient*, London, 1921.

—— *The Latin Orient*, London, 1921.

—— *The Latins in the Levant : History of Frankish Greece* (1204-1566), London, 1908.

PEARS, E., *The Fall of Constantinople, being the story of the Fourth Crusade*, London, 1885.

RODD, R., *The Princes of Achaia and the Chronicles of the Morea*, London, 1907.

SCHLUMBERGER, G., *Byzance et Croisades*, Paris, 1927.

—— *Les Principautés franques du Levant*, Paris, 1877.

—— *Mélanges d'archéologie byzantine : p. 87, Sceaux et bulles des Empereurs latins de Constantinople*, Paris, 1895.

—— *Récits de Byzance et des Croisades*, Paris, 1922-3.

VILLEHARDOUIN, G. DE, *La conquête de Constantinople*, edited by E. Bouchet, Paris, 1891.

CHAPTER X : BYZANTINE ASIA MINOR.

A certain number of the existing remains are described in Murray's Handbook and the works of Sir William Ramsay.

ANDERSON, J. G. C., *The Road-system of Eastern Asia Minor*, Journal of Hellenic Studies, London, 1897.

DIEHL, C., *Etudes byzantines*, Paris, 1905.

GARDNER, A., *The Lascarids of Nicæa*, London, 1912.

JERPHANION, G. DE, *Les églises rupestres de Cappadoce*, Paris, 1925.

MUSIL, A., *Kuseyr 'Amra*, Vienna, 1907.

PAPPADOPOULOS, J. B., *Theodore II Lascaris*, Paris, 1908.

BIBLIOGRAPHY

PERNOT, H., *Etudes de littérature grecque moderne*, pages 1-70, Paris, 1916.

ROTT, H., *Kleinasiatische Denkmäler*, Leipzig, 1908.

WROTH, W., *Catalogue of the coins of . . . the Empires of Thessalonica, Nicæa, and Trebizond in the British Museum*, London, 1908.

WULFF, O., *Die Koimesiskirche in Nicäa und ihre Mosaiken* (destroyed by the Turks in 1921), Strasbourg, 1903.

CHAPTER XI: BYZANTINE DEFENCE AND THE EASTERN INVADERS.

ANDRÉADÈS, A., *De la population de Constantinople sous les Empereurs byzantins*, Metron, Rovigo, Dec., 1920.

Cambridge Mediæval History, Vol. IV, chs. V, X, XX and XXI.

GIBBONS, H. A., *The Foundation of the Ottoman Empire*, Oxford, 1916.

LAURENT, J., *Byzance et les Turcs seljoucides*, Paris, 1913.

MIJATOVICH, C., *Constantine, the Last Emperor of the Greeks*, unreliable, but giving legends and details from the Slavonic Chronicle, London, 1892.

OMAN, C., *A History of the Art of War : the Middle Ages*, London, 1898.

PEARS, E., *The Destruction of the Greek Empire*, London, 1903.

SCHLUMBERGER, G., *Le siège, la prise et le sac de Constantinople par les Turcs, en* 1453, Paris, 1914.

—— *Récits de Byzance et des Croisades*, Paris, 1922-3.

CHAPTER XI: MISTRA AND TREBIZOND.

FALLMERAYER, J. P., *Geschichte des Kaiserthums von Trapezunt*. Munich, 1827.

MILLER, W., *Trebizond : the Last Greek Empire*, containing the only complete bibliography, London, 1926.

MILLET, G., *Inscriptions byzantines de Trébizonde*, Bulletin de Correspondence Hellénique, Paris, 1896.

—— *Les monastères et les églises de Trébizonde*, Bulletin de Correspondence Hellénique, Paris, 1895.

—— *Monuments byzantins de Mistra*, Paris, 1910.

Bibliography

Tozer, H. F., *A Byzantine Reformer : Gemistos Plethon*, Journa of Hellenic Studies, London, 1886.

Chapter XI : RUSSIA AND ITALY.

Kluchevsky, V. O., *History of Russia*, London, 1911.

Pares, B., *A History of Russia*, London, 1926.

Rostovtzeff, M., *Iranians and Greeks in South Russia*, Oxford, 1922.

Symonds, J. A., *Renaissance in Italy*, Vols. I and II, London, 1898.

Vast, H., *Le Cardinal Bessarion*, Paris, 1878.

Chapter XI : POPULAR LAMENTS AND SURVIVALS OF BYZANTINE TRADITION.

Abbott, G. F., *Songs of Modern Greece*, Cambridge, 1900.

Garnett, L. J. M., *Greek Folk-songs*, London, 1885.

Halliday, W. R., *Folk-lore Studies*, London, 1924.

Hesseling, D. C., *Histoire de la littérature grecque moderne*, Paris, 1924.

Legrand, E., *Recueil de poèmes historiques en Grec vulgaire*, Paris, 1877.

—— *Recueil de chansons populaires grecques*, Paris, 1874.

Passow, A., *Popularia Carmina Graeciae Recentioris*, Leipzig, 1860, from which, No. CXCVI, the poem at the end of this book is translated.

Pernot, H., *Etudes de littérature grecque moderne*, Paris, 1916.

Of greater assistance than books have been the advice and encouragement of Professor A. Andréadès, Mr L. Bower, Canon J. A. Douglas, the Archbishop Germanos, Metropolitan of Thyateira, Mr C. Hourmouzios, Dr W. Miller, Mr A. Pallis, General Phrantzes, *and particularly of* Mr J. Mavrogordato, *who revised the proofs.*

331

INDEX

INDEX

Architecture—
Antique, 33, 64
Byzantine, 33, 62, 83, 100, 187-
192 ; influence on West, 209 ;
Iranian influence on, 66 ; pen-
dentives, 190, 201 ; see also
St Sophia ; Professorships of, 71
Arezzo, frescoes at, 244; note on
Pl. XII
Argyropoulos, John, 306
Aristotle, 59, 210, 212-213, 295, 305
Arius, 168
Armenia and Armenians, 85, 91, 96,
134, 148, 174, 270
Arms and Defence Services—
Byzantine, 30, 92, 114, 126, 128,
268, 272-303 ; ambulance, 276;
bands, 206; baths, 249; cavalry,
273, 278; commissariat, 277;
communications, 276 ; during
last siege of Constantinople,
289-293 ; Emperor with, 249;
Engineers, 276; Marine, 85, 87,
279, 289; officers, 274; recruits,
96; salaries, 143-144; standards,
241 ; strength, 272-279 ; text-
books, 272, 275-276, 277 ; see
also Conscription, Greek Fire,
Mercenaries
Roman, 50
Turkish, 289 ; see also Cannon
Art, 187
Antique, 33, 63-65, 193, 196
Balkan, 192, 193
Byzantine, 62, 90, 100, 187-203,
209, 215-220 ; colour, 37, 190-
194, 197, 216 ; craftsmanship,
187, 196 ; cubism, 197 ;
enamels, 134 ; interpretational,
33, 37, 191-195 ; mosaics, 33, 37,
83, 134, 151, 188, 192, 193, 197,
198, 201, 203, 209-210, 226, 233 ;
notes on Pls. V and VIII ; painting, 37, 38, 107, 111, 151, 193-
194, 211, 216-220 ; Cretan school
of, 194, 217-220 ; Macedonian
school of, 194, 217-218 ; pattern
and design, 33, 189, 196;
periods, 188-195 ; relation to
Italian, 216-217; see also Italy,
painting in ; secular, 175, 191 ;
splendour, 37, 94, 152, 192,

Art—continued
194, 197-198, 209-210, 226-227 ;
transformed by Iconoclasm,170-
173, 176; see also Architecture
Early Christian, 188, 196
Interpretational, 33, 63, 90, 171-
173
Iranian, 64, 65-66
Modern, 171-172
Naturalistic, 63, 65, 171-173, 193,
217
Roman, 64
Russian, 192
Semitic, 65, 66-68
Serbian, 193
Artists, Byzantine, 193
Aryans, 10
Asia Minor, 8, 44, 47, 80, 96, 97, 100,
105, 108, 221, 250, 271, 278,
280, 283-285
Life in, 208, 229-234
Wealth of, 230-231
Askania, Lake of, 103 map, 105, 260
Astronomy, Study of, 206 ; note on
Pl. V
Athanasius, St, 154, 158
Athanasius of Athos, St, 160
Athens, 35, 47, 92, 103 map
Barony of, 102, 103 map
Brothels, 20
Church of, 164
Dukes of, 260
Pagan academy of, 56, 211
Athos, Holy Mountain, 33, 103 map,
134, 160-161, 216, 218, 221,
229, 252, 287
Attila, 78
Augustus, 45, 47, 226
Avars, 84
Azo of Bologna, 118, 122

B's, the Palæologus, title-page, 242-
243 ; note on Pl. VIII
Baalbek, 299
Bagdad, 87, 96, 142, 191, 205, 225,
270, 271, 272, 301
Bajazet, Sultan, 184, 225, 265, 283,
286
Baldwin I of Flanders, 102, 105, 140,
241
Baldwin II, 105, 106, 107, 259
Balearic Islands, 80

333

INDEX

INDEX

Index